TURKEY STEARNES AND THE DETROIT STARS

Wayne State University Press

TURKEY STEARNES AND THE DETROIT STARS

The Negro Leagues in Detroit, 1919-1933

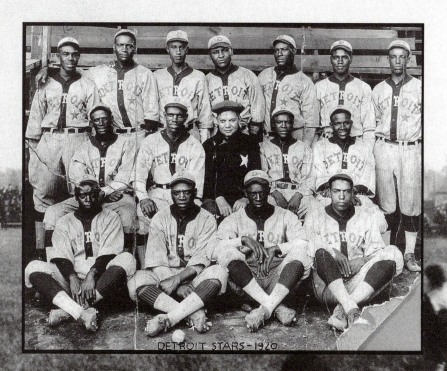

DETROIT STARS - 1920

RICHARD BAK

Great Lakes Books

A complete listing of the books in this series can be
found at the back of this volume.

Philip P. Mason, Editor
Department of History, Wayne State University

Dr. Charles K. Hyde, Associate Editor
Department of History, Wayne State University

Copyright © 1994 by Wayne State University Press,
Detroit, Michigan 48202. All rights are reserved.
No part of this book may be reproduced without formal permission.
Manufactured in the United States of America.
99 98 97 96 95 94   5 4 3 2 1

Library of Congress Cataloging-in-Publication Data

Bak, Richard, 1954–
Turkey Stearnes and the Detroit Stars : the negro leagues in
Detroit, 1919–1933 / Richard Bak.
p.   cm. — (Great Lakes books)
Includes bibliographical references (p.) and index.
ISBN 0-8143-2483-5
1. Stearnes, Turkey.   2. Baseball players—United States—
Biography.   3. Detroit Stars (Baseball team)   4. Negro leagues—
History.   5. Baseball—Michigan—Detroit—History.   I. Title.
II. Series.
GV865.S795B35   1994
796.357′092—dc20
[B]   93-34402

Designer: Mary Krzewinski

Baseball is a legitimate profession. It should be taken seriously by the colored player. An honest effort of his great ability will open the avenue in the near future wherein he may walk hand in hand with the opposite race in the greatest of all American games—baseball.

Sol White, 1906
History of Colored Baseball

There were a lot of great ballplayers came through Detroit with the Stars. I guess the names don't mean much now. Seems to me, a man can play ball that good, he ought to be remembered.

Ted "Double Duty" Radcliffe, 1992

Contents

★ Contents ★

Acknowledgments

I am indebted to the many men and women whose reminiscences and special knowledge of people and places made this book so much richer in detail: Eddie Batchelor, Jr., Gene Berlin, Bea Buck, Saul Davis, Lou Dials, Charlie Gehringer, John Glover, Fred Guinyard, Edgar Hayes, Haywood Henderson, Bill Hines, Charles "Red" House, Willie Horton, Willis "Ace" Hudlin, James Jenkins, Otis Johnson, Ruth Porter, Ted Radcliffe, Bobbie Robinson, Joyce Roesink, Bob Sampson, Nettie Stearnes, Jesse Walker, Fred Williams, and Fred "Sunnie" Wilson. I am also grateful to Jeannette Bartz, Pat Zacharias, and David Good of the *Detroit News;* Richard Harms of the Grand Rapids Public Library; and Dan Lori and Carole Marks for their kindnesses, both great and small, in locating photographs and contemporary newspaper items. My biggest debt is to Dick Clark, John Holway, Robert Peterson, Janet Bruce, David Katzman, and several other historians inside and outside of baseball, whose research and insights paved the way for this study. It's no exaggeration to say that this book is as much theirs as it is mine.

▲ Nettie Stearnes ponders her husband's exclusion from the Hall of
Fame: "Why isn't Norman in there? I wish I could answer that."
(Courtesy of Dan Lori.)

A Vote for Turkey

Even on the sunniest of summer afternoons, Norman "Turkey" Stearnes played the game he loved in the cool shadow of anonymity. Old-timers who ventured down to Detroit's Mack Park in the 1920s can tell you about the young black center fielder who would hammer a long home run one inning, then race to the fence to make a game-saving catch the next.

Although he was every bit as good as the white major-league stars of the era, Stearnes's exploits were unknown outside of the black community. Over time, his name has grown dimmer. The Negro leagues he dominated are long gone, as is the east side park at Mack and Fairview avenues he romped in. Owing to the Jim Crow practices of the "national pastime" then, traces of the man are practically nonexistent: a handful of grainy photographs, but no archival film, certainly no bubble gum cards. It's almost as if Turkey Stearnes never existed.

Almost.

"I remember one time I saw him hit a ball way over the stands at Mack Park," recalled his widow, Nettie Stearnes, pursing her lips at the memory. "Ooh-wee, that ball just went and went."

New research by baseball historians reveals that Stearnes—not his better-known black contemporaries such as Josh Gibson and Buck Leonard—hit the most home runs in Negro leagues history. The fact that other Negro leaguers have long since been admitted to the National

Baseball Hall of Fame in Cooperstown, New York, while her husband has been overlooked, is a continuing source of frustration to Nettie Stearnes.

"If anyone deserves to be in there, he does," said the retired school-teacher, who reserves a portion of her time and her modest Detroit home to keeping his name alive. A file cabinet in the living room contains correspondence with major-league baseball executives and Hall of Fame board members. "I'm writing all the time," she said. "Why haven't they noticed him? I wish I could answer that."

Nettie first became interested in Norman as a teenager in Alabama. The ballplayer was eighteen years older than Nettie and finishing his career with the Chicago American Giants. Nettie's uncle, Ted "Double Duty" Radcliffe, had been Stearnes's teammate in Detroit and Chicago. "My uncle played for the Birmingham Black Barons, and Norman and some other players would stay at our home when they played," she recalled.

The tall, thin ballplayer with the hollow cheeks and quiet manner filled in his past for Nettie. Growing up in Nashville, Tennessee, he had resisted offers to play ball professionally until he finished high school, aware that economics and his skin color would probably keep him out of college. He joined the Detroit Stars in 1923, spending his summers playing ball in the country's urban ghettos and his winters either working in an auto plant or barnstorming in Cuba and South America.

"They called him 'Turkey' because of the way he ran around the bases, flapping his arms," said Nettie. "The ballplayers used to have races before the games. Norman was fast. He'd win every time."

The one thing he never won was the recognition he deserved. Part of the problem is that an accurate statistical record of his achievements is just now being compiled by baseball historians. So far it shows a lifetime batting average of .352 in the black leagues and .313 against barnstorming white major leaguers. He led the league in home runs seven times and hit an astounding .474 in playoff games.

"Norman was very shy," said Nettie. "He'd play very well, then go right home after the game." Lacking a colorful personality, he never was a fixture in the storytelling that helped earn other Negro leaguers belated entry to Cooperstown in the 1970s and 1980s.

After he married Nettie and quit baseball in 1946, Norman labored in characteristic obscurity at the Ford Rouge foundry for twenty-five years. If he talked at all, it was about the game he had first played as a barefoot boy in Tennessee.

"His whole conversation was baseball," recalled Nettie. "That man loved the Tigers, he loved them all. He was never bitter. He said Al Kaline reminded him the most of the how he had played himself. He would go to all the games, even when he had to go to work the next morning."

Norman Stearnes died in 1979 at age seventy-eight. Since then, there have been infrequent queries from historians and recognition from the local Afro-American Sports Hall of Fame and Gallery. Nettie was given a small plaque with her husband's image and achievements on it. While the gesture is appreciated, she knows a small plaque buried in the clutter of a crowded fireplace mantel doesn't compare with one hanging alongside the large bronze tablets of Babe Ruth, Ty Cobb, and Ted Williams in the "big hall" of baseball's immortals, Cooperstown.

"I'd like to see Norman in there before I die," she said, motes of dust floating like knuckleballs in the sunlit room. "Not because of me or the children or the grandchildren, but for Norman. He deserves to be remembered."

Introduction

A Distant Diamond

When Fred and Bob Guinyard were growing up in Detroit's "Black Bottom" neighborhood in the 1920s, the perfect summer Sunday featured a pair of religious experiences. In the morning the brothers would attend services with their mother and father at Calvary Baptist Church on McDougall Street. Afterwards they would hurry home, change out of their "Sunday best," and then—assuming that they were successful in sneaking away from their parents—walk to the corner of Gratiot Avenue and Chene Street.

"That was a busy intersection, so it was easy to catch a truck," recalled Fred Guinyard, who still lives on the city's near east side. "We'd wait until one stopped at a red light, then hop on. We'd ride down Chene to Mack Park." The mischief didn't end once the Guinyard brothers jumped off the back of the truck.

"We'd wait until the game was on and then we'd sneak in," said Guinyard. "At least we *thought* we were sneaking in." Actually, as was often the case at Navin Field, where the Detroit Tigers played, gatekeepers usually saw little harm in letting youngsters into the park for free after the fourth or fifth inning, especially if their cherubic faces bore appropriately forlorn expressions.

Once inside, the brothers would plop down on a bleacher board

◄ Detroit Stars manager Bruce Petway and mascot "Johnie" at Mack Park in 1922.

15

and debate the relative merits of that afternoon's competition—the St. Louis Stars with Mule Suttles and Cool Papa Bell, say, or the Chicago American Giants with Willie Foster on the mound. Arguments and fantasy encounters were the order of the day. How would Ty Cobb do against the Stars' hard-throwing lefthander, Andy Cooper? Who hit the ball farther, Oscar Charleston of the Indianapolis ABCs or the Detroit Stars' resident slugger, Turkey Stearnes? And could either of them compare with the fabulous white home-run hitter, Babe Ruth? Or the Tigers' Harry Heilmann? Baking in the hot sun on a summer Sunday, inhaling the ballpark smells of perfume, grass, and smoke, so close to the action that they could listen to the ballplayers holler and laugh, it seemed the best of all possible ways to spend the Sabbath.

"It was a lot of fun," said Guinyard, remembering the likes of Turkey Stearnes, Pepper Daniels, and Andy Cooper. "The guys there could play baseball . . . *really* play baseball."[1]

That they could. Between 1919 and 1933, the Detroit Stars, the city's first black professional sports franchise, showcased some of the finest talent ever to grace a diamond in Detroit—first at Mack Park and then, beginning in 1930, at Hamtramck Stadium. Although they are now all but forgotten, in their time the Stars were an integral part of the city's black culture.

"On Sundays," former Black Bottom resident Lawrence Carter once recalled, "Mack Park would be jam-packed to watch the Stars play the Kansas City Monarchs with their peerless pitcher Bullet Rogan, the Pittsburgh Homestead Grays with the legendary home-run hitter Oscar Charleston, or maybe the Cuban All-Stars.

"Across Gratiot at St. Antoine near Beacon was 'Brosher the Biscuit King.' Brosher was . . . a fervent booster of the Detroit Stars. When they won, Brosher, a stompin' down good piano player, would celebrate with music and eats. It was a great time."[2]

Organized in early 1919 by Rube Foster of Chicago, the Stars began scheduled play in the following spring as a charter member of Foster's Negro National League. Foster placed black-owned franchises in several of the North's emerging ghettos, including Detroit's Black Bottom, a neighborhood of some sixty square blocks on the lower east side. For the next thirteen summers, until the Great Depression forced the club to fold midway through the 1933 season, the Stars provided Detroit's rapidly expanding black community one of its few entertainment options in a racially polarized city.

"We used to fill that Mack Park on Sundays," said Ted Radcliffe, who played three seasons for the Stars. "They'd be lined up on the streets when we opened the gates. We could only get seven or eight thousand in the place, but there were some days that we'd outdraw the Tigers."[3]

The wobbly wooden park at Mack and Fairview seemed to be the place to go for many of Black Bottom's residents. The Stars not only offered them entertainment, community, and a short respite from life's daily indignities, they represented a rare example of successful black entrepreneurship at a time when most opportunities were closed to men and women of color. For the Detroit Stars and the rest of the Negro National League were the inevitable by-product of Jim Crow America, which by the turn of the century had in place a suffocating network of discriminatory customs and laws that kept blacks isolated, impoverished, and economically and socially enslaved. In Detroit this meant that the thousands of newly arrived members of "the Great Migration" north drank at designated water fountains, worked menial jobs, and slept four to a bed in tumbledown back-alley shacks rented at exorbitant prices. In a climate where black men in the South were still being lynched with impunity, where a black dentist in Detroit had to fend off a murderous mob because he had moved into a white neighborhood, the major leagues' unofficial color bar was hardly thought exceptional—except by those whose livelihoods and legacies were irreversibly affected by it.

"If we'd only been given the opportunity, a lot of us would have made the majors," insisted one-time Stars infielder Ray Sheppard. "This isn't bragging, but over ten years I hit .300 or better each year." According to Sheppard, the proof that Negro leaguers were at least equal in talent to their white counterparts was apparent in the frequent exhibition games between the two sides, when black squads usually gave better than they got. According to available scoresheets, black nines won about 60 percent of these interracial matches in the first half of the century.[4]

Modern fans might wonder just how good Negro-league[5] teams like the Detroit Stars and individual Negro leaguers really were. Over the years, many knowledgeable players, fans, owners, and sportswriters have insisted that top-notch black clubs like the Chicago American Giants, Kansas City Monarchs, and Pittsburgh Crawfords probably were as good as the champion white teams of the period, such as the New York Yankees, St. Louis Cardinals, and Philadelphia Athletics. Respected white sportswriters—like Harry Salsinger of the *Detroit News,* who once wrote that "the level of the game in the Negro leagues is easily on a part with that being played at Navin Field"—were convinced that baseball's color bar was depriving the game of some of the country's finest talent.[6]

The Detroit Stars were never quite as good as the top Negro-league teams of the 1920s. A second-tier team that usually played winning, competitive ball, it qualified for the Negro National League playoffs only twice, losing each time. In terms of talent, most years the Stars probably resembled an outstanding Triple-A farm club or a so-so, second-division major-league team. But certain individual Stars, including Norman "Tur-

17

key" Stearnes, the most storied Star of them all, could have cracked the starting lineup of any big-league nine.

"You can talk all you want to about the players from the Negro leagues that made the Hall of Fame and they deserved all of it," said Ted Radcliffe. "But unless Turkey Stearnes is in there, too, ain't none of them should be there. He played in Detroit at the same time as Ty Cobb and Harry Heilmann and Heinie Manush and Charlie Gehringer were with the Tigers and all four of them ended up in Cooperstown. But I saw him play and back then Turkey Stearnes didn't have to care for nobody."[7]

Neither did Edgar Wesley, the Detroit Stars' slugging first baseman of the early 1920s, who may have been as good a power hitter as anyone then or now. In terms of size, strength, and achievements, Wesley was roughly comparable to the Detroit Tigers' powerful first baseman of the 1990s, Cecil Fielder. Wesley led the Negro National League in home runs three times (1920, 1923, and 1925) and in batting average in 1925 with a .424 mark. By that time Stearnes had joined the lineup, giving the Stars a one-two punch as dangerous as any in the game. Had they been allowed to play in the major leagues, Wesley's and Stearnes's statistics—even allowing for the superior everyday pitching they would have faced— could reasonably have been expected to fall in the range of a .300 batting average with higher-than-normal home run and slugging figures. Skeptics should know that, in a three-game exhibition series between the Detroit Stars and St. Louis Browns played at Mack Park in the fall of 1923, Wesley hit three home runs against the Browns' front-line pitching— which had been good enough to carry St. Louis to a second-place finish in the American League the year before.

Black teams, which normally carried only fourteen or fifteen men on a roster, had notoriously thin pitching staffs and mediocre reserves. These weaknesses would have become glaring over the course of a long season in the American or National league. Of course, that's assuming that entire Negro-league squads would have been allowed into the majors, a circumstance which not even the most fanatical integrationist of the 1920s ever dreamed would happen. A more realistic scenario, one that the major leagues ultimately chose to follow in the late 1940s with Jackie Robinson and the subsequent first wave of black ballplayers, would have had individual blacks slowly introduced into all-white lineups. Organized baseball's failure to desegregate earlier not only deprived fans like the Guinyard brothers of some classic matchups, it allowed the story of men like Turkey Stearnes and Edgar Wesley to go largely unchronicled.

Over the last twenty years, the story of American's Negro leagues is being slowly, painstakingly pieced together. This is due to the pioneering efforts of Robert Peterson, John B. Holway, and Donn Rogosin, among others, who recorded the memories of many early Negro leaguers before these players passed away. As might be expected, these oral histories are an uneven mix of fact and fable. However, thanks to the continuing hard work of researchers and historians scrolling through miles of microfilm, tabulating ancient boxscores, and weeding out apocrypha, a more accurate portrait of the Negro leagues is emerging. Since many boxscores and game reports were either never kept or have yet to be uncovered, most Negro leaguers' individual statistics will remain fragmentary and subject to perpetual updating and revising.

The growing scholarship so far has revolved around famous teams like the Kansas City Monarchs, Chicago American Giants, Homestead Grays, and Pittsburgh Crawfords. These clubs enjoyed substantial coverage in the local black press, which in the case of the *Pittsburgh Courier* and *Chicago Defender* also served as national black weeklies. Lesser known teams like the Detroit Stars have so far been overlooked—not for lack of interest, but often because of the frustrating paucity of original source material. For example, only a few scattered issues of the *Detroit Contender* and other black weekly newspapers survive from the early 1920s, making it next to impossible to find contemporary human-interest accounts of the Stars. The three major white Detroit dailies of the period—the *News, Free Press,* and *Times*—either published box scores of the Stars' games selectively or not at all. *Free Press* sportswriter Eddie Batchelor once wrote a long piece on Mack Park for the weekly *Detroit Saturday Night,* but features and profiles of individual players and owners were otherwise unheard of.

As a result, this story of the Detroit Stars often is necessarily more anecdotal than comprehensive, with many questions about finances and ownership, for instance, largely left unanswered. On the positive side, a handful of former Stars, ranging in age from eighty-five to ninety-one, were found, as was a smattering of relatives and fans. One, Saul Davis, has his reminiscences set down in narrative form in a chapter entitled, "The Way It Was." The Batchelor piece also is presented this way. At times the effect is impressionistic rather than linear history, but even that is more than already exists on the subject of the Detroit Stars.

Most of what *is* available, including statistics, has been put to use. With the permission of Dick Clark, chairman of the Negro leagues committee of the Society of American Baseball Research, an all-time roster and seasonal and career performances of the Stars have been extrapolated from the committee's research. These names and numbers can be found in the back of the book. This lengthy statistical section—the first every published for a single Negro-league team—serves to put some badly needed flesh on the bones of such vanished Stars as Edgar Wesley, Ed Rile, Clarence Smith, and John Jones. But it still leaves one aching for scraps of personal information. For example, readers can discover that first baseman Ed Rile hit .351 during his four seasons with the Stars and also starred on the mound. What remains a mystery is when or where he was born and died. Until recently baseball historians couldn't even agree on what hand he threw with. This for a pitcher who won as many as fourteen games in a single eighty-four-game season!

The passage of time practically guarantees that most of the men who wore a Detroit Stars uniform between 1919 and 1933 will remain as mysterious as Ed Rile. Nonetheless, aging contemporaries such as Nettie Stearnes and Fred Guinyard insist that they deserve to be remembered, a sentiment with which the author wholeheartedly agrees. This book is meant to be a first step in preserving their memory.

Chapter One

FOLLOWING THE NORTH STAR

Two youngsters—one black, one white—stood on a dusty street in turn-of-the-century Detroit, awkwardly sizing each other up.

"I'm English, Dutch, and Irish," said the white child. "What are you?"

Replied the black child, "I'm nothin'."

Variations of this apocryphal story abound, but all serve to illustrate the overwhelming sense of worthlessness and inferiority that afflicted most black Americans at the dawn of the twentieth century. A bloody civil war had ostensibly given the race its freedom a generation earlier. But long after emancipation, blacks remained victims of a systematic oppression, both physical and psychological, designed to keep people of color subordinate—or, in the vernacular of the day, "in their place."

Blacks' place in Detroit's history reaches back to shortly after 1701, when Antoine de la Mothe Cadillac, with the help of one hundred French soldiers and traders, built the initial stockade, Fort Pontchartrain, near the river. Detroit was an important outpost as France and England fought to build competing empires in the vast North American wilderness. During the first half of the eighteenth century, blacks occasionally appeared

◄ Streetsweepers in downtown Detroit, circa 1900. At the turn of the century blacks usually were restricted to the most menial, poorest paying jobs. (Courtesy of the Burton Historical Collection of the Detroit Public Library.)

in Detroit, sometimes as free men, but more often as slaves. Following its defeat in the Seven Years War, France surrendered the fort to the British in 1760. The French were allowed to keep their own slaves but were required to return to their British owners those who had been captured in battle.

The transatlantic slave trade, which had started in earnest in the early 1600s, boomed with the expansion of the plantation system in the southern colonies. Between ten and twenty million men, women, and children—no one knows the exact number—were transported, under whip and gun, from Africa to the Western Hemisphere in the three centuries leading up to the American Civil War. About one in four were shipped to the United States.[1]

A contemporary document vividly describes the scurrilous conditions of the slave ships, where captives were chained ankle to ankle in the dark, pestilent cargo holds and forced to lie for weeks in their own excrement: "The height, sometimes, between decks, was only eighteen inches; so that the unfortunate human beings could not turn around, or even on their sides, the elevation being less than the breadth of their shoulders; and here they are usually chained to the decks by the neck and legs. In such a place the sense of misery and suffocation is so great, that the Negroes . . . are driven to frenzy."[2] It has been estimated that as many as one in three blacks failed to survive the dreaded "middle passage."

If this human suffering ever pricked the consciences of those involved in slave trafficking, the large profits to be made, coupled with the manpower shortage that threatened colonial tobacco and cotton planters, nonetheless guaranteed its expansion. On the eve of the American Revolution there were 170,000 slaves in Virginia alone, roughly half the population. Many of the signers of the Constitution owned slaves. One, James Madison, boasted that he could make $257 annually on each slave while paying only $13 for his keep. Another founding father, Thomas Jefferson, gave new meaning to the term by siring a family of bastards with a young slave named Sally Hemings.[3]

Interested buyers in western regions such as Detroit could order slaves from eastern brokers with a specificity usually reserved for restaurants. In 1760 the firm of Phyn & Ellice in Schenectady, New York, offered a menu of "negro lads" costing from eighty to ninety pounds each, while more reasonably priced "wenches" went for between sixty and seventy pounds apiece. "Upon your arrival at Philadelphia, please advise us by letter . . . if you can purchase for us two negro lads from fifteen to twenty years . . . ," Phyn & Ellice wrote a procurer in 1771. "They must be stout and sound, but we are indifferent about their qualifications, as they are for a Frenchman at Detroit."[4]

Several prominent Detroiters, whose names today adorn street signs in what has become an overwhelmingly black metropolis, were eighteenth-century slaveowners. Joseph Campau had as many as ten working his narrow ribbon of farmland. His favorite was the one called "Crow," who delighted the citizenry by performing acrobatic tricks on the steeple of St. Anne's Church on Jefferson Avenue.

Not all were as clever or well-received as Crow. "We have received two negro boys," Phyn & Ellice informed a Mr. Levy in 1770. "[The] oldest will do for Mr. Stirling, at Detroit, as is entered in our Order book. But we are entirely at a loss what to do with that fat-gutted boy, having orders for none such for any of our correspondents, and we don't by any means want him for ourselves."[5]

Another letter to John Porteous (who, along with Alexander Macomb and the above mentioned James Stirling, ran the leading dry goods store in Detroit) informed him that Phyn & Ellice had "contracted with a New England gentleman for some green negroes to be delivered here the first of August, and then your wench will be forwarded, together with a negro boy, in case she may sometime hereafter choose a husband. We apprehend he will be useful to you . . . or you can dispose of him as you find best. The price is fifty pounds each."[6]

In 1782 there were 179 slaves in Detroit, including 101 women. Perhaps half of these were American Indians. According to historian Silas Farmer, Native Americans such as the Pawnees "made excellent servants and commanded high prices."[7] Black or red, these prisoners of color faced long years of unremitting labor and daily humiliations, with small hope that tomorrow would offer anything better. Those who ran away were hunted like wild game and returned to face the bullwhip; those who dared to fight back often faced inventive torture and death.

Because of their gender, servant girls were doubly damned. They represented much needed help for the ceaseless, backbreaking domestic chores and, far more often than is commonly supposed, an unwilling sexual partner for the master, his sons, or a friend stopping by to share some tobacco and whiskey. In a remarkable narrative from the early 1800s, a servant named Linda Brent remembers turning fifteen as "a sad epoch in the life of a slave girl. My master began to whisper foul words in my ear. Young as I was, I could not remain ignorant of their import. . . . My master met me at every turn, reminding me that I belonged to him, and swearing by heaven and earth that he would compel me to submit to him. If I went out for a breath of fresh air, after a day of unwearied toil, his footsteps dogged me. If I knelt by my mother's grave, his dark shadow fell on me even there. The light heart which nature had given me became heavy with sad foreboding."[8] In those instances where rape led to pregnancy, little, if any, social stigma was attached to the unpunished perpetrator of the outrage. Detroit, like most American communities, had its share of mulatto offspring—distinctive by their yellow-hued skin—sprinkled throughout its multicultured, frontier population.

For reasons that were more economic than humanitarian, slavery died in the northern states even as it flourished in the South. The Ordinance of 1787 banned slavery in the Northwest Territory. However, since the region was not yet under American control, the law did not affect Detroit. When the British finally turned over the town to the Americans in 1796, there were about ninety black slaves among the community of some 2,200 people. Many of them had been captured during raids into Kentucky during the Revolutionary War and brought to the North. Since the Jay Treaty of 1794 allowed British settlers to retain all personal property acquired prior to American control, many citizens held on to their slaves well into the early years of the nineteenth century. Detroit's official census in 1810 revealed seventeen slaves, and as late as 1830 there were still thirty-two in Michigan. By 1836, however, one year before Michigan was admitted into the Union, all slaves in the soon-to-be state had either died or been manumitted by their owners.[9]

The opening of the Erie Canal, which provided a water route from the overcrowded East to the cheap, open spaces of the western frontier, made Detroit an important port in the 1830s. The city quickly grew into a substantial mercantile center, its population increasing almost tenfold in twenty years, from a mere 2,222 in 1830 to 21,019 in 1850. Beyond the physical ramifications of this population increase—a growth in manufacturing and shipping facilities, and a doubling of the city's size to almost six square miles—the "Yankee invasion" of New Yorkers and New Englanders helped transform Detroit into one of the more enlightened cities in the North. Many of the Yankees brought with them a reformist zeal that included among its goals the abolition of slavery.

On one occasion in 1833 a large crowd of mostly black Detroiters—armed with rocks, clubs, and pistols—surrounded the jail on Gratiot, where the sheriff was waiting to transport a pair of runaway slaves, Thornton Blackburn and his wife, back to their owner in Kentucky. A sympathizer was somehow able to exchange clothes with the imprisoned woman, allowing her to flee to Canada. The husband was freed the following day when another mob attacked the sheriff as he attempted to transfer his prisoner onto a steamboat. During the assault, the sheriff was seriously wounded. With emotions running high, Governor Lewis Cass called out the militia. Several blacks were arrested for "riotous conduct," but they were eventually released.[10]

The following year Detroit's first anti-slavery society was organized by Erotious Parmalee Hastings, a leading citizen and justice-loving Presbyterian for whom Hastings Street—destined to one day become the city's major black thoroughfare—had been named a few years earlier. The abolitionists' constitution declared that "slave-holding is a crime in the sight of God, and that the duty, safety, and best interests of all concerned require its immediate abandonment." The society faded away, but its spirit remained strong, as Detroit evolved into the northernmost terminus on the storied "underground railroad."[11]

The railroad was a secret network of houses, churches, barns, haystacks, attics, cellars, and other hiding places stretching from the southern states north to Canada. Several Detroit-area communities—including Farmington, Wyandotte, Pontiac, Rochester, Plymouth, Mount Clemens, and Birmingham—were way stations on this clandestine freedom road, over which an estimated fifty thousand escaped slaves traveled between 1830 and 1860.

There were also several stations in Detroit, including the city's first two black churches: St. Matthew's Episcopal at Woodward and Holbrook, and Second Baptist on Croghan (later Monroe), which was founded in 1836 by thirteen former slaves. "On any night of the week, the church could expect the arrival of passengers on the railroad," explained Arthur M. Woodford. "The pastor would receive a note from one of his members which might read: 'Pastor, tomorrow night at our 8:00 meeting, let's read Exodus 10:8.' In Underground language, that meant 'Conductor No. 2 will be arriving at 8:00 p.m. with ten slaves, eight men and two women.'"[12]

The busiest Detroit station was the livery stable of Seymour Finney, who operated the Temperance House at the corner of Woodward and Gratiot (today the site of the Kern Block). Finney's stable was a block away at State and Griswold, where the Detroit Bank & Trust Company branch office now sits. A bronze plaque on the bank's wall marks the spot where countless escapees were fed and hidden by day, then spirited away at night across the Detroit River in canoes and barges. Today many of Ontario's black citizens can trace their heritage back to those frightened but determined fugitives.

One was George Hatter, a runaway slave from Bluefield, an obscure mountain town just north of the Virginia state line. He was nineteen years old that hot summer day in 1837 when he said goodbye to his brother Frank and set off for freedom. Hatter "came to a break in the mountains and found a cave where he spent the rest of the day," goes the family tale of his escape. "That night he came to a meadow and jumped on a horse that was grazing there. He rode all night, following the North Star. . . . Always, toward the North Star." Near Clearfield, Pennsylvania, a Quaker farmer hid Hatter for a week, then furnished him with a fresh horse and food. Continuing his journey, Hatter was accosted by a white man, who brandished a wooden club and called him a "runaway nigger." Hatter pulled out a pistol the sympathetic Quaker had given him and announced that if he moved, he would blow the man's brains out. "He didn't have any untoward experiences after that," the tale continues. Hatter crossed at Niagara Falls and settled in South Buxton, Ontario, where he prospered and lived the life of a free man. In 1910, Hatter's son moved to Detroit and opened a used furniture store at St. Antoine and Macomb, in the heart of the growing black community. His descendants still live in the city.[13]

☆

On the eve of the Civil War, Detroit had a population of more than 45,000 people. This included 1,402 blacks, or about three percent of the population. They were settled on the near east side, within a half-mile radius of Campus Martius (Kennedy Square today), in the rows of old building stock that ran between St. Antoine and Beaubien from Gratiot Avenue to the river. The area, whose streets followed the property lines of the original French "ribbon" farms, had been known by early settlers as "Black Bottom" because of the rich topsoil. The name gained new currency as the racial composition of the near east side changed. Eventually the term "Black Bottom" came to encompass the entire black community, even as it spread east and north of the original area.[14]

The scenery and morality of Black Bottom became more frayed the closer one got to the river. Sandwiched between Jefferson and the waterfront was a hodge podge of warehouses and tumbledown shacks that included dozens of flophouses, brothels, and saloons. Until these "disorderly houses" were gradually displaced by small factories and businesses during the 1870s, this area constituted the city's vice district, the Potomac Quarter. Operated and frequented by social rabble of all colors, the quarter was so notorious that on several occasions indignant citizens took the law into their own hands and torched the worst offenders.[15]

On fashionable East Congress Street, near St. Antoine, was the neatly kept house of William Webb, a black active in the smuggling of escaped slaves. It was there, on the evening of March 12, 1859, that two of the leading historical figures of the time, John Brown and Frederick Douglass, met.

Brown, the wild-eyed, bearded abolitionist, had arrived earlier in the day with fourteen fugitive slaves from Missouri. By either design or coincidence, the noted orator Douglass also was in town. After delivering a lecture, Douglass met with Brown and several local black leaders at Webb's place, where Brown outlined his radical plan to lead a series of armed slave revolts throughout the South. Brown then crossed into Canada, picking up recruits for his famous, failed occupation of the federal

▲ A street peddler and his young companion rest in front of a Black Bottom grocery store. Until the First World War, blacks constituted only a tiny percentage of Detroit's population. (Courtesy of *The Detroit News*.)

arsenal at Harpers Ferry, Virginia. Brown and several of his companions were convicted of murder, treason, and promoting slave insurrection and were hanged. Brown—eloquent, passionate, and probably insane—was vilified by the South but became a martyr to the North.[16]

Union troops marched to war in the spring of 1861 singing, "John Brown's body lies a-mouldering in the grave," but the issue at hand was race, not slavery. Thirty years earlier, French magistrate Alexis de Tocqueville had passed through Detroit on his famous trip across America. He observed that the "prejudice of race appears to be stronger in the states that have abolished slavery than in those where it still exists."[17] Although Detroiters in the main were willing to accept freedmen into the community, they repeatedly defeated attempts to grant them the right of suffrage. Abraham Lincoln was just one of many at mid-century who, far from looking to extend citizenship to blacks, openly expressed the wish that they could somehow be transported back to Africa. This, of course, was an impossibility. One way or another, blacks and whites would have to find a way to co-exist, either as slave and master or as free men sharing a common destiny. De Tocqueville predicted that friction between the races would be the cause of the "future dangers of the United States."[18]

On March 6, 1863, just a few weeks after blacks had celebrated the Emancipation Proclamation at the Second Baptist Church, an ugly event proved de Tocqueville correct. A mulatto named Thomas Faulkner had been arrested on charges that he had raped two girls, one of whom was white. As he was being led away from court, a crowd of demonstrators, many of them Irish immigrants, tried to separate Faulkner from the armed escort. The provost-guard fired into the attackers, killing one. The frustrated mob turned its fury elsewhere, surging through the black neighborhoods, burning property and attacking residents at random.

"I could see from the windows men striking with axe, spade, clubs, &c, just as you could see men thrashing wheat," went one contemporary account. "A sight the most revolting, to see innocent men, women, and children, all without respect to age or sex, being pounded in the most brutal manner."[19] Scores of blacks were hurt, and two died of their injuries. The girls later admitted that they had lied, and in early 1870 Faulkner was pardoned after spending nearly seven years in prison.

That spring some fifteen hundred Detroiters gathered to celebrate the ratification of the Fifteenth Amendment, which guaranteed the vote to all male citizens, black and white. The interracial crowd paraded through downtown streets, then packed the Opera House for speeches and entertainment. George De Baptiste posted a whimsical notice to all "stockholders" of the underground railroad on his storefront, which had served as a way station. "This office is closed," it declared. "Hereafter all stockholders will receive dividends according to their merits."[20]

But constitutional amendments, much like Faulkner's pardon and the ex-railroader's inside joke, rang hollow. In the wake of war, courts and legislators looked to mend fences by restoring the delicate balance between national and state authority. By the end of the century a series of decisions had stripped away much of the federal government's ability to protect the civil liberties of former slaves. The most shocking decision came in 1883, when the Civil Rights Act of 1875 was declared unconstitutional. The essence of the U.S. Supreme Court's cumulative decisions between 1873 and 1898 was that Congress had the "power to restrain

▲ This nameless Alabama sharecropper may very well have joined the "Great Migration" of southern blacks to northern cities during the first three decades of this century. (Courtesy of Carole Marks.)

states but not individuals from acts of racial discrimination and segregation."[21] The resultant doctrine of "separate but equal" was only half-right, as white supremacists in and outside of government worked overtime to make blacks second-class citizens.

At the turn of the century, blacks in Detroit were not nearly as bad off as those in the post-Reconstruction South. Such familiar southern tactics as convoluted poll taxes, designed to keep blacks from voting, and indiscriminate lynchings, designed to terrorize, were not part of Detroit's landscape. In fact, in 1885 Michigan had passed a civil rights statute nearly identical to the federal act that had been overturned two years earlier.

However, the legal guarantees failed to stop almost all aspects of everyday life from developing along caste lines. The Detroit Board of Education resisted the 1867 School Integration Act for years. When it finally capitulated, the cash-strapped board spent practically its last dollar replacing double desks with single desks, so that black and white children would not have to sit next to each other. Similarly, local restaurants and theaters had "colored only" sections, while most hotels and barber shops continued to bar blacks. Those who chose to challenge segregation almost always lost their cases in court.[22]

Since blacks constituted a tiny percentage of Detroit's population (only 1 percent in 1910, when the city had grown to 466,000 people), the majority of whites had little daily contact with blacks. When the races did mix, behavior was predicated on a set of unwritten rules. Blacks never entered the house of a white through the front door. Waiters, house servants, delivery men, and others in the service trades were drilled to say "Yes sir" and "No ma'am" when speaking to whites, assuming that they had been spoken to first. Those who were cautious knew to step off the wooden sidewalk and into the mud to allow a crowd of whites to pass. "To be a good Negro in some men's estimation, one must lose his self-respect," complained attorney Walter H. Stowers in 1903. "He must cringe and crawl and fawn in the presence of the 'superior race' or he is a bad actor and must be dealt with by men who have red blood in their veins and often on their hands, too."[23] The all-white police force was no help, ignoring or often precipitating random acts of violence against ordinary black citizens.[24]

As dispiriting as these daily tribulations were, blacks might have found them easier to swallow if they had been allowed into the economic mainstream, the path to social advancement that waves of immigrant groups had traditionally followed. A young, emerging economic power, America offered real opportunities, but it was the new arrivals from Germany, Italy, Russia, Hungary, Greece, Lithuania, Sweden, and Poland who, because of their skin color, were better able to take advantage of them. Never mind that most could not speak English, and many had had less formal schooling than urban blacks. In the 1870s labor agents crossed the Atlantic to recruit thousands of Poles for the city's booming stove works, ignoring the capable blacks in their own backyard. By 1900, more than 70 percent of the city's black males worked in unskilled or service jobs, three times the rate of foreign-born whites. Even a traditional black occupation, barbering, had been usurped by Italian and Greek immigrants.[25]

With a few exceptions, Detroit's blacks performed the most menial, poorest paying jobs. In 1900, nearly nine of every ten black women who worked were employed as house servants, a physically draining job that often required being on call around-the-clock, six days a week. Of the city's 1,186 telephone operators, all were white females. Of the city's 2,081 store clerks, only one was a black woman.[26] Meanwhile, their husbands and sons broke their backs on the docks and construction sites, performing manual labor that helped reinforce age-old racial stereotypes. A newspaper story in 1896 described a coal-refueling station on the Detroit River as a "city plantation" where laborers "pass day after day, eating and sleeping, working and playing, apparently as happy and jolly as though they were back on the old plantation itself."[27]

At the heart of such stereotyping was the principle of white supremacy, or, as one U.S. senator at the time put it, "the divine right of the Caucasian to govern the inferior races."[28] This was supported by the pseudoscientific studies of the day and helped explain not only racism at home, but U.S. imperialism in Cuba, Hawaii, and the Philippines, where Americans sought to pacify and convert "our little brown brothers." No matter where one turned—daily newspapers, popular journals and magazines, scientific books, Sunday lectures—the notion that the Anglo-Saxon race was superior to all others was being presented, and accepted, with little debate. In 1896, for example, a reporter for the *Detroit Sunday News-Tribune* described a gang of black laborers repairing asphalt on Lafayette Avenue. "There is a curious fitness in the fact that the asphalt laying is in the hands of negroes," he wrote, "for the asphalt, of course, is tar black, and the men who handle it have something of the same distinguishing tint. But there is another and a deeper reason. Such work is hard, hot and difficult, and the negro, coming of a tropical race, is fitted by nature to do the necessary hauling and pulling, without undue physical prostration."[29]

Discrimination, far from preventing the formation of a black middle class, helped encourage it. In the last two decades of the nineteenth century, businesses in Black Bottom moved away from servicing a white clientele and concentrated on meeting the needs of their own growing community. A business district developed along St. Antoine and adjoining streets, including black-owned hotels, restaurants, grocery stores, tailor shops, drug stores, funeral homes, saloons, pool halls, and newspaper, real estate, and insurance offices. (By the early 1900s a vice district also was in place. Known as "The Heights," it ran along the lower end of Beaubien, St. Antoine, and Hastings.) Although 85 percent of the city's blacks lived in Black Bottom, others had settled in an area twenty blocks north of Gratiot known as "Kentucky." There also existed an upper class of physicians, attorneys, politicians, and clergymen, who lived in spacious brick homes on Canfield, Alfred, Adelaide, and Frederick and moved in circles that were foreign to the average black. While a small elite group

33

of "respectable" blacks were nervous over the prospect of losing their hard-won status among whites and thus distanced themselves as much as possible from ordinary blacks, other professionals threw themselves into social activism.[30]

The most notable member of the latter group was Robert A. Pelham, Jr., who started writing for the *Detroit Post* while still in grade school and later became an independent distributor of the newspaper. In 1883 the twenty-four-year-old Pelham, his brother Benjamin, and three others established the *Plaindealer,* the city's first black paper. Among its many causes the *Plaindealer* advocated the use of the term "Afro-American," hoping that blacks would eventually become recognized as just another of the city's many hyphenated ethnic groups. "The word 'Negro' as commonly used in America and as scientifically applied means everything low and degraded," the paper explained.[31]

Before it folded in 1894, a victim of a national depression, the *Plaindealer* had achieved a circulation of 2,500 and a reputation for incisive, if often ironic, coverage of racial matters. One such example was in 1891, when Mayor Hazen Pingree made several municipal appointments. "Mayor Pingree sent in ten new appointments to the council last Tuesday evening," the *Plaindealer* reported. "All of them good men and all of them confirmed. The only good man the Mayor has found among the Afro-Americans was given the position of chimney sweep. Long live Mayor Pingree!"[32]

Pelham—who, like several other local blacks, also was very active in Republican politics—left Detroit in 1900 for a federal position as a census clerk in Washington, D.C. There he earned a degree from Howard University and carved out an impressive career as an inventor, demographer, and publisher. Thus Detroit's leading black advocate missed the social tremors of the new century as the city breathed its first whiffs of gasoline.[33]

It's easy to imagine that Detroit was somehow predestined to become the automobile capitol of the world, but in the early years of the twentieth century Buffalo, Cleveland, or Indianapolis could just as easily have become the Motor City. What ultimately turned the "automobile game" in Detroit's favor were the presence of certain industries, such as the manufacturing of railroad cars and marine gasoline engines, which could be easily adapted to car production; fortuitous shipping lanes on the Great Lakes; large numbers of skilled tradesmen; and ready capital in the pockets of a few idle gentlemen—sons of lumber and real estate tycoons—who saw fun, adventure, and riches as dividends for investing in a visionary mechanic or two.

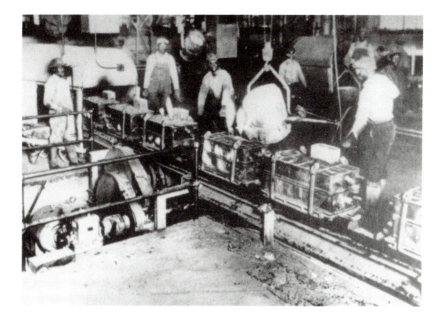

▲ During the First World War, a manpower shortage brought tens of thousands of southern blacks to Detroit's factories. As always, like these Ford foundry workers, they found themselves in the dirtiest and most dangerous departments.

Avenue, near the Belle Isle bridge, in 1899 by Ransom E. Olds. Here vehicles were slowly, expertly handcrafted on sawhorses and sold to the wealthy for $2,382 apiece—or roughly what the average workingman made in four years. By 1915, however, Henry Ford's moving assembly line, five-dollar day, and cheap but reliable Model T had revolutionized the industry and permanently changed the face of Detroit. As the city's reputation for high-wage, low-skill jobs spread rapidly throughout the country and abroad, hundreds of thousands of people poured in. Between 1910 and 1920, whatever small-town characteristics Detroit may have retained from Robert Pelham's day were obliterated by cement and exhaust, as the population doubled to just under one million and the city expanded by leaps and bounds. Three of every four citizens were either immigrants or their children. Most of these families owed their livelihood to one of the countless soot-stained factories cranking out a particular four-wheeled version of the American dream: Ford, Dodge Brothers, Graham-Paige, Hudson, Packard, Essex, Hupmobile, Chevrolet, Detroit Electric, Cadillac, Saxon, Liberty, Maxwell-Briscoe, and Scripps-Booth, to mention just a few. As the country entered the First World War, about 140,000 factory workers in the city were producing one million cars a year.[34]

Initially, few of them were black. But the situation changed dramatically when the war put many whites in khaki and temporarily turned off the faucet of immigration. All told, 65,000 Detroiters served in the war, a large percentage of them autoworkers. The manpower shortage forced the auto companies, and all of the other northern industries that were making huge profits by producing war-related goods, to reconsider their hiring policies. By 1916, labor agents were spreading the word in small towns throughout the south: "Anybody who wants to go to Detroit"—or Cleveland or Pittsburgh or Chicago—"come and see me."

At first only a few hesitant sharecroppers, tenant farmers, and domestic servants took up the offer. But the trickle turned into an absolute flood when letters and newspapers described the high wages and fairer treatment to be found in northern cities. "Of course everything they say about the North ain't true," one man wrote his family, "but there's so much of it true don't mind the other." A Mississippian wrote home: "I should have been here 20 years ago. I just begin to feel like a man." Countless blacks sold their meager belongings for a train ticket north. "Farewell," said one sign chalked on the side of a railroad car. "We're Good and Gone." The phenomenon that came to be known as the Great Migration wasn't peculiar to Detroit; cities throughout the north continued to be swamped with newcomers from Mississippi, Kentucky, Alabama, Georgia, Louisiana, the Carolinas, and other points south. In Philadelphia, for example, the black population grew from 84,000 in 1910 to 134,000 in 1920. In Chicago, the same period saw a gain from 44,000 to 109,000. But nowhere was the percentage of increase more dramatic than in the Motor City, where the black community experienced a sevenfold growth, from less than 6,000 in 1910 to more than 41,000 a decade later.[35]

Industrial wages doubled and tripled the incomes of former sharecroppers, who just a few weeks earlier had been eking out a hardscrabble existence on some dusty Georgia farm. But, unsurprisingly, auto bosses continued to reserve the higher paying skilled trades and semi-skilled jobs for whites. Blacks found themselves in the dirtiest, hottest, and most dangerous departments: the foundry, for instance, where one black was placed after being hired by Graham-Paige. "The furnaces for melting the iron [were] so hot that within five minutes my clothes would stick with dirt and grease," he recalled. Only three or four whites, all Poles, worked alongside the blacks. "Their faces looked exactly like Negro faces. They were so matted and covered with oil and dust that no skin showed."[36]

The one exception to the hiring rule was Henry Ford, whose pater-

▲ As Detroit's black population exploded after the First World War, a housing crisis quickly developed. Most southern immigrants were squeezed into the dilapidated, unsafe structures of the near east side, as this 1919 photograph illustrates.

nalism made him a hero in Black Bottom. As the city's biggest employer and one of the country's wealthiest men, Ford—who believed that "dominance is an obligation"—could afford to indulge his interest in sociological experiments. These included a "Sociological Department" that sought to Americanize workers and their families, and the widely ridiculed "Peace Ship" of goodwill ambassadors that sailed to Europe in 1915 in hopes of ending the war. Ford's solution to the problem of "Negrophobia" (and his own company's manpower shortage) was to hire about ten thousand blacks between 1917 and 1925 at the massive Rouge plant in Dearborn. "The Negro needs a job and this it ought to be the desire of our industrial engineers," he said.[37]

Unlike other auto bosses, Ford hired blacks in all classifications, including the coveted tool-and-die trades, and paid them the same wages as their white counterparts. Ford, a master of public relations, often attended service at black churches and contributed financially to their support. For many men, wearing a Ford work badge on Sunday was a matter of intense personal pride and an enviable social distinction.[38]

Thanks in large part to Ford, half of Detroit's black male workforce was drawing a paycheck from the auto industry in 1920. But a crushing housing problem and increased poverty and misery were the by-products of their relative prosperity. Blacks' wages were watered down by the exorbitant rent they were forced to pay for substandard housing in what had turned into an overcrowded ghetto. The majority of Black Bottom's residents (which through the 1930s still included large numbers of foreign-born Italians, Greeks, Jews, and Poles) went to bed in tiny, windowless row houses and rickety, one-story frame houses, with no guarantee that in the morning a greedy landlord wouldn't inform them that their rent had been raised—again. Many were forced to live in the stables, outhouses, and other wobbly sheds that had been thrown together in the filthy service alleys that criss-crossed the near east side. Others slept on pool tables or inside bathtubs. Despite the already packed quarters, most blacks had no choice but to take on boarders to help make ends meet. One social worker discovered a woman who shared her three-room flat with two *families* of renters. Of course, no one chose to live this way. But white hostility and illegal housing covenants kept blacks from moving into the better neighborhoods.

The press of flesh promoted a high crime rate and regular outbreaks of tuberculosis, pneumonia, and syphilis. But to the rough, peasant-type blacks fleeing the poverty and flagrant racism of the South, sweet optimism outweighed any possible surprises the North might hold. "To die from the bite of frost," the *Chicago Defender* proclaimed, "is far more glorious than at the hands of a mob."[39] Between 1917 and 1919 an estimated 25,000 single black men took that advice and moved to Detroit, all looking for work in what Tennessee farmhand Charles Denby called the land of "milk and honey and pearly gates."[40] By the spring of 1920, remembered John Dancy, nearly one thousand people were arriving weekly in trains from St. Louis and Cincinnati, "not knowing what they would do when they got here, having no direction, not knowing where they would sleep, who they were going to see, or who would be interested in them."[41]

One member of the Great Migration was Oscar Lee, who as a resourceful young man in the spring of 1919 took a passenger train from Birmingham, Alabama, as far north as his money would allow him. That turned out to be Cincinnati. There he sneaked aboard a coal tender and rode that to Toledo, where a railroad detective chased him off. Walking over to a truck stop, Lee overheard a driver talking of a run he was making to the Hudson Car Company in Detroit. Lee crawled under the canvas and rode in the cool darkness for a couple of hours or so, until the truck was standing in traffic in Cadillac Square. As Lee recalled, it was May 15, in the middle of the afternoon, when he finally concluded his three-day exodus to the promised land. He jumped off the truck, peeled off his overalls, and stood there, amidst the honking and commotion of downtown, in his forty-dollar suit. "I wasn't dirty," he said. "I wasn't raggedy. I had 10 cents in my pocket. I was 17 years old. I felt real good."[42]

Chapter Two

THE FATHER OF BLACK BASEBALL

The Detroit Stars and the Negro National League were born in the tumultuous years immediately following the First World War, a period scarred by intense racial violence. In 1919 alone, more than a score of race riots broke out in American cities. In Longview, Texas, whites took over the city, murdering blacks practically at will. Armed veterans chased blacks through the streets of Washington, D.C. The worst rioting occurred in Chicago, where blacks and whites battled each other for days. The strife blew like a terrible, hot wind through the city's embattled south side, past the ballpark of one of the country's great black entrepreneurs, an overweight, middle-aged visionary named Andrew "Rube" Foster.

Foster had been dodging the flames of bigotry for all his forty

◄ Andrew "Rube" Foster, owner and manager of the Chicago American Giants, in about 1918. Gone is the chiseled physique of his younger days, a victim of organized baseball's color bar. "Five or six years ago, I think I'd have been a first-class pitcher," Foster told a reporter. "But I found then I'd gone as far as I could go and that there was no hope of getting into the big league, so I kind of let myself go." (Courtesy of Dick Clark.)

years, but, true to his nature, he was able to see beyond the smoke and the chaos that clouded America's postwar horizon. Born on September 17, 1879, in Calvert, Texas, the asthmatic son of a preacher, he had split his Sundays between church and the ballfield, leaving home and school after the eighth grade to pursue a career in baseball. Headstrong but congenial, the strapping Foster came of age during a time when America had capitulated almost wholly to racism. This meant untold incidents moving down life's segregated highway, but Foster kept his eyes on the prize. From his professional start as a raw seventeen-year-old pitcher for the Fort Worth Yellow Jackets to his acknowledged status today as "one of the five or six most towering figures in the history of American baseball,"[1] Foster's remarkable story was characterized by boundless energy and optimism, and perseverance in the face of great odds.[2]

Although the average baseball fan has never heard of him, Foster's accomplishments were many. In addition to being one of the finest pitchers ever—one whose mound credentials alone would qualify him for anyone's hall of fame—in 1910 he organized one of the truly great early black teams, the Chicago American Giants. By the time of the First World War he was arguably the most successful baseball boss outside of the white major leagues. In trying to emulate the big leagues, Foster created the first enduring association of black teams, the Negro National League, in 1920. Not only was he the league's creator, he was its glue, holding it together with money, savvy, and the sheer force of his personality. The league died when Foster died, but from its limited success came other black leagues, whose players were ready when organized baseball finally became integrated. Without Foster, declares historian John Holway, "there might never have been a [Jackie] Robinson—or a Willie Mays or a Hank Aaron, also products of Foster's league. All baseball, black and white, is in his debt."[3]

Foster could be hard, fearless, and dictatorial, but he was not a hateful or vindictive person. Because of his religious upbringing, he tended to see the best in people, black or white, even after lapses in judgment boomeranged on him. He could be almost effeminate in his camaraderie; his favorite form of endearment was "darling," a term he used even with crusty, world-weary ballplayers. Foster was, however, a practical man. He instinctively knew that the elevation of his race depended on results, not rhetoric. If he could create a black major league that paralleled the success and reputation of the American and National leagues, it not only would provide employment for hundreds, maybe thousands, of his race, it would help disprove the popular characterizations of his people as shiftless, slow-witted, and unable to tend to their own affairs. This concept of self-help contrasted sharply with the eloquent speeches of W. E. B. Du-

Bois, an educator whose Niagara Movement advocated social reform through agitation. In his response to institutional racism, Foster was more akin to Booker T. Washington, the other leading black social scientist of his day, who thought racial harmony depended on accommodation, not confrontation, with white society. Foster, the eighth-grade dropout, was a man of action, not a philosopher. But what he proposed would prove of tremendous benefit to many blacks, especially hundreds of vagabond ballplayers desirous of a regular paycheck.

☆

The roots of baseball's historic racism usually are traced to an incident involving Adrian "Cap" Anson, captain of the National League Chicago White Stockings and the foremost player of his time. One July day in 1887, the White Stockings were preparing to play a game against Newark of the Eastern League when it was drawn to Anson's attention that Newark's star pitcher, George Stovey, was not a dark-faced French-Canadian as he had been reported to be but a light-skinned black. "Get that nigger off the field!" Anson reportedly yelled, threatening a boycott. With the prospect of a handsome gate in jeopardy, Stovey was removed and the game went on as scheduled.

Shortly afterwards, International League owners voted to ban the future signings of black players. While the ruling didn't affect the handful of blacks then playing on four of the league's ten teams, within three years all had been chased out, some by teammates who ostracized them, others by fans who chanted "Kill the nigger" during games. Anson's celebrity endorsement of apartheid gave other circuits in organized baseball the confidence to slam the door as well. After pitcher-outfielder Bert Jones was forced out of the Kansas State League in 1898, almost fifty years would pass before a black would be allowed to play on an integrated club in organized ball.[4]

The history of black-white competition in Detroit is less remarkable. During the 1850s and 1860s, as baseball replaced cricket as the city's favorite field sport, teams were organized around similar occupations or neighborhoods. Printers, clerks, and warehousemen all fielded their own nines. There is no record of a wholly black team in the city during this time, but it seems likely that, with a highly concentrated population of 2,235 blacks on the near east side by 1870, some existed. They would have played among themselves or competed in challenge matches with the various ethnic neighborhood teams.

During the sport's amateur era, the city fielded a variety of athletic clubs that, like all such organizations of socially conscious young men, were restrictive in who they admitted. The first of these—called, naturally enough, the "Detroits"—operated from 1858 through the early 1870s. It was composed of middle-aged citizens, several of them cricket players, who could afford the time and expense of representing the city in "foreign" matches in places like Cleveland and Pittsburgh. The Detroits were members of the National Association of Base Ball Players (NABBP), a New York-based organization of more than one hundred clubs that was trying its best to keep the game on an elitist, gentlemanly plane. And gentlemen didn't play baseball matches against blacks, as the NABBP made clear in turning down the application of a black Philadelphia nine at its 1867 convention. "If colored clubs were admitted there would be in all probability some division of feeling," the nominating committee explained, "whereas, by excluding them no injury could result to anyone." The NABBP then went on to write the game's first specific color line into its constitution.[5]

The NABBP was succeeded by the National Association of Professional Base Ball Players, which in 1871 became the country's first major league. The league employed a "gentleman's agreement" to bar blacks rather than a formal written rule. This unwritten pattern of discrimination was accepted without debate by its successor, the National League, when it began play in 1876.

While the first avowedly professional team surfaced in Cincinnati in 1869, Detroit waited another ten years before some eastern professionals were imported to serve as a "house team" for a brand new sports enterprise called Recreation Park, located near Brady and Brush streets in the heart of what is now the Medical Center. Two years later the city was awarded a franchise in the National League, and professional baseball was off and running in Detroit. The Wolverines, as they were called, won the National League pennant in 1887. That year they also played an exhibition game against the Cuban Giants (actually a group of black New York waiters) without incident. The Wolverines prevailed, 6–4, scoring their winning runs on four errors in the eighth.[6]

The Detroit franchise disbanded in the fall of 1888, but in 1894 a new team, the Creams, started play in Ban Johnson's reorganized Western League. It played for two years at League Park at Lafayette and Helen, then moved to a new facility built at Michigan and Trumbull. By now known as the Detroit Tigers, the team became a charter member of the American League in 1900. Thanks to the lockstep, racist mentality of organized baseball, none of these teams ever fielded a black player, although they played occasional exhibitions against all-black teams. Detroit's Western League team, for instance, played a couple of games against the Page Fence Giants in the fall of 1895—with disastrous results, as we shall soon see.

As the conspiracy to keep blacks out of baseball's mainstream solidified in the 1890s, blacks were forced to organize their own teams and leagues. Several, including the Cuban X-Giants of New York and the Chicago Unions, enjoyed considerable popularity and press coverage, particularly since most of their games pitted them against local white nines. The leagues, however, were held together with little more than spit and baling wire. Typically, a black league would debut with great fanfare and dissolve several weeks later, unloved and underfinanced.[7] Black teams remained dependent on white promoters to book their games. Many of these booking agents were unscrupulous, making off with the gate receipts or otherwise cheating blacks. To be a black ballplayer was to be eternally criss-crossing the country, moving from opportunity to circumstance.

One of the most successful of the early black teams was the Page Fence Giants of Adrian, Michigan, a community about fifty miles southwest of Detroit. The Giants were organized in September 1894. While corporate sponsors provided the money, George "Bud" Fowler, a forty-seven-year-old barber who had spent most of the last twenty-two years pitching and playing second base for a succession of eastern and midwestern teams, provided the inspiration.

Fowler's experiences prior to coming to Adrian were typical of the seventy or so blacks who played in nineteenth-century organized baseball before the door slammed shut. He was born in 1858 in upstate New York and grew up in Cooperstown. He first raised eyebrows in 1878, when he beat Boston of the National League, 2–1, in an exhibition game. He went on to pitch that summer in the International Association, the first minor league. Between 1879 and 1882 he played for several semipro and independent teams, finally catching on with the Stillwater, Minnesota, club in the Northwestern League. The following year *Sporting Life* described Fowler as "one of the best general players in the country, and if he had a white face he would be playing with the best of them. . . ."[8]

Instead, prejudice forced him to move from team to team, a total of fourteen, in nine different leagues, over a single seven-year span. The most eventful stop was Binghamton in the International League, where Fowler found himself purposely muffing throws to avoid the flashing spikes of sliding whites. Remembered one player: "I could not help pitying some of the poor black fellows. . . . Fowler used to play second base with the lower part of his legs encased in wooden guards. He knew that about every player that came down to second base on a steal had it in for

▲ In the late 1890s, the Page Fence Giants of Adrian, Michigan, were one of the most successful teams—black or white—in the country. Second from left in this 1897 team photo is second baseman Charlie Grant, who in 1902 nearly made it into the major leagues as "Charlie Tokohama." To sidestep local Jim Crow ordinances, the team traveled in a custom Pullman coach with the name of their sponsor emblazoned across it. (Courtesy of the Bentley Historical Library, University of Michigan.)

him."[9] In June 1887, Fowler was cut loose by Binghamton after his white teammates refused to take the field with him.

It had always been the peripatetic Fowler's ambition to organize his own ball club—to guarantee his employment, if nothing else. In the summer of 1894, by now playing for a team in Findlay, Ohio, he enlisted the aid of a pair of white businessmen, L. W. Hoch and Rolla Taylor, in finding sponsorship. The trio entered into a surprisingly favorable formal agreement with the Page Fence Company of Adrian and an unidentified Massachusetts bicycle manufacturer. Page Fence, creators of "the barbed wire that changed the West," was the major investor. The two companies agreed to bankroll the enterprise for purely promotional purposes. All profits and full operational control remained with the club, which began its first full season of play the following April.

Assisted by a full-time business manager, Augustus S. Parsons, the Giants traveled throughout the Midwest in a specially outfitted railroad car emblazoned with the principal sponsor's name. Page Fence agents often accompanied the team, serving up sales pitches and writing orders in the cities along the route. Besides serving as a mobile advertisement for the company's products, the handsome brown railroad car allowed the company to neatly sidestep local Jim Crow practices by giving the players—who were each paid about one hundred dollars a month—a place to eat and sleep. To help make life more comfortable on the road, a porter and a cook also accompanied the team.

The Giants lacked affiliation with any organized league, making them a permanent road team. They played about 140 games a season in cities and villages throughout southern Michigan, northern Ohio, and northern Indiana, drawing crowds that ranged in size between 800 and 7,100 people. According to Tom Powers, the average game attendance was about 1,500—a healthy figure.

Most matches were with white semipro teams representing the local community, and they presented little trouble, at least in terms of the score. Even the extras occasionally got into the act—the cook once belting out five hits against the Romeo, Michigan, team. However, the Giants often were victims of prejudice, both subtle and blatant. Newspapers regularly referred to the Giants' "watermelon battery" of pitcher George Wilson and catcher Vasco Graham, while umpires were "invariably home players, and hate[d] to see a colored team beat a white one," observed Rolla Taylor.

As part of the bargain, the Giants were expected to blend showmanship with craftsmanship. They would bicycle down Main Street before every game (giving their Massachusetts-based sponsor something for its money) and ham it up for the locals on the field, a minstrel show in flan-

▲ Between 1894 and 1898 the Page Fence Giants barnstormed throughout the countryside, taking on all comers. Here the Giants are playing an unnamed midwestern opponent sometime around 1897. Because of organized baseball's unofficial color bar, black teams remained unaffiliated to any league and thus depended on barnstorming to make a living. (Courtesy of Dick Clark.)

nels. Grant "Home Run" Johnson, a young shortstop from Findlay, Ohio, once cartwheeled around the bases after hitting a ball into the stands. Pitcher Billy Holland, who loved playing to the grandstand, was described as "funnier than an end man in a minstrel show."[10]

Despite the clowning, the Page Fence Giants were a force to be reckoned with. In 1895 they compiled a 118–36 record, twice losing to the National League Cincinnati Reds before finishing the season on October 9–10 in Detroit against a congregation of Western League players. Several Detroit players chose to skip these final games, but there was little doubt among the white professionals as to which team would come out on top.

The first game was played on a cold afternoon at League Park, which kept the crowd—and the witnesses—to a minimum. The Giants' first baseman, George Taylor, set the tone of the game in the bottom of the first inning when he drove the first pitch served for a home run. Reported the next day's *Detroit News:* "Some of the Detroit professionals did not show up on account of the cold weather, but judging from the way the Giants went after the leaguers from start to finish it is doubtful if the result would have been changed had the regular lineup participated. Some Detroiters present expressed belief that the Giants 'are the best team in Michigan.'"[11] The Giants won that game, 18 to 3. The Detroiters came back the following day with a lineup fortified by five National Leaguers. The Page Fence Giants buried them, 15 to 0.[12]

However, as countless other teams have learned, winning alone does not guarantee survival. Although they posted a record of at least 125–12 by the end of the 1897 season, including an 82-game winning streak, the Giants were starting to fail at the gate. Bad weather was partially to blame, but hard economic times and the fading novelty of watching the Giants play also bit into attendance. Newspaper accounts of the team's activities rapidly dwindled over the following year. The Page Fence Giants finally disbanded sometime in 1899, derailed by a depressed economy and their own success.[13]

The players scattered around the map, with some, like Home Run Johnson and George Wilson, graduating to such top-flight black teams as the Philadelphia Cuban X-Giants and the Leland Giants. Bud Fowler surrendered to stereotypical expectations, forming the All-American Black Tourists, who showed up for games in dress suits, opera hats, and silk umbrellas.[14] But the most intriguing post-Page Fence career was that of Charlie Grant, a light-skinned second baseman who in 1902 just missed becoming the first twentieth-century black in the major leagues.

Grant, the son of a Cincinnati horse trainer, left Adrian for Chicago, where he helped solidify the infield of the Columbia Giants. Like most black players, he spent the winter months working as a waiter, baggage handler, or bellhop. In early 1902 he was employed at the Eastland Hotel in Hot Springs, Arkansas, where John McGraw's American League Baltimore Orioles were staying during spring training. McGraw, unlike many of his managerial counterparts, would have readily fielded blacks if he could. Observing the talented young bellhop at play one day, McGraw schemed to get him on Baltimore's roster.

"Charlie," he told Grant, "I've been trying to think of some way to sign you for the Baltimore club and I think I've got it. On this map there's a creek called Tokohama. That's going to be your name from now on, Charlie Tokohama, and you're a full-blooded Cherokee."

Sporting Life breathlessly described Charlie Tokohama as "a phenomenal fielder" who was "between 21 and 23 years of age." Charles Comiskey, owner of the Chicago White Sox, wasn't fooled. He noticed the black fans cheering a bit *too* enthusiastically for Tokohama during spring training games. If McGraw "really keeps this Indian," declared Comiskey, he would install "a Chinaman" at third base. Neither happened. Grant was found out and cut from the team, and thus organized baseball remained free of blacks.[15]

☆

At the same time that the Page Fence Giants were rolling through the Michigan countryside in their customized coach, Andrew Foster was hopping freights and choking back dust in Texas, looking for opportunities to showcase his gifted right arm. In 1897 Foster signed with the Fort Worth Yellow Jackets, where the husky and cocky six-footer quickly became their ace pitcher. By 1901 he was playing in Hot Springs, Arkansas. At twenty-one, he had already been pitching batting practice to major leaguers in spring training for four years.

That year Foster headed north with Frank Leland, owner of the black Leland Giants. Offered forty dollars a month by the Philadelphia-based Cuban Giants, Foster eagerly jumped ship in 1902. He did so again in 1903, this time to the crosstown Cuban X-Giants. Around this time Foster earned his nickname by besting the American League star, George "Rube" Waddell, in an exhibition match in Philadelphia. He also pitched the X-Giants to a five-games-to-two playoff victory over the Cuban Giants in the "Colored Championship of the World," black baseball's first world series. Foster won four of the games and batted cleanup.

The Cuban Giants improved their chances the following year when the club induced Foster and practically the entire X-Giants roster to jump clubs. Once again, Foster starred in the post-season competition, leaving his sickbed to pitch the Giants to a playoff win over his old team.

In 1906 the Cuban Giants, who competed in Philadelphia's otherwise all-white city league, left town practically en masse after Foster quit in a salary dispute. Foster and seven of his teammates moved to Chicago to play for the Leland Giants. The transplanted Philadelphians claimed the city semipro championship. They ended the season with a four-game sweep of the City All-Stars, who featured several major leaguers playing under assumed names. Foster pitched and won all four games.

Chicago's city league was developing into the most ambitious and strongest in the country—an irony, given that Chicago was also evolving into the most segregated city in the country. All-white and all-black semipro teams competed in the league, and some teams featured integrated lineups. Foster quickly came to dominate this league, first as pitcher and manager, then as owner and promoter.

▲ The powerful Philadelphia Giants of 1906 featured several outstanding players from the early years of black baseball, including pitcher and clean-up hitter Rube Foster (standing second from right) and Charlie Grant (standing, center). That year the team moved almost en masse to Chicago to form the heart of the Leland Giants.

As Foster led the Leland Giants to another pennant in 1907, a Chicago paper called him "the greatest baseball pitcher in the country; that's what the greatest baseball players of white persuasion who have gone against him say."[16] That year Leland won 110 games and lost but ten. The following spring it became the first black team to train in the South.

Over the winter of 1909–10, Foster and John Schorling, Charles Comiskey's son-in-law, won a legal battle with Frank Leland over ownership of the Giants. Foster renamed the team the Chicago American Giants and acquired the White Sox's old park at 39th and Shields for a home field. For fifty cents, fans could get a box seat and free ice water and watch perhaps the finest black team ever assembled do their thing.

That "thing" was to win—123 times in 129 outings that first season. It wasn't unusual for crowds of 20,000 people to gather on a Sunday morning to watch the American Giants battle white semipro teams like the Gunthers and the Logan Squares, which had big leaguers such as the Cubs' Johnny Kling catching or Joe Tinker playing shortstop—under assumed names, of course. Heavyweight champ Jack Johnson might even show up to hand out souvenirs. On one Sunday in 1911, Foster's Giants outdrew the city's two major league clubs.

The Chicago American Giants' fame spread far and wide. They traveled to California one winter, barnstormed through the South, and spent some off-seasons in Cuba, long a popular destination for migratory ballplayers. They always went first-class. Dave Malarcher remembered his first glimpse of the team, in 1915 in Louisiana, with awe. "I never saw such a well-equipped ball club in my whole life!" Malarcher, who later replaced Foster as field manager, told John Holway: "I was astounded. Every day they came out in a different set of beautiful uniforms, all kinds of bats and balls, all the best kinds of equipment.

"The American Giants traveled everywhere, as you know," continued Malarcher. "No other team traveled as many miles as the American Giants. When Rube gave them the name American Giants, he really selected a name. That was a good idea, because it became the greatest ball club that ever was. That's right; the way he played, the way he equipped his team, the way he paid his men, the way he treated his men, the miles that they traveled."[17]

Sometime about 1916 or so, Foster surrendered his regular mound duties to younger pitchers. He was still an effective hurler, but he was growing old and gaining weight. He continued to direct action from the bench; in fact, he was as respected for his managerial skills as he was for his pitching ability. Foster knew the game inside and out, which made him an unquestioned field tactician and an effective disciplinarian. Under his tutelage, Malarcher, Pete Hill, Bruce Petway, and Oscar Charleston all turned into successful Negro-league skippers.[18]

Of course, Foster's Chicago club wasn't the only notable black team of the era. The years surrounding the First World War saw the emergence of a number of strong clubs, including the Indianapolis ABCs, the Lincoln Giants and Lincoln Stars (both based in New York), St. Louis Giants, Brooklyn Royal Giants, and Bacharach Giants. A very competitive squad represented the army's 25th Infantry Unit in Huachuca, Arizona, including several players who would one day form the nucleus of the Kansas City Monarchs. There were many more, though none more interesting than the All-Nations team.

This multicultural team was the brainstorm of J. Leslie Wilkinson, a white Kansas City businessman. In 1912 he and a partner organized a squad of blacks, whites, Indians, Cubans, Asians, and Mexicans. The lineup even included a woman, advertised as "Carrie Nation" (after the famous hatchet-wielding temperance leader), who played second base. Sponsored by a succession of white merchants, they barnstormed across several midwestern states in a specially designed Pullman coach. Traveling along were an orchestra and a wrestling team, which made the All-Nations' arrival in a community an event not likely to be soon forgotten

▲ The arrival of a black professional team to play the home nine usually was cause for great excitement. Here the Peterson Union Giants of Chicago pose before doing battle with Milwaukee's Kosciusko team sometime around 1910. As always, racial sensibilities required the taking of separate team photographs. (Courtesy of the Golda Meir Library, University of Wisconsin.)

BASE BALL!!

FEDERAL LEAGUE PARK
SEPTEMBER 24-5-6
ORIGINAL A. B. C.'s
VS.
WORLD'S ALL NATIONS

Heralding the First Appearance of The World's All Nations
The Great Donaldson will Positively Pitch 1 of These Games

Composed of Hawaiians, Japanese, Cubans, Filipinos, Indians, Chinese, direct from their native countries

JOHN DONALDSON
The Greatest Colored Pitcher in the World. Donaldson pitched 65 games last season, winning 60 of them.

JOSE MENDEZ
The Crack Cuban Pitcher, who defeated the Detroit Tigers, "American League Champions," 1-0, 10 innings, fanning Ty Cobb and Sam Crawford.

BLUKOI---The Giant Hawaiian, considered by critics to be the best 2nd baseman outside of Organized Base Ball.

PRIETO---The Sensational Cuban Pitcher, who won every game he pitched at Havana, Cuba, in 1915.

Traveling in Their Own Private Hotel Car
WILKINSON & GAUL, Sole Owners

by the local citizens. Games were followed by a dance and wrestling matches, after which the novelty act gathered up its portable bleachers, canvas awnings, and fences, and hit the tracks for the next small town. The All-Nations played ball as well as they entertained, defeating the Chicago American Giants on at least two occasions. When the All-Nations broke up in 1918, Foster snatched some of the best players—including Jose Mendez, Christobal Torriente, and John Donaldson—for his own team.[19]

For all their demonstrated skills on the diamond, most of the era's black teams lacked the business acumen to avoid being repeatedly exploited by the network of white owners and promoters who controlled the playing fields and arranged the games. "The colored people practically know nothing of baseball and the theories upon which it is based," said sportswriter and former player Dave Wyatt in 1917. "He [sic] knows less of the business side."[20] Wyatt's complaint didn't extend to the Chicago American Giants, however, who were universally recognized as the epitome of a successfully run black team.

Sometime over the winter of 1918–19, Rube Foster decided to expand operations beyond his home base. Since 1910, Chicago's black population had increased by 65,000, accounting for much of Foster's success, and he correctly foresaw similar opportunities in the country's other emerging ghettos. With his connections, reputation, and money, he judged himself the best man to unite the growing but disparate number of independent black teams into one grand association. Ideally, the success of such a venture would make his fortune, of course, but it would also pave the way for blacks to eventually gain their rightful place alongside white major leaguers. In early 1919, Foster installed a satellite operation in Detroit.

☆

Detroit was a logical choice. It was a favorite stop of Foster's American Giants, which regularly played semipro teams in and around the city. Separated by a half-day's train ride, the growing, heavily industrialized metropolises had much in common, not the least of which was a mushrooming black community with a demonstrated passion for baseball.

Foster installed John T. "Tenny" Blount as a baseball promoter in Detroit. Little is known of Blount, who has been referred to in some

◀ A 1916 barnstorming poster heralds the upcoming clash of two of the country's strongest black nines: the Indianapolis ABC's and the All-Nations.

circles as the city's "numbers king." That's not entirely correct, because during the 1920s the acknowledged bosses of what some called "nigger pool" were a character named "Rooster" Hammond, who ran the floating Alabama-Georgia house; John Roxborough, who would co-manage heavyweight champion Joe Louis in the 1930s; and his sometimes-partner, Everitt Watson, whose real estate office at 1905 St. Antoine was really a front for a smorgasbord of illegal activities.[21]

Numbers preceded the Detroit Stars by several years as a widely followed, black-controlled pastime. It was a simple, inexpensive game to play, which accounted for its popularity among the urban poor. A bettor put down money—usually a penny or a nickel, although "shooters" would gamble a quarter or more—on a specific three-digit number. The winning numbers were typically determined by the pari-mutuel figures of the winning prices paid in various horse races. At odds of 600 to 1, even a winning penny bet paid off six dollars, which represented a couple of days' wages for most blacks. Since bettors faced odds of 999 to 1, the difference gave the bankers their profits. The numbers' close cousin was called "policy," another daily lottery whose winning numbers were drawn from a lottery wheel. Operators supplemented their income by selling dream books, dope sheets, and other gambling aids.

Individually, the books and daily bets amounted to no more than streetcar fare for the players; collectively, however, they could add up to several thousand dollars a week for the bosses. Even allowing for the customary overhead—paying off winners and the police—numbers and policy operators could pull in a tidy profit. Some ranked with funeral home owners as the most affluent members of the black community. Outside of the pulpit, few people disapproved of anyone being an operator or a player. In black neighborhoods across the land, numbers racketeers represented a rare example of success and, more important, a source of liquid capital. The history of the Negro leagues, particularly in Detroit, is filled with such men.

From what can be pieced together about Tenny Blount from this distance, it appears that around the time Foster chose him to promote black baseball in Detroit, he was a man in his thirties with an unremarkable past. Using listings in the city directory and some fuzzy recollections, it can be conjectured that Blount had worked as a waiter just prior to Foster setting him up in business. Perhaps he had also worked as a writer or pickup man, writing or collecting wagers and delivering the money to the policy "bank," then graduated to running his own small numbers racket. Although published reports usually referred to Blount as the Stars' owner, he was in essence their business manager, scheduling and promoting games, arranging transportation, and taking care of all the other odds and ends inherent in running a business. The extent of Blount's capitalization in the team is unknown, but was probably no more than a token investment.

Policy banks took big losses on occasion, so bettors needed to trust racket men not to "swing with the kitty" instead of paying off. In this regard, Blount came across as someone who was as good as his word. He "was one of the squarest men," recalled one of his players. "I never worked for anyone better. If you worked, you got paid. Nothing but the best."[22] His greatest asset may have been his very light skin, which allowed him to "pass" in white society. This was an important consideration in turn-of-the-century America, whether one was a black waiter hoping to work in a downtown white hotel or a black promoter looking to arrange a game with the owner of a white baseball team. Black newspapers of the day were filled with advertisements for Nadinola Face Powder, Dr. Fred Palmer's Skin Whitener, and other makes of bleaching cream.

In 1919 Blount was living on Gratiot Avenue near Rivard, a couple of blocks south of the haberdashery of John A. Roesink. A thirty-eight-year-old Dutch Jew who had arrived in Detroit from Grand Rapids in 1900, Roesink had already established himself as one of the foremost promoters of athletics in the city. On several occasions Roesink brought the Boston Braves, New York Giants, Philadelphia Phillies, and Brooklyn Dodgers to Detroit to play his S & S team, which won the state semipro championship fourteen times in fifteen years. In 1920 he would be responsible for introducing professional football to the city, his Heralds team lasting two seasons before folding. He also was a friend of Detroit Tigers owner Frank Navin. In 1914, when the Federal League was looking to install a baseball team in Detroit, Roesink won Navin's gratitude by refusing to rent or sell Mack Park, the east side park that he owned. Roesink's fanciful signs (which, as a former display and advertising manager, he designed himself) could be seen around Navin Field and throughout the central business district.[23] Like all Hastings Street merchants, Roesink had daily contact with blacks. "Oh, John Roesink was a household word in the black community," recalled one Black Bottom resident.[24] Thanks to the Detroit Stars, whom he would one day own, he was destined to become even better known.

The Stars' playing site for the next decade would be Mack Park, located at Mack and Fairview avenues in the middle of a white, working-class neighborhood about four miles east of downtown. Many of the families in the area were of German stock, the fathers and sons working at Stroh's and the several other Gratiot-area breweries that, with the onset of prohibition, were now engaged in making such products as ice cream and near-beer.

▲ Rube Foster's Chicago American Giants were the most successfully run black team of the early twentieth century. Foster stocked the
Detroit Stars with several of his Chicago players, including outfielder
Jimmie Lyons (bottom row, second from left) and pitcher Bill Holland
(bottom row, extreme right). Also pictured is Oscar Charleston (back
row, second from right) a gifted center fielder that was often referred
to as the "black Ty Cobb." (Courtesy of the National Baseball Library, Cooperstown, New York.)

Mack Park, built in 1914, was a shaky, single-decked, wooden struc-
ture typical of the pre-war era. Its bleachers and theater-style seats could
accommodate perhaps 6,000 people. Overflows could be placed in roped-
off areas of the outfield and along the foul lines, giving the park a maxi-
mum capacity of perhaps 9,000. The inviting outfield fences added to the
coziness; right field, for instance, was but 325 feet away from home plate.
Under the right-field stands were clubhouses and living quarters for the
caretaker and his family. On game days the narrow streets surrounding
the park were congested with traffic; like everywhere else in the city that
put the world on wheels, parking space was at a premium. The park was
home for many sandlot baseball, football, and soccer teams. Southeastern High School, which opened in 1917, was close by. For the next sev-

eral decades, until the park was torn down in the urban renewal frenzy of the 1960s, Southeastern would use the grounds for most of its athletic activities.[25]

Blount and Roesink came to a lease agreement. In exchange for an unspecified rent (traditionally a share of the gate receipts in the range of 15 to 25 percent), the Stars were allowed to use the park whenever they wished. Hayes Wheel, Detroit Creamery, Murray Manufacturing, and other top-flight industrial teams scheduled games against the new kids on the block.

Foster stocked the Stars with players whose contracts he, not Blount, held. This was an important technicality. From the beginning Foster felt that if his dream league was to succeed, he needed the freedom to unilaterally shift players to and from franchises in an attempt to balance competition. Foster also operated a team in Dayton, Ohio, under similar arrangements. While John Matthews was technically the owner of the Dayton Marcos, he, like Blount, was little more than a figurehead. Foster owned both clubs, possibly right down to the bats and the balls.

The Stars were nattily dressed in white uniforms with navy blue pinstripes and navy trim. Roesink, who as a men's clothier provided uniforms for the several sandlot teams he sponsored, and who is remembered by relatives as being a talented artist, may have designed as well as manufactured the uniforms. "DETROIT" was spelled out in red letters across the front of the blouse, except for the "R," which was white and stood out on the navy blue placard. A large red star was sewn over the left breast.[26] As was the custom then, there was no identifying number on the back of the blouse. Instead, starting lineups and substitutions (along with scoring decisions and other pertinent ballpark information) were announced by a man with a megaphone. Some of the players were already familiar to the fans, having previously appeared in Detroit as barnstormers. As was the case at Navin Field across town, fans in even the most distant seats learned to pick out favorites by their size, throwing motion, batting stance, or other mannerisms.

The lineup for the inaugural edition of the Detroit Stars included some of the best known names from the early days of black baseball. The field manager was J. Preston "Pete" Hill, considered by many to be the first great black outfielder. Hill was nearly thirty-nine years old in 1919, but still highly regarded for his physical skills and tactical ability. He had started with the top-flight Philadelphia Giants in 1904, joining Rube Foster in Chicago two years later. He had played left field for the Chicago American Giants since the team's formation in 1910, serving as captain and helping to run the team on the field. Cumberland "Cum" Posey, who owned the Homestead Grays, described Hill as "the most consistent hitter of his time," someone who hit equally well against righthanders and southpaws. "He was the backbone, year in and year out, of great ball-clubs," said Posey.[27]

Jose Mendez, a thirty-year-old native of Havana, was a gifted right-handed pitcher who once came within one out of no-hitting the Cincinnati Reds in an exhibition game in Cuba. Blending a quality curveball with a smoking fastball, Mendez hurled twenty-five straight scoreless innings against the Reds in the eleven-game series, of which Cincinnati won only four. Unfortunately for Mendez, he didn't have a similar success against the Detroit Tigers during their two tours, losing four of five decisions.[28] After his arm went dead in 1915, Mendez joined the All-Nations team as a shortstop and manager, moving on to Chicago in 1918. Mendez's all-around talent once made New York Giants manager John McGraw say he'd give $50,000 for Mendez—if only he was white.

Mendez was complemented by southpaw John Donaldson, a tall, slender Missouri native who had previously starred on the All-Nations club with Mendez. Utilizing a whiplash curve, he was a strikeout artist who had once pitched three straight no-hitters. Donaldson's hitting ability made him a regular outfielder on days when he wasn't pitching.

Joining Mendez and Donaldson was a thirty-one-year-old righthander named Frank Wickware. Born in Coffeyville, Kansas, in 1888, Wickware broke into the Negro leagues with the Leland Giants in 1910. Three years later he was matching fastballs with the great Walter Johnson, beating the legendary Washington speedballer in two of three exhibitions. In a sense, Wickware was "exiled" to Detroit, since his fondness for drinking exasperated Rube Foster, as it did the managers of the several other ball clubs he played for during his stellar career. But Pete Hill thought enough of him to start him most games in 1919, forcing Mendez to shortstop and Donaldson to the outfield.

Catching this trio of aces was Bruce Petway, a thirty-six-year-old backstop and native of Nashville, Tennessee. Petway dropped out of medical college to concentrate on baseball. Starting with the Leland Giants and Brooklyn Royal Giants in 1906, he moved on to Philadelphia and then Chicago. Like Pete Hill, Petway was an original member of Foster's American Giants in 1910. During his nine seasons with Foster he perfected the technique of throwing the ball to second from his haunches.

Probably no white person in Detroit, outside of the Tigers' clubhouse, knew of Petway's major claim to fame. During the Tigers' exhibition series in Cuba in 1910, the catcher had twice gunned down the great Ty Cobb trying to steal second base. Under normal circumstances, getting thrown out attempting to steal is no embarrassment; in 1915 alone,

▲ The inaugural edition of the Detroit Stars line up inside Mack Park in 1919. From left: unknown, unknown, Frank Warfield, unknown, Pete Hill, Jose Mendez, Tenny Blount, Frank Wickware, Jose Rodriquez, unknown, Bruce Petway, John Donaldson, and Sam Crawford.

Cobb would get nailed a record thirty-eight times in American League play. But being thrown out by one's social inferior, as Cobb saw the matter, was humiliating. According to legend, the Tiger star was so upset he swore never to play against blacks again—a vow he kept.[29]

Because of the lack of surviving black newspapers, exactly what the citizens of Black Bottom thought of Detroit's first professional black baseball team has been lost to time, although it's safe to assume the Stars inspired considerable pride in a community unaccustomed to cheering for any pro team other than the all-alabaster Tigers. The Stars certainly didn't excite the local dailies, which offered little more than occasional line scores of the Stars' contests. The first published mention of the Stars showed the Detroiters defeating Maxwell's, a white semipro team, by a score of 8 to 4 on April 19, 1919. For the entire season, the fragmentary record has the Stars winning four of seven games against black teams and five of six from white semipro squads, including a fifteen-strikeout, shutout performance by Wickware.

Without a league schedule to hinder their movements, the Stars barnstormed freely, even entering the Michigan Semi-Pro Tournament that Roesink's S & S team had long dominated. It's not known if Roesink sponsored the Stars in this annual, single-elimination competition, which attracted many of Michigan's top nines. According to an advertisement placed in a tournament guidebook, the Stars entered and won the tournament each year through 1923. There are no attendance figures for any of the Stars' contests, but the club obviously met Foster's expectations in what amounted to a trial run for the Negro National League.

While Foster's personal hopes soared during the summer of 1919, America's race relations plummeted to an all-time bloody low. That year race riots erupted like so many brush fires in Knoxville, Tulsa, Philadelphia, Washington, and more than a score of other cities across the map. The genesis was the increased friction between blacks and whites in transitional neighborhoods and the fierce competition for the limited number of postwar jobs. An air of hostility and xenophobia prevailed during this "Red Summer." Suspected Bolsheviks were rounded up and deported without due process, while labor organizers were ostracized as radicals. Native-born Americans agitated for an end to unlimited immigration from eastern and southern Europe, a wish that would soon be fulfilled. Labor unrest resulted in more than four million workers going on strike. When workers walked out of several auto plants in Detroit, the Urban League's Employment Bureau provided employers with black strikebreakers. This created white-on-black violence outside several factories. At least one black strikebreaker was killed.[30]

The "Negro problem" swallowed up even returning veterans. Some 360,000 blacks had served in the U.S. armed forces during the war, including Lieutenant Charles S. Smith, Jr., the son of Bishop Charles S. Smith of the African Methodist Episcopal Church in Detroit. While overseas, their eyes had been opened to America's hypocrisy, said Bishop Smith in a letter to the National Negro Press Association in early 1919. "Far better that our sons should die and be buried in France, the glorious land of 'Liberty, Equality and Fraternity,' than to return to find America unsafe for them, though they have made the world safe for democracy," he wrote.[31] In the first twelve months after the war, more than seventy blacks were lynched across the country, including several veterans in their uniforms.[32]

Chicago experienced a slaughter that surpassed any within its many meat packing plants. On a hot Sunday afternoon in July, a black youth swam into the segregated waters of Lake Michigan, was hit by a rock thrown by an angry white, and was drowned. This touched off an orgy of shooting, looting, bombings, and arson on the south side by

◄ Foster created the Detroit Stars against a backdrop of intense racial violence, most of it caused by overcrowding in growing urban centers and competition for the limited number of postwar jobs. In 1919 alone, race riots erupted in more than a score of U.S. cities. In this series of photographs, a white mob chases down a black man during that summer's riot in Chicago and stones him to death in his own back yard.

members of an Irish athletic club called Ragen's Colts. Black veterans brought their service revolvers out of the closet and fought back, over-turning streetcars and destroying white property. James T. Farrell cap-tured the mindlessness of the moment through the experiences of his character, a young punk named Studs Lonigan.

> Studs Lonigan gripped a baseball bat, and swung as if stepping into a pitch. He said that when he cracked a dinge in the head, the god-damn eight ball would think it had been Ty Cobb slamming out a homer off Walter Johnson. Red Kelly unsheathed a hunting-knife, and vowed that he was ready. Andy Le Gare tried to tell everyone that in close fighting they should kick the niggers in the shins. Tommy Doyle said the niggers were never going to forget the month of July, 1919. Studs said that they ought to hang every nigger in the city to the telephone poles, and let them swing there in the breeze. Benny Taite said that for every white man killed in the riots, ten black apes ought to be massacred. Red said that the niggers had caught Clackey Merton, from Sixty-first Street, down in the black belt, and slashed his throat from ear to ear. . . .
>
> Young Horn Buckford suddenly appeared and breathlessly said that there was a gang of niggers over on Wabash Avenue. Studs, Red, Tommy, Weary, Kenny, and Benny Taite led the gang along Fifty-eighth Street, over to Wabash. For two hours, they prowled Wa-bash Avenue and State Street . . . searching for niggers. They sang, shouted, yelled defiance at the houses, and threw bricks into the windows of houses where they thought niggers lived. They were joined by other groups, men and kids. The streets were like avenues of the dead. They only caught a ten-year-old Negro boy. They took his clothes off, and burned them. They burned his tail with lighted matches, urinated on him, and sent him running off naked with a couple of slaps in the face.[33]

That ten-year-old boy had the virtue of being fictional. In reality, thirty-eight people were killed and another five hundred injured. Most of the victims were black. The Chicago riot was one of twenty-five that erupted that year across the United States. Detroit, which had experi-enced a six-fold increase in its black population during the decade—the highest in the nation—was not one of them. In fact, Foster and his club were in Detroit when the riot broke out. When they returned home on August 3, they discovered the tents and stacked rifles of the Illinois National Guard on their ballfield.[34]

What effect, if any, the tumult swirling around his home base had on Foster's plans is unknown. Certainly the prospect of violent social change hadn't discouraged him; the surprising militancy of the Chicago blacks who had fought back may have even secretly pleased him. Whatever his train of thought, it was a fact that he now had teams in place in three cities, all apparently drawing well enough at the gate. Their success, fueled by the expectation that the country's black urban population centers would continue to grow in size, purchasing power, and assertiveness, convinced him that the time was ripe to launch a wholly black league that was professional in practice as well as name. Sometime over the winter he called for an organizational meeting of leading black club owners, promoters, and sportswriters. Events would justify Foster's confidence and daring. Unlike the short-lived Negro leagues of the past, which had stayed on the scene scarcely long enough for anyone to note their passing, this one would prove so successful that even whites would have to stand up and take notice.

Chapter Three

A LEAGUE FOR EVERY RACE-LOVING MAN

If Rube Foster was the superstitious type, one couldn't tell it by his choice of date for launching his dream league. On Friday, February 13, 1920, he and a select group of midwestern club owners and sportswriters gathered inside the Paseo YMCA in Kansas City, Missouri, and hashed out the details of creating the first viable organization of black baseball teams.

After a day of debate, the constitution of what was officially called the National Association of Colored Professional Base Ball Clubs was drafted that evening by attorney Elisha Scott of Topeka, Kansas, and four sportswriters: Cary B. Lewis of the *Chicago Defender;* Elwood Knox of the *Indianapolis Freeman,* and A. D. Williams and Dave Wyatt of the *Indianapolis Ledger.* The constitution provided for the creation of the Negro National League (NNL), a western circuit that was envisioned as the first of many associated black leagues to follow. The document also addressed several of the problems and practices that had helped undermine previous attempts to organize black teams. Provisions were made to suspend players who jumped contracts to sign with another team; to fine managers who petulantly pulled their teams off the field in the middle of a game; and to discipline anyone guilty of "ungentlemanly" conduct.

The following day, club owners reviewed and then signed the constitution. Each team put up $500 as a franchise fee.[1] In addition to the Chicago American Giants, Detroit Stars, and Dayton Marcos (all essentially owned or financially controlled by Foster), other members of the eight-team league included:

- the Indianapolis ABCs, originally sponsored by the American Brewing Company and now headed by C. I. Taylor, who possessed one of the keenest diamond minds in the game. Foster strengthened the club by shifting outfielder Oscar Charleston, arguably the greatest black player ever, from his American Giants to the ABCs.
- the Kansas City Monarchs, owned by J. Leslie Wilkinson, the sole white in the original group of owners. While Foster would have preferred an all-black operation in the beginning, it was impossible to ignore "Wilkie," creator of the famous All-Nations team and one of the fairest promoters, black or white, in the country. He also held the lease for the American Association Park in Kansas City, the only suitable playing field in what Foster considered a key Negro-league city.
- the St. Louis Giants, owned by Lorenzo S. Cobb.
- the Cuban Stars, operated by Alex Pompez, Harlem's leading black gangster. The Stars, as their name indicates, were a collection of talented Latin players whose home base was New York. Lacking a playing site, they were a permanent road team for much of their existence. However, in 1921 they would become the first full-time black tenants of a major-league park, renting Cincinnati's Redland Park for $4,000 a year.
- the Chicago Giants, owned by Joe Green. The club was an outgrowth of the Chicago Leland Giants of pre-war days, on which Green and Foster had starred. As a player, Green had once impressed sportswriter Ring Lardner by trying to score from third base on a broken leg—demonstrating the kind of grit and determination that a young league would need to survive.[2]

Foster was elected president of the league, which for the next several years would be run out of his Chicago office, or wherever else he happened to hang his hat. Administrating the league was a daunting, full-time task that Foster handled in addition to running his Chicago club on and off the field. (Tenny Blount, who attended the meeting as Detroit's representative, soon was given additional duties as NNL vice president, a position he would hold for the next several years.)

Foster's organization was modeled as much as possible after the white American and National leagues, since 1900 the country's top two circuits. Like their major-league counterparts, NNL players were to have written contracts with franchise owners and be paid a regular monthly salary. They were also to be bound to their club by a reserve clause. (Heretofore, black players had usually worked with verbal agreements, making it easy for unscrupulous promoters and owners to cheat them and creating a situation where players were constantly jumping clubs for better offers elsewhere.) An equitable distribution of gate receipts was also worked out: 45 percent for the home club, 35 percent for the visitors, 15 percent for park rental, and 5 percent to the league for operating expenses.[3]

Down the road, Foster envisioned a second black major league in the East, as well as a system of farm clubs that, like the white leagues, would feed prospects to the majors. Foster's ultimate goal, reported the *Indianapolis Freeman,* was to "pave the way for [the black] champion team eventually to play the winner among the whites"[4] in a true world series. He certainly wasn't lacking in confidence, as evidenced by the motto that adorned the league's stationary: "We are the Ship, All else the Sea."

The first NNL season officially opened on May 2, 1920, with a game at Washington Park in Indianapolis, where the ABCs beat the Chicago Giants, 4 to 2. The Detroit Stars and the rest of the league launched their seasons on or shortly after the same date.

The Stars' roster had changed dramatically between seasons, as Foster redistributed talent around the league to help balance competition. Manager Pete Hill, catcher Bruce Petway, and infielders Edgar Wesley, Frank Warfield, and Joe Hewitt remained. But gone were Jose Mendez, Hurley McNair, Jose Rodriquez, John Donaldson, and Sam Crawford (to Kansas City), Dicta Johnson (to Indianapolis), and Dave Malarcher, Jelly Gardner and Frank Wickware (to the Chicago American Giants). Despite the turnover, the Stars ultimately finished second to Foster's Chicago club, which was declared the winner of the single-division pennant. Although no official standings were compiled for the season, research shows the Stars with a 35–22 league record to date.

Detroit's mound staff was headed by the beefy Negro-league veteran Bill Gatewood, a savvy control pitcher who led the league with fourteen wins, and Bill Holland, a nineteen-year-old Indianapolis native whose right arm produced eleven victories. Foster had moved Jimmie Lyons from St. Louis to Detroit, and the speedy, lefthanded-hitting outfielder responded to his new surroundings with a .404 average and twenty-two stolen bases, both tops in the league.

Anchoring the lineup was Edgar Wesley, who led the circuit in

▲ The 1920 Detroit Stars. Top row, from left: Bill Holland, Edgar Wesley, Bruce Petway, Charlie Harper, Bill Gatewood, unknown, and unknown. Middle row, from left: Buck Hewitt, Pete Hill, Tenny Blount, Jimmie Lyons, and Andy Cooper. Bottom row, from left: unknown, William Force, Orville "Mule" Riggins, and unknown. (Courtesy of the National Baseball Library, Cooperstown, New York.)

home runs with ten. Wesley, a fine glove man for his size, was generally considered the best all-around first baseman of the NNL's early years, good enough to serve as a role model for future Negro-league star George Giles. According to Indianapolis catcher Larry Brown, the powerful, deadpanned Wesley was one tough customer—at bat or on the base paths. While most people recall Wesley's explosive line drives knocking the knots off the wooden outfield fences, Brown remembered the left-handed slugger storming home plate one day with such abandon that he jumped up and cut his chest protector: "My mask went one way, my glove went the other way and the ball went up in the stands."[5]

The odds are that it landed in the lap of a wildly applauding fan. Despite a severe postwar recession in 1920–21, which cut auto production in Detroit and thus affected local pocketbooks, the first couple of NNL seasons saw huge crowds of the curious, the proud, and the fashionable making their way into Mack Park and other parks all around the circuit. Sunday crowds in 1920 averaged about 5,000 fans, including large numbers of whites in Kansas City, Chicago, and Indianapolis. The excitement was contagious.[6] According to John Glover, in those first heady years a Negro National League game was as much a social affair as a sporting event. "I really wasn't that great of a baseball fan," said Glover, whose family moved from Alabama to Detroit in 1919, when he was nine years old. "A lot of us were going because that's where the crowd was going." Those who didn't enter the park stood outside and gabbed, gawked, hawked goods, placed bets, or shot craps. *Being there* was what was important to many, stressed Glover.[7]

For those who could afford the fare, the Super-Six Taxi Company on St. Antoine kept cars at the ready. "Benny Ormsby, Joe Mack, Walter Dues, Rob Christian and other black private taxi drivers shuttled the St. Antoine sports and their lady friends to Mack Park," remembered Lawrence Carter.[8] The less affluent arrived via streetcars. "At that time, Mack Park was considered way out of town," said Glover. "We used to take the Mack streetcar down, and if you were the least athletically inclined you could hop off the car before the conductor came through and collected fares."[9] The immediate postwar years were bereft of black sports figures, said Fred Guinyard, another young fan. The controversial prizefighter Jack Johnson "was the only notable black athlete in the news at the time. You had to go to Mack Park to see any others."[10]

The following year, as the Stars embarked on a brand-new season, the weekly *Detroit Contender* reminded its black readers that the importance of the Stars and the Negro National League transcended mere wins and losses, and that their continued success depended upon unflagging public support:

> Saturday, May 7, marks the opening of the Negro National League for the season of 1921 in Detroit. Behind this opening should be the concentrated support of every race man in Detroit. In this support should be good-will, finance, influence and presence of every race-loving man. The league should be considered your personal league; if it succeeds you should feel that you have succeeded; if it fails, you should consider it a personal failure. Your heart should vibrate sympathetically with the heart of the league. If the league succeeds, the race succeeds; if the league fails, the race fails.
>
> You should realize that this is one of the largest organized movements ever advanced by our group, and that our ability to put over large projects will be measured largely by the way we handle this one.
>
> Last season's baseball was prosperous because of abnormal conditions, but this season it will be given the acid test. If you are reluctant

▲ One of the finest eating establishments in all of Black Bottom was the Pittsburgh Inn on St. Antoine, pictured here one July day in 1920. That summer a hungry ballplayer could order a T-bone steak for fifty-five cents and pie for a dime. Coffee and tea were free. (Courtesy of Manning Brothers, Photographers.)

in giving of your support, you are lending aid to its failure. Now, attention, fans! Forward march! Eyes right! While we pass in review the opening of the Negro National League.[11]

League play began with a Saturday contest against the powerful Bacharach Giants, who were coming off a successful winter season in Cuba. But, as was customary, the Stars' true opening day was always the first Sunday in the schedule, when exhausted laborers had had a chance to recoup their energy (and cash Saturday's paycheck). The pre-game parade of players, fans, and local dignitaries and merchants was guaranteed a crowd and level of festivity that would be missing on any other afternoon of the week. For years NNL teams competed for a loving cup that was awarded to the club with the largest opening-day crowd. As far as is known, the Stars never won it. But throughout their history, Sunday crowds at Mack Park—opening day and otherwise—generally were five to ten times larger than those at weekday games, a pattern of attendance common throughout organized baseball before the advent of night ball.

The Stars broke out of the chute in 1921 with eighteen wins in their first twenty-two games, including a five-game sweep of the Chicago Giants. Rookie William Force compiled thirteen wins and hit well as an outfielder when he wasn't pitching, while Bill Holland added twelve victories. The fading Bill Gatewood won just six games, but occasionally starred on the mound. On June 6 he no-hit the Cuban Stars at Mack Park, walking two and striking out ten in a 4–0 victory. Three days later he threw another seven shutout innings against the Cubans, surrendering but two hits. However, injuries limited Edgar Wesley to just thirty-three games and sidelined Pete Hill for much of the year. Worse, before the season Foster had "traded" for the talented Jimmie Lyons—a fine point, since Foster owned Lyons's contract. The deal helped Chicago cop a second straight pennant. The Stars, meanwhile, stumbled home fourth, although they continued their domination of white semipro teams, winning eleven of twelve exhibitions.

Many of the problems that would hound the league throughout its entire existence were apparent from the very start. The most serious was the scheduling, which proved a nightmare. Since no NNL club owned its own ballpark, it was necessary for each team to rent a city park or minor-league field. The park could only be used when the white tenant was on the road. In this respect, the Stars were lucky; their lease allowed them to use Mack Park whenever they wanted. St. Louis had a similar arrangement. But other black teams were forced to work around the schedules of the white club owners. Still other teams—the Chicago Giants in 1920–21 and the Cuban Stars in 1920, 1922 and 1923—were permanent road teams for most of their existence, their "home" games played at a variety of sites. The result was a wildly disparate number of games played by each club. In 1921, for example, the Detroit Stars played sixty-four league games, compared to eighty-one for Kansas City and a mere forty-two for the Chicago Giants.

Equally confusing was the recordkeeping. Unlike the major leagues, the Negro leagues never fully appreciated the value of statistics in creating fan and media interest in the progress of favorite teams or individuals. "Owners will put out large amounts of money for uniforms, automobiles, and buses, pay high salaries to managers and business agents . . . , but the majority will not spend 60¢ or a dollar for a score book," a black weekly once complained. The owners were "deaf, dumb and blind to the fact that status is based on records of performance, good or bad."[12]

Coverage of the Stars by Detroit's three major dailies was always spotty and usually confined to a box score or a simple line score. Most games were just ignored completely. Sports coverage in those days centered on major-league baseball, collegiate football and track and field (especially the University of Michigan and the University of Detroit), boxing, and sandlot baseball. The relative silence surrounding the Stars' activities probably wasn't wholly racist in nature, since attempts by white promoters to establish professional football in the city at the time also received scant attention.[13] How the Stars may have been viewed had the NNL regularly released accurate, up-to-date information on batting leaders or pennant races is conjectural. Edgar Hayes, who broke in as a sports reporter with the Hearst-owned *Detroit Times* in 1924, maintained that the paper's editor "was opposed to giving blacks coverage of any kind."[14] That attitude actually was changing by then, but not to the extent of covering a "colored league" that couldn't even agree on how many games a particular team had won or who its batting and home run champions were.

The uneven record keeping baffled the Detroit Tigers' star second baseman, Charlie Gehringer, who barnstormed against Negro leaguers in the 1920s and 1930s. "I don't know how well he did, since I never did read his statistics," Gehringer once said of black slugger Walter "Buck" Leonard. "I don't know how well they were kept. I'm surprised they kept any at all."[15]

Most league games were scored by a local reporter, but even then there was no certainty that the game account and statistics would ever find their way to the league office for tabulation. One year the NNL hired a reporter, Harry Sinclair, to travel around the league and file stories and scores, but the following year he was dismissed as an extravagance.[16] In the mid-1920s the Stars had a young volunteer scorekeeper, Russell Cowans, who grew up to become a sportswriter and Joe Louis's first publicist. Too often, though, yesterday's starting pitcher or a bored reserve kept score. While players had a general idea of how well they were doing, their estimations were a devil's brew of league games, exhibition matches, and tall tales. Hard evidence of a player's performance in NNL play was lacking until researchers started tabulating old existing box-scores in the 1970s. All of the batting champions, pitching leaders, and other statistics used in this account were determined decades after the fact.

Showboating and rowdyism also were problems at times. Like their fans, the vast majority of NNL players were transplanted Southerners. As a rule, these "countrified" blacks were more raucous than old-line urban blacks in their behavior. Foster told the *Chicago Defender* that "colored baseball players are harder to handle than the white player. It seems to

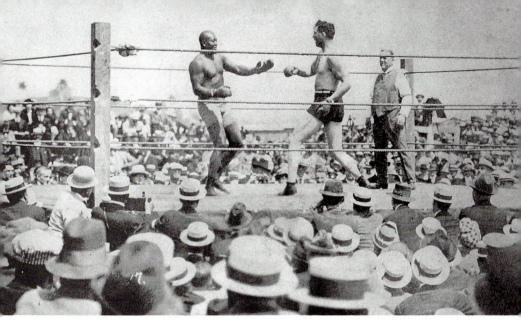

▲ Controversial prizefighter Jack Johnson (above, left) was the first
black heavyweight champion of the world, holding the title from
1908 until his defeat to Jess Willard (shown here) seven years later
in Havana, Cuba. During his reign the outspoken Johnson outraged
America by marrying a white woman and generally refusing to con-
form to racial stereotypes. In 1912 he was convicted of violating the
Mann Act; that is, transporting a woman across state lines for "lewd
or immoral purposes." He escaped to Canada when Rube Foster, a
fellow Texan, disguised him in the uniform of a Chicago American
Giant during a road trip through upstate New York. Johnson finally
surrendered to authorities in 1920 and served a year in jail. (Courtesy of the National Portrait Gallery, Smithsonian Institution.)

be characteristic of our race to act according to the size of attendance. . . ."[17] A hotly contested game, particularly when staged in the suffocating confines of a small, packed park, often inspired fistfights and
pop-bottle showers.

A competent umpiring crew generally could keep order, but compe-
tence often was sorely lacking. League rules called for the use of two
officials—one stationed behind the plate and the other at first base—for
each league game. (One was satisfactory for exhibitions.) Through 1922
the home team was responsible for providing the umpires. These were
always white and their decisions frequently favored the home club
(which, after all, was paying them). Rhubarbs were inevitable. The lack
of discipline reflected poorly on the league, so in 1923 Foster hired six
black umpires, whose salaries were paid by the league. For the next
three years he arranged to have a pair on hand for every NNL contest.[18]

With most of these problems requiring immediate action, Foster ran the league like an enlightened despot. During a league meeting before the 1921 season, for example, he reportedly disbanded the ailing Dayton franchise while its owner napped; when he woke up, he discovered that his players had been shifted to a new Columbus franchise and to other needy NNL rosters.[19] Whatever else one thought of these kinds of unilateral actions, there was no arguing that Rube Foster *was* the Negro National League. He adjudicated disputes, manipulated rosters, juggled schedules and playing dates, arranged advertising, wired money to teams that went broke on the road, pondered franchise shifts and suffered their failures, and fended off critics while sweating a thousand and one details. "Many a time I have sat in his offices and observed him direct managers in other cities of the league as to the proper pitchers to assign to certain games," remembered one sportswriter. "No star twirler was used to the limit before a small Saturday crowd, with prospects of a good Sunday attendance, while Rube was bossing baseball."[20]

On the diamond his Chicago American Giants were easily the class of the league, winning games while disdaining the long-ball philosophy that Babe Ruth was popularizing in the white major leagues. Foster's strategy emphasized the cerebral, rather than the muscular, aspects of the game. His players employed the bunt, the hit-and-run, the bunt-and-run, the double steal, the squeeze play. It was not unusual for six or seven or even eight players in a row to lay down a bunt. During one memorable game between Chicago and Indianapolis, played on the Fourth of July in 1921, Foster's Giants were trailing 18–0 in the seventh inning when he ordered his men to start bunting. The improbable rally, which included eleven consecutive bunts and two grand slams, allowed Chicago to tie the score before the game was called on account of darkness. It was a throwback to the dead-ball era, when bat control was everything and the unexpected was the order of the day.

"The Chicago American Giants had the smartest players you ever saw," Cool Papa Bell told John Holway. "They used to run on a base on balls. If they had a man on third and the batter walked, he'd just trot easy-like down to first, and the man on third would just sort of stand there looking at the stands. At the last minute, the batter would cut out for second as fast as he could go, the coach would yell, 'Heh, look at that!' the pitcher would whirl around, the guy on third would light out for home, and like as not they wouldn't get anybody out."[21]

Indicative of the shaky financial underpinnings of most NNL franchises, three clubs—the Columbus Buckeyes, Chicago Giants, and St. Louis Giants—dropped out of the league before the 1922 season. They were replaced by the St. Louis Stars, Pittsburgh Keystones, and Cleve-

▲ The Kansas City Monarchs featured some familiar faces when they first visited Detroit in the summer of 1920. Top row, from left: John Donaldson, Sam Crawford, Rube Currie, Jose Rodriquez, Zack Forman, unknown, George Carr, and "Bullet Joe" Rogan. Bottom row, from left: Jose Mendez, unknown, Bartolo Portuando, Dobie Moore, "Jaybird" Ray, and Hurley McNair. Donaldson, Crawford, Rodriquez, Mendez, and McNair had all played the 1919 season with the original Detroit Stars. (Courtesy of the National Baseball Library, Cooperstown, New York.)

land Tate Stars. That year the Chicago American Giants won their third straight pennant, finishing comfortably ahead of Indianapolis. The Detroit Stars finished third, winning forty-two league games while dropping thirty-two.

The Stars did so without two veterans, who had left to assume managerial duties elsewhere. Pete Hill went to Milwaukee, an independent black team, and was replaced by Bruce Petway, whose creaking knees and battered digits had just about finished him as a daily catcher. Bill Gatewood moved on to the St. Louis Stars. There he instructed a young pitching staff to acquire control by repeatedly throwing at objects. "Just like a shooting gallery: you got to aim, you got to pick a target," one of his students, Bill "Plunk" Drake, later said. "If you want to throw at a man's knees, you aim at his knees. . . . It requires practice, just practice. I got so I could wake up in the morning and throw in a quart cup."[22]

Of greater cultural significance, Gatewood that summer created one of the Negro leagues' great nicknames when he pegged rookie pitcher James Bell to start a game against Detroit. "Wake up, wake up,"

Compliments of

DETROIT STARS

Michigan Semi-Pro.
Champions

1919-20-21-22-23

J. TENNY BLOUNT, President

▲ As this advertisement in a tournament guidebook indicates, the
Detroit Stars were a force on the local semipro scene. After dropping
a game to Murray Manufacturing in 1919, the Stars remained unde-
feated against Detroit white semipro teams at least through the summer of 1923.

teammates shouted as Bell slept in his Pullman berth. "Lookee here, you're on this train sleeping and this headline says you're going to pitch in Detroit." Far from being nervous, on June 26 the young Mississippian outdueled Charles Wilson, 6–5, in ten innings in front of a hostile crowd at Mack Park. Bell even contributed a home run to his cause. "He's so cool he doesn't get excited," players on the St. Louis bench marveled during the game. They started calling him "Cool" Bell. That wasn't quite good enough for Gatewood. "We've got to add something to it," he said. Thus was born the marvelous moniker of a future Hall-of-Famer: James "Cool Papa" Bell.[23]

Detroit benefitted from Columbus's demise, picking up speedy Clint Thomas, who divided his time between second base and center field. Batting from the right side of the plate, the twenty-three-year-old Kentucky native compiled fourteen- and fifteen-game hitting streaks en route to a .346 batting average. In a memorable performance against Kansas City on May 14, he slammed out a double, triple, and two home runs in an 18–5 rout of the Monarchs. Once again the pitching corps was led by Bill Holland (a league-high sixteen victories) and William Force, who won ten games and hit .304 with three home runs as an occasional outfielder. Force's finest moment came the day after Cool Papa's performance, when he quieted St. Louis with a 3–0 no-hitter.

Coming into his own in his third season with Detroit was Andy "Lefty" Cooper, who compiled a 14–5 record with four shutouts. Born in Waco, Texas, on March 4, 1896, the 6-foot-1, 210-pounder had made a name for himself on the U.S. Army's all-black 25th Infantry Regiment team prior to coming to Detroit. The smiling, broad-chested Cooper wasn't averse to brushing back hitters with his good fastball, a tactic that over the years would help make him the Stars' all-time leader in nearly every pitching category.

Another bright spot was backstop Leon "Pepper" Daniels, playing his first of eight seasons in Detroit. "Well, he was a good catcher, pretty smart, Daniels was," a future batterymate, Willie Powell, once recalled. "Now there's a man didn't come to the ball park without his chewing tobacco."[24] Or, if it could be helped, a woman. By all accounts, Daniels was a night owl and one of the team's premier ladies' men.

The Stars' roster included several other young but solid front-line players, including shortstop Orville "Mule" Riggins, a former coal miner from southern Illinois, and outfielders John Jones and Clarence Smith. Together with a young, grim-faced center fielder from Nashville who would join Detroit the following spring, this nucleus of talent would give the Mack Park faithful something to cheer about for most of the rest of the decade.

Chapter Four

THE WAY IT WAS: EDDIE BATCHELOR

The Detroit Stars' home games occasionally were attended by white sportswriters from the local newspapers, some of whom undoubtedly considered a trip to Mack Park to be "slumming." Their reportage—or lack of it—usually reflected that attitude. Of the three major Detroit dailies, the Free Press *reported on the Detroit Stars fairly often, the* Times *only haphazardly, and the* News *not at all. One interested viewer was E. A. "Eddie" Batchelor, a respected newspaperman who appreciated all levels of the game, from sandlot to the major leagues. When he could manage time away from his family, editorial duties, and considerable freelance work, Batchelor occasionally coached local nines, such as the amateur Detroit Athletic Club.*[1]

The following piece by Batchelor first appeared in a 1922 issue of Detroit Saturday Night, *a well-regarded, slick-paper weekly that didn't survive the depression.*[2] *The story, originally headlined "Afro-American Rooters Are the Best Part of the Show at Mack Park," suffers from the stereotypical journalistic conventions of the day, such as quoting blacks in an Uncle Remus dialect. Despite its faults, it is easily the most even-handed and comprehensive account of the Stars and Mack Park published in the local white press in the 1920s.*[3]

Whatever the national game of baseball may lack in technical excellence when played by the Afro-American it makes up in the vigor of the rooting. A blind man could enjoy the games at Mack Park, where the Detroit Stars perform on an average of about four days a week. The show on the field is well worth while in itself, for the pick of the black teams of the country are brought here. But the show in the grandstand and bleachers is even better.

It is hard to tell just where the Negro National League, of which Detroit is one of the eight members, would rank as compared with the best white professional teams. There are some players in the circuit who might make the majors if they were white. So far as fielding and baserunning are concerned, there are half a dozen who could shine in any company. Whether the best hitters would fare consistently well if opposed to the "smart" pitching that is found in the big leagues is hard to say. It would take an actual test to prove it. In exhibition games against white teams composed all or in part of major leaguers, the unbleached stars have acquitted themselves with credit. But that does not necessarily mean that they would be able to hold up through a long season.

Whether the Negro league is up to the standard of say a Class B team composed of white men is beside the point, however. The important fact is that in the Negro league there is the keenest kind of competition and the fastest kind of baseball. You can usually see a game at Mack Park that will produce about as many sparkling plays as one at Navin Field, and invariably you will hear rooting that even the bleacherites at Trumbull and Michigan would find it impossible to equal.

The Mack Park crowd is intensely partisan but at the same time good-humored. There is more "kidding" than "panning." Only the star who is having a bad day is made the target for the sort of abuse that "Babe" Ruth and Ty Cobb receive on foreign grounds. Recently the home-run king of the circuit, one Oscar Charleston, of the Indianapolis A.B.C. team, played here and whenever he came to bat he was "booed." When he hit, which was frequently, the "boos" changed quickly to cheers. When he struck out, the crowd went into ecstasies. This man Charleston, by the way, is a ball player in any company. He has made 24 home runs this season up to date and has a big batting average aside from the circuit wallops. He can field and throw as well and is a flash on the bases.

This Negro National League gets the pick of the race, but it is the only circuit of any importance to which the black man is eligible. There are probably not more than twenty top-notch clubs in the whole country bidding for the services of the colored stars, as against the many hundreds of white nines which share the cream of the talent.

The league is rather a loose-jointed affair in a way, with a schedule

▲ "A blind man could enjoy the games at Mack Park," wrote Eddie Batchelor. The Detroit Stars assemble before a 1921 game inside the cozy wooden park at Mack and Fairview avenues. (Courtesy of the National Baseball Library, Cooperstown, New York.)

that is not always equitable in the number of games one club plays against another. In a recent standing, for example, Kansas City had played 64 games and Cleveland only 40. The dates are so arranged as to keep a team at home when the major league or American Association club representing its town is on the road. There are, however, numerous conflicting dates and the Negroes draw fairly well even when the white leaguers are competing with them. In Detroit this is true partly because Mack Park and Navin Field are so far apart that they might almost be in different cities. Furthermore, on Sundays the Tigers draw such crowds that some fans prefer to go to Mack Park and be sure of finding a seat. When the Navin Field grandstand is double-decked and the Tigers can care for more people on their big days, the Negro team undoubtedly will experience a drop in attendance.

The circuit is composed of Detroit, Chicago, Indianapolis, Pittsburgh, St. Louis, Cleveland, Kansas City and the Cuban Stars, the latter being constantly on the road. At last accounts, the American Giants, of Chicago, managed by "Rube" Foster, were in first place. Games are played on Saturdays and Sundays in all the cities where Sunday ball is permitted and in some of the towns on a couple of week days as well.

When not booked with league teams, the eight clubs fill in with exhibitions. There are several fast Negro teams in the independent ranks, notably the Bacharachs and the Lincoln Giants of New York, and Hilldale, from Philadelphia.

The pitching in general probably is the weakest point in the league. There are several excellent pitchers, good enough perhaps for any company, but no club seems to have enough stars to round out a very good staff. It is what might be termed a "curve ball" league. Every pitcher seems to throw more curves than a white man's arm would stand and this may be why their average performance isn't equal to the other departments of the game. Wilbur "Bullet" Rogan, of Chicago, is said by some judges to be the best hurler in the league. Detroit has two very good ones in Bill Holland and William Force, and a capable left-hander in Andy Cooper. James Jeffries, a little southpaw, with tremendous speed, is the Indianapolis ace apparently, or at least he looked very good in the recent Detroit series. Phil Cockrell, of the Hilldale club, last Sunday pitched a no-hit game against the American Giants, a hard-batting aggregation.

Every player in the league seems to have an iron arm. The throwing is of real big league calibre, both in speed and accuracy. The infielders seem to be able to throw from any position and it is practically impossible for even the fastest runners to beat out anything that is handled cleanly. Probably the most spectacular fielder in the league is Leon Day, second baseman of the Indianapolis team. The writer never saw a better stop than he made in one of the recent games against Detroit, and he made numerous others that would have featured any game. He can go to either side, has a wonderful pair of hands, and an accurate arm.

Most of the catchers are fine throwers, as indeed they have to be to cover up a very general tendency among the pitchers to give baserunners a flying start. This, by the way, seems to be one of the most conspicuous faults in the moundsmen. They don't hold 'em on. Bruce Petway, the Detroit manager, in his prime, was one of the best catchers that ever lived, white or colored. He is getting old in baseball now but is still a star. They used to compare him to Lou Criger when that great backstop was his best. He was a "ringer" in build and action for Lou and suffered nothing in comparison as a thrower. Poindexter Williams, another Detroit catcher, handles a pitched ball as well as anybody living, and is full of pepper.

Another fine catcher is Raleigh "Biz" Mackey of Indianapolis, who not only handles his pitchers capably, but is a superior thrower and one of the best hitters in the league, a left-handed slugger who is so dangerous that they pass him as often as they do "Babe" Ruth with men on the bases.

Valentin Dreke, of the Cuban Stars, is called by the "dopesters" the best outfielder in the league, everything considered. He can't have very much on Charleston and Christobel Torriente, the latter of the American Giants. Torrienti used to be one of the great hitters of the game, with as fine a position at the plate and as nice timing and power in his swing as

▲ The Indianapolis ABCs in 1921. Oscar Charleston, "a ball player in any company," stands in the center. Other identifiable players include outfielder Crush Holloway (standing at extreme right) and catcher George "Tubby" Dixon (sitting at extreme right). Both later played for Detroit. (Courtesy of the National Baseball Library, Cooperstown, New York.)

anyone ever seen outside the big leagues. The writer has seen him hit the ball over the center field fence at Mack Park in the days when baseball was played with a sphere much less lively than the oversized golf ball that is now used.

Almost all of the outfielders can "go and get them" in big league style. They cover ground, are very sure of any ball that they get their hands on, and when it comes to throwing hard and accurately, ask no odds of anyone. In one of the recent games here, two men were thrown out at the plate from deep left, plays that would have been features anywhere.

The teams usually play a smart brand of ball, though inclined to run a little wild on the bases. The head-work of the majority of the batters is hardly up to the standards of other departments, however. They chase a lot of bad balls and let a lot of good ones curve over. This may be due in part to the irrepressible instinct to play to the grand stand. Long hits are sure to bring applause and home runs usually cause a cash shower. The man who crashes one over the fence parades in front of the stands, gathering up coins and sometimes bills lavished on him by the delighted public.

The banter of the rooters must be rather trying on visiting players, even more so than abuse would be. Always some leather-lunged wag is roaring remarks calculated to upset the equilibrium of the enemy and the enemy's adherents. The duels between rivals' rooters are often classics.

"Boy, you does a heap o' hollerin' but you don't bet no money. I keeps capital behind my club all the time," bellowed one Hastings street sport to a shouter who had been encouraging the visiting team.

"Capital! Man you ain't seen nothin' yit. How much does you want to bet," replied the other, exhibiting a roll that a giraffe would have to stand on tip-toes to see over.

"Huh, that ain't no bankroll? You's got a corn-cob in the center of them bills," replied the first gambling man.

A batter in his effort to knock the ball out of the lot took such a "healthy" that he fell down.

"Good Lawd, that man don't mean NOBODY no good," bawled an excited partisan. "He's got evil in his heart."

In a tight situation, the batter had three balls and two strikes.

"Don't lose him boy," shrieked a fan to the pitcher. "If you ain't goin' to git him for me, tell me whar he's at and I'll go git him myself."

"Now let's do a little air-tightin'," advised another enthusiast when the home team took a lead of one run. "Let's air-tight 'em this innin' and git some mo' runs in the next."

In spite of their intense interest in the games, the Negro fans are much kinder to the umpires than the white. They "razz" the arbiters a little when a particularly bad decision is rendered, but do not cherish the generally hostile attitude that is characteristic of the Caucasian rooter. The players, too, accept the verdicts with comparatively little kicking. Perhaps the fact the fans do not extend to the home athlete who imagines he has a grievance the same sympathy that the big league spectators give has something to do with this attitude. At Mack Park, a player, even a very popular player, who makes a kick without extreme provocation, is likely to be told by the crowd to "git back and play ball." The umpires here are white men and they have plenty of authority to maintain discipline. One day this week, Charleston, the home-run king, who is described as "ve'y tempermental," threw the ball over the stand as a means of registering disapproval of a decision. He promptly got the gate and the crowd "rode" him as long as he remained in sight.

▲ Detroit newspaperman Eddie Batchelor and his son, Eddie, Jr.

The Sunday crowds represent "*le dermer cri*" sartorially. In fact they are a couple of jumps beyond it. All the youth, beauty and chivalry of local African aristocracy is there to see and be seen. The latest "modes" and the most advanced fashions in "nobby suitings for young men" are on view. The finest examples of the painters' and decorators' art, and jewels that would put the Kohinoor to shame enhance the beauty of the belles. Gallons of perfumery and tons of powder are expended on this great social event. No wonder the athletes have hard work heeding the admonition to "keep out of the grandstand." No wonder they sometimes sacrifice team work to the desire to do something that will bring individual favor in beauty's eyes.

Next to a wardrobe that is at least a year ahead of the Rue de la Paix designers or of the "Tony Togs" tailors, the most important thing in preserving or enhancing one's social standing as a rooter is to arrive in a large automobile. A white man may chug up to the park in a Ford and get away with it, but the elite of Catherine street must be better mounted. Coupes and runabouts of any make are merely tolerated and touring cars are slightly below par. To be in at all, Mr. and Mrs. George Washington Thompson must have a limousine. It may be a limousine of the period when automobile coach work was running to Queen Anne effects or even to the Garfield administration architectural lines, but it must have an imposing size and a large carrying capacity.

The co-operative ownership of a limousine is recognized as good form. There was one standing at the gate last Sunday of the vintage of 1909 or thereabouts, upon the door of which were painted in a most entrancing scroll the initials "A.B.C. *and* E.F.G.," telling the world that the owners of these initials were equal proprietors of the vehicle. Etiquette makes it necessary for the limousine customers to arrive late and leave early, just as the occupants of the diamond horseshoe are expected to do at the Metropolitan. In fact, Mack Park in many ways occupies the same place in the social life of Detroit that the opera does among the Park avenue set in New York.

The crowd is by no means confined to the Afro-American. White fans make up an appreciable proportion of the attendance, some drawn by their interest in the game and some by their desire to hear the comedy that sparkles through the whole performance. Many Tiger fans transfer their allegiance to the Negro league when the Navin Field aggregation is out of town.

It is a boisterous, merry, but thoroughly well-behaved crowd. Nobody seems to take the game so seriously as the average patron of the major league contests. The players to be sure fight tooth and nail, putting more bite into their efforts than many of the big leaguers do when there is nothing much at stake. All the teams are great front-runners and sometimes there is not much fight on the part of the one that is handed a bad handicap in the early innings. But so long as the score remains reasonably close, you are sure to see a battle all the way. Late-innings rallies are even more numerous than they are in the major leagues, possibly due to the fact that the pitchers crack under the strain of throwing so many curve balls and the managers are not so quick to change them as they are where staffs are larger and relief men more reliable.

On Sundays when the Tigers are away and a good attraction is booked for Mack Park, there is usually an overflow crowd. Last Sunday more than 6,000 paid to see a double-header and ground rules were necessary.

Fans of an older generation will remember when the Page Fence Giants of Adrian were among the best semi-professional teams in the country. They were a sterling bunch of sluggers and tales are still told of the tremendous hits made by their "clean-up" men. Negro teams were very scarce in those days and the Adrian nine was able to get the pick of the African fence-busters.

"Rube" Foster, who is now president of the Negro National League and manager of the Chicago club, is regarded by old-timers as the best pitcher of his race that ever lived. They say that he could have played on any team in the world but for the color line. He is an enormous man with the shoulders and arms of a gorilla and when he was "right" the batter was lucky to see his fast ball, much less hit it. "Rube" quit playing years ago but his knowledge of the game is one of the important factors in keeping his club out in front in the present race.

Three Sad Sports

In a recent game at Mack Park between the Detroit Stars and the Cleveland Negro champions, the tide had gone very much against the local Afro-Americans.

Three Forest City sports, wearing clothes that could be both seen and heard, had kept rubbing it in by loud and raucous rooting and jeering. Finally the tide of battle turned. Detroit staged a rally and went into the lead. The dusky home partisans were not slow to avenge the indignities heaped upon them by the visiting shouters.

Finally the Cleveland trio could stand it no longer, but betook themselves and their canes and their spats, and their diamonds to the exit. As they were filing out, a large and strong-lunged Detroiter arose and shouted:

"People, three spo'ts from Cleveland paid their way over here to see the ball game. They has just left the park, askin' kin anybody tell 'em the way to the Michigan Central freight yards."

Chapter Five

SHINING BRIGHT

The Pittsburgh Keystones and Cleveland Tate Stars dropped out of the Negro National League after the 1922 campaign and were replaced by the Toledo Tigers and Milwaukee Bears, neither of whom would finish the 1923 season. These and the alarming number of other franchise shifts and failures that would follow underscored the fundamental imbalance of the league. Competitive teams stood to gain the most at the gate, both at home and on the road, while the weaker clubs ran out of money at the same time fans ran out of interest. Rube Foster's Chicago American Giants had won the pennant in each of the first three seasons, a streak that Kansas City would break in convincing fashion in 1923. But in nearly every case through 1924, the pennant race was over by mid-summer. To maintain enthusiasm and to keep the turnstiles humming, Foster eventually settled upon the idea of split seasons. Starting in 1925, the winner of the first-half schedule would play the winner of the second half to determine the overall league champion.

For all of its problems—some of which were serious, indeed—by 1923 the Negro National League was being held up in the black press as a model of achievement. Attendance, while not as great as it had been in

◄ Detroit fans got their first taste of Turkey in the spring of 1923, when Norman "Turkey" Stearnes arrived from Nashville as the Detroit Stars' center fielder. Stearnes immediately established himself as one of the league's premier players.

the first couple of seasons, had leveled off to an acceptable average of 1,650 a game.[1] Half of the original NNL cities—Chicago, Detroit, Kansas City, and St. Louis—retained franchises, and these for the most part remained strong and profitable. The league as a whole employed perhaps 400 to 500 people on a regular basis, including players, managers, umpires, drivers, secretaries, and park personnel. Just as important, the dollar turned over several times within the black community. Printers received orders for scorecards and advertising placards, restaurants and hotels catered to teams and their fans, clothiers manufactured or repaired uniforms, and taxi drivers did a land-rush business on Sundays. All this eased somewhat the age-old complaint about blacks not supporting their own businesses. One historian estimates that for every NNL dollar spent, as much as seventy-five cents stayed in the hands of blacks.[2]

At the end of the 1923 season the NNL published some financial data, the only year for which such information is available. Total gate receipts were $197,218, of which 5 percent ($9,860.90) went to Foster for running the league. Other expenses included:

- $101,000 for players' salaries
- $25,212 for rail fares
- $9,136 for board and streetcar fares
- $7,965 for baseballs
- $7,500 for advertising
- $7,448 for umpires
- $4,164 for miscellaneous expenses.

Total expenses were $162,425, leaving a profit of $34,793 to be divided equally among the seven remaining NNL clubs. (The Toledo Tigers had disbanded on July 15.) Each share was $4,974.28.[3] Considering that a hearty dinner of boiled smoked ox tongue and string beans could be had at the Pittsburgh Inn on St. Antoine for fifty cents (pie was a dime and the coffee was free), this was a decent profit. A club owner could buy an entire infield with that amount.

Foster's success was a double-edged sword: in 1923 it helped inspire a group of independent eastern club owners to establish a rival circuit. Officially labeled the Mutual Association of Eastern Colored Clubs, the Eastern Colored League (ECL) consisted of the Brooklyn Royal Giants, New York Lincoln Giants, Baltimore Black Sox, Havana Cuban Stars, New York Bacharach Giants, and the Hilldale club of Darby, Pennsylvania.

Imitation may be the sincerest form of flattery, but Foster wasn't buying that. In 1921 Foster had made the Bacharach Giants and Hilldale affiliate members. This guaranteed playing dates for NNL clubs when they headed east, and games for eastern clubs when they ventured west. The agreement also kept the signatories from raiding each other's rosters. However, it evolved that few NNL clubs could afford the long trip east. This didn't please Hilldale owner Ed Bolden, who also was piqued that his team's victories didn't count in the NNL standings. When Bolden withdraw from the league in 1922 in protest, Foster refused to refund the thousand dollars he had deposited as good-faith money. Bolden responded by helping to organize the ECL, serving as the chairman of its six-man committee of commissioners, and announcing player raids on the NNL.

Despite the bad blood between Foster and Bolden, what really steamed Foster about the new league was the presence of four white owners, particularly Nat Strong, the most powerful booking agent in the East. In addition to operating the Brooklyn Royal Giants, Strong booked games for all but one of the other five teams. The white-controlled ECL was a league, all right, said Foster. But calling it a "colored league" was like calling "a street car a steamship."[4]

As Foster fumed and fretted, the ECL signed several established NNL players for its inaugural 1923 season. Detroit was badly hurt, losing its top pitcher, Bill Holland, to the Lincoln Giants and two starters, Clint Thomas and Frank Warfield, to Hilldale. Thomas and Warfield would help Hilldale capture the first three ECL pennants (1923–25). If the Stars were hobbled by the loss, the Indianapolis ABCs were crippled. By 1924 ten ABC players, including five starters, had defected. These included stars Oscar Charleston and Biz Mackey. Foster shipped several Chicago players to Indianapolis in an attempt to hold that team together.

Clint Thomas's defection wound up not harming the Stars as much as expected. In early 1923, Tenny Blount signed a slender, hollow-cheeked youngster from Nashville, Tennessee, who possessed all the ingredients necessary for a long, successful professional baseball career. Not the least of these was an imaginative nickname.

Norman "Turkey" Stearnes was born May 8, 1901, and grew up playing ball barefoot on the sandlots of Nashville. There are a couple of versions regarding the origin of his nickname. His wife thought it was because of the way he flapped his arms as he ran the bases, but Stearnes always maintained that it was because of the pot belly he had when he was a child. Turkey was one of five children whose father died when Turkey was about fifteen. To supplement his mother's seven-dollar weekly wage as a cook, he "had to go to work to help," he once recalled. "I just did any job that popped up, taking care of hogs and cows and anything like that. I worked at a grocery store, driving a wagon, delivering groceries. I worked at the Baptist Publishing Board, a janitor mostly, running errands."[5]

When he wasn't working or attending school, Stearnes played weekends for local teams. In 1921 he traveled to Alabama to play for the Montgomery Grey Sox in the Southern Negro League (SNL), which had been organized the year before. Batting leadoff because of his speed, Stearnes led Montgomery to a four-game sweep of his hometown Nashville Elite Giants for the pennant. The following summer he played for the Memphis Red Sox. Because of the generally impoverished nature of the Southern Negro League, northern managers and owners had come to regard it as an unofficial farm system.[6]

In 1922 Bruce Petway scouted Stearnes at Memphis and, liking what he saw, offered him a contract to come to Detroit. To Petway's surprise, Stearnes turned him down. "He begged me to come up here in '22," said Stearnes, "but I couldn't make it. . . . I at least wanted to finish high school, because I knew I couldn't go to college."[7] Although Stearnes was twenty-one years old when he finally earned his high school diploma, it was an achievement that at the time still eluded well over half of all Americans, black and white. In fact, many parents ended their children's formal schooling when they turned fourteen, the magical age at which they could secure working papers and start contributing to the family welfare. Justifiably proud of his accomplishment, Turkey Stearnes then felt free to sign with Detroit.

Physically, the slender recruit didn't fit the profile of the classic power hitter. He stood but 5 feet, 9 inches tall, and his weight hovered around 165 pounds. Most of his power was generated by his broad shoulders and a whiplike swing. Stearnes threw and batted lefthanded. His odd stance—right foot splayed, the toe pointed skyward—called to mind another emerging power hitter of the day, Al "Bucketfoot" Simmons of the Philadelphia Athletics. All similarities ended at the batter's box, however. Unlike the fiery, lusty Simmons, Stearnes was detached, colorless, and coolly efficient. As such he became the perfect embodiment of the Detroit assembly line, dependably delivering clutch plays in conveyor-like fashion.

In addition to his hitting, Stearnes was an excellent fielder. Although he had been pitching and playing first base in Memphis, the Stars shifted him to center field. It was as if he had been playing there all his life. In fact, in terms of defense, some respected Negro leaguers rate him ahead of the expected choice, Hall-of-Famer James "Cool Papa" Bell, as the all-time best at that position. "Everybody knows that Cool Papa Bell was the fastest man," said Ted Radcliffe, who played with and against both men. "But Cool Papa Bell couldn't field with Turkey Stearnes. He was faster, but Turkey Stearnes was one of the best fly ball men."[8] Stearnes patrolled the center field grass throughout his entire Negro-league career, even when he was in his forties, his speed and reflexes giving him a range that few outfielders possessed.

Stearnes was in center field when the Stars opened the 1923 NNL season on April 29 with an 8–7 loss to Indianapolis. Typically batting third in the order, in front of another humorless slugger, Ed Wesley, Stearnes was a lethal combination of speed and power. In a 7–6 win over Toledo on May 31, he hit for the cycle—the only Star ever to accomplish the feat. On June 17, he legged out three triples in a 12–5 thrashing of Milwaukee. On four separate occasions he hit two home runs in a game. Mack Park's tall right-field fence, which was topped with a wire screen, required better-than-average "lift" to clear it. "You got to hit a tall fly ball," is the way Stearnes once described it.[9] While Mack Park was a friendly environment for left-handed pull hitters like Stearnes, over the years he would prove that he could hit the ball to all fields and out of any park.

"He had a funny stance, but he could get around on you," remembered the legendary pitcher, Leroy "Satchel" Paige, whose longevity made him perhaps the best authority on Negro-league hitters. "He could hit it over the right field fence, over the left field fence, or center field fence. I pitched to him on the outside low, where he'd have to pick it up to hit it over the fence, or else he'd hit it on the ground. If you didn't pitch it in the right place to him, he would just hit the ball out of that park just about every time he came up. He was one of the greatest hitters we ever had. He was as good as Josh [Gibson]. He was as good as anybody ever played baseball."[10]

The cheap baseballs that the Negro leagues used didn't lend themselves to tape-distance blasts. Nonetheless, one of Turkey's homers sailed some 470 feet out of Mack Park. Another traveled an estimated 500 feet at cavernous Compton Park in St. Louis, clear over the car barn that sat in the far reaches of left field. It came off a curveball delivered by the Stars' ace hurler, Ted Trent. "The wind was blowing that day, and the ball curved about 30 feet," Stearnes later recollected. "The umpire said the last time he saw it, it was in foul territory. They beat us, 1–0."[11]

Stearnes finished his rookie season with a .353 average, fifteen doubles, thirteen triples, and seventeen home runs (which tied Ed Wesley for the league lead) in the fifty-seven league games so far uncovered by researchers. His .741 slugging percentage set a new team record. Stearnes later estimated that he had hit "about 50-some" home runs in 1923, but that tally obviously included the many exhibition matches the Stars played to fill in the NNL schedule. At any rate, round-trippers were

◄ Three Mack Park favorites of the 1920s. Outfielder John Jones (left) hit .302 during his seven seasons in Detroit, while first baseman Edgar Wesley (center) led the NNL in home runs three times before jumping to Harrisburg of the rival Eastern Colored League. He returned to Detroit and captured the 1925 batting title with a .424 mark. Of shortshop Orville "Mule" Riggins (right), one Chicago paper wrote: "He is a flashy handler of difficult rolling grounders, a slashing hitter and possesses one of the great throwing arms in baseball."

worthless "if they didn't win a ball game," Stearnes believed. "It didn't make any difference if I hit four or five over the grandstand, it didn't make any difference to me, as long as I hit them to try to win the game. That's what I wanted: to win the game. Wanted to win. As long as I was winning, I wouldn't think about it."[12]

Stearnes would play nine seasons in Detroit, longer than anybody else. He would leave holding nearly every Stars single-season and career batting mark, including most home runs in a game, season, and career. The most remarkable quality of Stearnes's career (which would stretch well into the 1940s with various other black clubs) was a brilliant consistency. He hit well in league games and exhibition games against whites, and was particularly devastating in postseason play. According to some Negro leaguers, Stearnes was a sucker for an off-speed pitch, and others claimed a high fastball could always do him in. If that was the case, there must have been a sore lack of good off-speed and high-fastball pitchers, both black and white, during this period, because the numbers and the memories reveal him to be one of the finest hitters of all-time.

"Turkey Stearnes was a master of the long ball," remembered Lawrence Carter, "though he often struck out. Standing at the plate with his chest protruding, he was one of the darlings of the crowd. 'Hit that ball,

Turkey Breast! Hit it, baby!' some chick would cry out. When Turkey swung and missed, it would set up a Pentecostal wind in Mack Park."[13]

Bob Sampson, a native Georgian whose family emigrated to Detroit in 1917 when he was seven years old, painted an equally vivid picture of Stearnes. "He had features like an Indian," he said. "A pointed nose and high cheekbones. He was always ramrod straight. And he was silent." Sampson, then a high school track star at Cass Tech, used to watch in fascination as Stearnes worked out winters inside the gymnasium at Hastings and Vernor Highway. Push-ups, sit-ups, laps around the gym—all with barely a word spoken to anyone. "You could go up to him and say something to him, but he wouldn't talk. Never seen anybody like him."[14]

According to several Negro leaguers, Stearnes was a sterling conversationalist when it came to himself or his bats. After making an out, he'd often sit on the bench, holding his bat and mumbling, "They say I can't hit. Why can't I hit?" and "I hit that good, but he caught it. Next time I'll get one."[15] Fans and players remember Turkey regularly chatting with himself in the outfield.

"He was a peculiar fellow," concluded Sampson. "But he sure could play the game."[16]

The following season, 1924, the Stars lost one-half of their powerful one-two punch when Wesley jumped to the Harrisburg (Pennsylvania) Giants of the ECL. The Stars signed Bill Pierce to play first base. Pierce responded with a .335 mark, which included a sixteen-game hitting streak and a 5-for-5 performance against St. Louis. He also clubbed thirteen triples in just fifty-eight games, tying Stearnes's team mark of the previous year. Stearnes compiled seventeen- and nineteen-game hitting streaks on his way to an exceptional sophomore season: a .346 average and another home-run crown, this time with ten. However, before the season William Force had also bolted to the East, leaving a hole in the rotation. The staff gave up 6.18 runs per game, including eleven losses in which the opposing team scored in double digits. Six regulars hit over .300, but the pitching killed Detroit's chances. The Stars finished a distant third to Kansas City, which won a second straight NNL pennant and the right to face the ECL representative, Hilldale, in the first Colored World Series.

The scheduled best-of-nine series was not Foster's idea. Although his Chicago club had concluded each of its pennant-winning seasons of 1920, 1921, and 1922 with an informal postseason "championship series" against an eastern team, the practice had ended with the formation of the Eastern Colored League and the bitter feud with the NNL that had ensued. But the idea of an official World Series to determine a national

THOMAS COCKRELL BRIGGS WARFIELD STEVENS

▲ Several members of the Hilldales, champions of the Eastern Colored League, shown prior to the first game of the 1924 Colored World Series against the NNL's Kansas City Monarchs. The Hilldales had been bolstered the year before by the acquisition of former Detroit Stars Clint Thomas (at extreme left) and Frank Warfield (fourth from left).

black champion was too appealing to Kansas City owner J. L. Wilkinson, who independently issued a challenge to Ed Bolden. The owner of the Hilldales eagerly accepted, leaving Foster with little choice but to go along. The emollient intercession of Kansas City secretary Quincy Gilmore, several sportswriters, and others interested in seeing the two major Negro leagues end their differences helped Foster, Bolden, and their respective leagues reach a rapprochement of sorts. While the two men would never truly like or trust each other, they stiffly posed for photographers as the first Colored World Series opened October 3 in Philadelphia's Shibe Park.

It was a memorable, hard-fought series, as exciting as that year's fall classic between the New York Giants and Washington Senators, which went down to the twelfth inning of the seventh game before the Giants finally pulled out a victory. In the opener of the Colored World Series, the Monarchs' Bullet Joe Rogan defeated Hilldale's spitballer, Phil Cockrell, 6 to 2, in a classic confrontation of two great pitchers. But Hilldale came back to win the second game big, 11 to 0. The venue shifted to Baltimore for the next two games, to Kansas City for games five through seven, and then to Chicago for the final three contests.

After nine games, each club had won four times. (One game had ended in a twelve-inning, 6–6 tie.) The deciding game was played on a cold, blustery afternoon in Chicago. For eight innings the 2,500 chilled fans watched Jose Mendez, Kansas City's aging and ailing manager, match goose eggs with Holsey "Scrip" Lee, Hilldale's young submarine pitcher. Finally, in the ninth, Kansas City pushed across five runs against Lee, giving the Monarchs the game and bragging rights as "World's Colored Champions."[17]

The series was judged a financial, as well as an artistic, success. Crowds averaging about 5,000 for the ten games had produced more than $52,000 in gate receipts. After expenses were deducted, more than $23,000 was distributed. Kansas City was awarded the winner's share of 42 percent (about $9,800), of which Wilkinson received about $4,900 and each Monarch player $308. The loser's cut of 28 percent (about $6,500) produced $3,250 for Bolden and $193 for each Hilldale player. Lesser shares were sprinkled among various officials and the second- and third-place teams in each league.[18] The Detroit Stars received 2 percent, roughly $460, for finishing third. If Tenny Blount followed the customary 50/50 split between owner and players, that means Kansas City's victory was worth approximately fifteen dollars to each Star.

Given these share-outs, the Stars undoubtedly hungered after some real money in 1925. Stearnes had another fine season, but even he had to take a back seat to Ed Wesley, who returned from Harrisburg and put

▲ Looking west from the intersection of Lafayette and St. Aubin, in the heart of Black Bottom. This photograph was taken on June 30, 1925, two days after Andy Cooper's no-hitter at Mack Park. The red-hot Stars were playing at home that afternoon against the Indianapolis ABCs, which may account in part for the relatively empty sidewalks. (Courtesy of Manning Brothers, Photographers.)

up some incredible numbers. Throughout his career hard play had always made Wesley susceptible to injuries, and 1925 was no different. After gathering four hits in a 19–10 pasting of Birmingham on August 4, a broken ankle caused him to miss the final third of the league schedule. It put the skids on what was developing into a phenomenal season. Wesley had started the campaign by hitting safely in his first eighteen games; another eighteen-game streak saw him collect thirty-nine hits in sixty-seven at bats—a .536 clip—including eleven home runs. Overall he hit .424, good enough to win the batting championship. Stearnes, who played twenty-eight more games than Wesley, managed to tie his teammate for the league lead in home runs, with eighteen. However, Wesley slugged the ball at a .810 clip; in the long history of the Detroit franchise, not even Turkey would ever be able to top that.

The mound staff was marginally better in 1925, with Andy Cooper winning his first nine decisions. Victory number nine came in the second game of a doubleheader against Indianapolis on June 28, when he twirled a 1–0 no-hitter that was called after seven innings because of darkness. The following afternoon he picked up a save in the Stars' 8–7 victory over the ABCs—then was sidelined by a broken leg until August 1. During his absence from the boxscores the Stars lost ten of twenty-one games. After the team regrouped in August, five straight losses to St. Louis sent the Stars reeling back into the middle of the pack. All told, Detroit wound up winning just nine of twenty-six games with St. Louis and Kansas City, the league's top two teams.

Detroit Stars vs. Chicago American Giants
1925 Playoff

Chicago won series, 4 games to 2

DETROIT PITCHING

Player	GP	GS	CG	Won	Lost	IP	H	R	BB	SO	RPG	ShO
Hampton	2	2	2	1	1	18	11	5	3	7	2.50	1
Newsome	1	1	1	1	0	9	2	0	1	1	0.00	1
Morris	1	1	1	0	1	9.1	7	6	1	4	5.79	0
Bell	1	1	1	0	1	9	8	7	7	6	7.00	0
Cooper	1	1	1	0	1	8	8	5	1	1	5.63	0
Totals		6	6	2	4	53.1	36	23	13	19	3.88	2

DETROIT BATTING

Player	Pos	Games	AB	H	Avg.	2B	3B	HR	SB
Clarence Smith	1B-OF	6	25	7	.280	2	0	0	2
Riggins	SS	6	25	3	.120	0	1	0	0
Pryor	3B	6	25	5	.200	0	0	0	0
Stearnes	CF	6	23	8	.348	2	1	1	0
Hampton	OF-P	5	21	0	.000	0	0	0	0
Bell	P-OF	6	21	4	.190	0	0	1	1
Jones	2B	6	19	4	.210	1	1	0	0
Daniels	C	5	18	3	.167	0	0	0	0
Wesley	1B	3	10	2	.200	0	0	0	0
Kennard	C-PH	2	4	1	.250	0	0	0	0
Morris	P	1	4	2	.500	0	0	0	0
Petway	RF	1	4	1	.250	0	0	0	0
Cooper	P	1	3	1	.333	0	0	0	0
Newsome	P	1	3	1	.333	0	0	0	0
Cleo Smith	2B	1	1	1	1.000	0	0	0	0
Totals		6	206	43	.212	5	3	2	3

The 1925 season was the first to feature Foster's idea of a split season, with Kansas City winning the first-half schedule (which ran from May to early July) and St. Louis the second-half (which ran from mid-July through September). In a thrilling best-of-seven playoff that went the limit, Bullet Joe Rogan shut out St. Louis, 4–0, on a bitterly cold day in Chicago. This gave Kansas City its third straight NNL pennant and a berth in the Colored World Series against Hilldale, the ECL champions.

Interestingly, Chicago and Detroit staged their own playoff at the end of the season. On September 19 in Chicago, Foster's team scored a ten-inning, 6–5 decision over the Stars. Chicago won again the following day, 5–1, before Lewis Hampton—who had won five games and hit .353 bouncing between the mound and the outfield for the Stars—blanked them, 4–0, on Sunday. The series shifted the following weekend to Detroit, where Chicago won 7–2 and 5–2 before being shut out, 5–0, by seldom-used Omer Newsome in the meaningless finale.

In its way, the playoff foreshadowed the contrived postseason tournaments that have come to characterize modern sports. Its stated purpose was to determine which team would receive the several hundred dollars in third-place money that the Colored World Series between Kansas City and Hilldale was expected to produce. The real intent, of course, was to produce more revenue. So even though Chicago wrapped up the best-of-seven series in five games, an additional sixth game was played to take advantage of an open Sunday date at Mack Park.

In this sense the losing Detroit players may have come out ahead of their Kansas City and Hilldale counterparts, who staged a flop of a rematch. The Monarchs were routed, five games to one, and only $6,000 in profits was distributed. "We could have made more in two games [of barnstorming] than we'll get out of the whole series," moaned one Kansas City player, whose pay for two weeks of work and travel was a pitiful $57.64.[19] The Stars, assuming that they received a percentage of the gate for their six-game set with Chicago, could hardly have done worse and probably did much better. Such were the economic vagaries of the Negro National League, even during the height of its popularity.

Chapter Six

BLACK AND WHITE AND RED ALL OVER

From early spring through late autumn, Negro leaguers played a long, grueling schedule of official league games and exhibition matches. The Detroit Stars, like all NNL clubs, typically started action in late March or early April, holding spring training in Nashville or New Orleans or some other warm-weather southern site (when they could afford to) and playing their way into shape against local semipro squads and other black professional teams. Although the league schedule started the first week of May and ran through the middle of September, it seemed twice as long to the players, who saw the off days in their schedule filled in with as many exhibition games as an owner or promoter could arrange. These were played wherever an opponent and a diamond could be found and usually numbered between 75 and 125 games each season.

"Saturday, Sunday, Monday, Tuesday we'd play league games against Chicago, Kansas City, and them," Turkey Stearnes told John Holway. "Wednesday and Thursday we'd play exhibition games with the white kids. We used to work Canada, all those places, the little leagues they got over there. Sometimes we'd go 300 miles. Everybody thought they could beat us, until they found out."[1]

If the Stars were at home, they might arrange a date with a team from one of the very competitive industrial leagues in the city, such as Detroit Creamery or Lasky Jeweler.[2] Perhaps a semipro squad from Alma, Lansing, or Toledo would be in town for a game or two. Or, since barnstorming remained the primary source of most clubs' livelihood, the Stars might find themselves bumping along the countryside in a procession of dust-caked touring cars, on their way to games in a series of towns whose names they would soon forget—assuming that they ever knew them. Because of local Jim Crow customs and ordinances, restaurants and hotels were off-limits to Negro leaguers on the road. The players would pack sandwiches and, if need be, curl up in the back seat or even under the stars, their uniform roll a handy pillow.

On the road, the arrival of a black professional team engendered considerable excitement and curiosity, not only in isolated hamlets, but even in comparatively more worldly locales. "The Detroit Stars will be quartered at the [black] Hotel Milton during their stay in the city and will be entertained in many ways by colored residents of the city . . . ," reported the *Grand Rapids Herald* in May 1928, as the Stars stopped in that western Michigan city for a couple of games against the local Fox Colored Giants before continuing on to open a league series in Chicago. "Mgr. Walter Coe says he will proudly show the Detroit Stars one of the finest and best kept playing fields in the country." Coe assured fans that the home grounds, Ramona Park, "will be in gala day attire."[3] As expected, the Stars "played like a well oiled piece of machinery behind good pitching and showed themselves major leaguers in every movement." The Detroiters won both games, 6–3 and 12–7, as the Fox Colored Giants "gave an exhibition of what a baseball team can't do when it has an off day and is facing opposition that outclasses it. . . ."[4]

The Stars might occasionally struggle against an inspired factory team, especially one whose lineup included a couple of ex-big leaguers, but they almost never had any trouble handling town teams. The usual scenario was to score big in the first few innings and then coast. To maintain interest—and also because most of their opponents were white—the Stars refrained from running up the score. If a shutout was imminent, a few discreetly delivered "fat" pitches, misjudged fly balls, or errant throws would allow the locals to score a run or two. Had they wanted to, the Stars almost always could have buried their opponents in an avalanche of runs. But there was nothing to be gained by embarrassing the local nine and offending the patrons. That would have been bad for business. And Negro-league baseball was, after all, first and foremost a business. Whatever the locale or the circumstances, the sole criterion for playing any exhibition match was the prospect of a good gate, and that depended on at least the illusion of competitiveness and cordial relations between the races.[5]

The most intriguing matchups occurred in the fall, after the white and black major leagues had completed their seasons. These interracial affairs were part of the customary postseason barnstorming tours that were so economically important to most professional ballplayers. During the 1920s, only a handful of superstars drew the kind of salaries that are taken for granted by even journeyman players today. In 1926 Ty Cobb earned $50,000 as player-manager of the Detroit Tigers, and his counterpart on the Cleveland Indians, Tris Speaker, was paid $35,000.[6] Babe Ruth, already a cultural icon, was easily the best-compensated athlete of his day, drawing a salary of $80,000 in 1930 and tens of thousands of dollars more in endorsements.[7] But these were isolated cases. More typical were the Detroit Tigers' Harry Heilmann, a four-time batting champion who averaged about $10,000 during the decade, and Charlie Gehringer, a gifted second baseman who broke into organized ball for $3,500 in 1924. Gehringer worked winters in a downtown department store to make ends meet.[8]

At that, the major leaguers still had it all over the Negro leaguers. Monthly salaries among blacks averaged between $135 and $175 during the early 1920s.[9] That amounted to between $810 and $1,150 when projected over the six-month NNL season—approximately what a white Class B minor-leaguer made. However, more gifted players could expect to make twice that amount. If adequate compensation was not forthcoming, players like the Stars' Bill Holland, Frank Warfield, and Edgar Wesley showed little compunction in "jumping" to a club in a rival league that offered an extra twenty-five or fifty dollars a month. In 1926, the Negro National League and Eastern Colored League, looking to end the escalating bidding war that threatened to bankrupt them, experimented with a salary cap of $3,000 a month.[10] With most rosters carrying about fifteen players, that worked out to an average monthly salary of $200. Although figures are not available, it's likely that even an established star like Turkey Stearnes never made more than $300 to $400 a month—$1,800 to $2,400 a year—in Detroit. Thus, barnstorming was an economic fact of life for most ballplayers, who received a share of the gate receipts. And some of the most lucrative match-ups, the ones that usually produced the greatest crowds, involved head-to-head competition between blacks and whites.

In 1923 the Detroit Stars and St. Louis Browns clashed in three contests that drew up to 6,000 fans to Mack Park each afternoon. The Browns had just wrapped up the regular season with a weekend series

▲ On October 8, 1923, in their first game against white major leaguers, the Detroit Stars shocked Dave Danforth, a sixteen-game winner for the American League's St. Louis Browns, by overcoming a six-run deficit to win. "Some folks said it couldn't be done," reported the *Detroit Times*, "but now they are really convinced." (Courtesy of George Brace.)

against the Tigers at Navin Field. Although they had finished in fifth place with a 74–78 record, the Browns were fielding basically the same team that had come within a whisker of winning the American League pennant the year before. The lineup had proven .300 hitters in shortstop Wally Gerber and outfielders Ken Williams and Baby Doll Jacobson. The pitching staff featured the slants of Ray Kolp, Dave Danforth, and Elam Vangilder. There were some notable absences, however. Future Hall-of-Famer George Sisler, who had hit .420 in 1922, had missed the entire 1923 season with a sinus infection and was replaced at first base by the very ordinary Dutch Schleibner. Urban Shocker, a twenty-game winner, chose to skip the series, as did a pair of .300 hitters, shortstop Marty McManus and outfielder Jim Tobin. To take up some of the slack, the Browns added Cleveland shortstop Bill Wambsganss to their lineup for the three games.

For this, their first opportunity to test themselves against a white major-league team, the Detroit Stars hedged their bets by importing a pair of ringers: Oscar Charleston of Indianapolis and John Beckwith of Chicago. Charleston's credentials can be summed up by his nearly universal reputation as "the black Ty Cobb." And the brooding Beckwith, who stood 6-foot-3 and weighed 230 pounds, was the very image of menace, with a bat in his hand and a perpetual scowl on his face. This was as volatile a pair of sluggers as existed anywhere in the game. Manager Bruce Petway sandwiched them in the fourth and fifth spots in the batting order, between Stearnes and Wesley. To put these additions in perspective, it would have been like the Browns inserting Babe Ruth and Ty Cobb into their lineup. But this is to take nothing away from what the Stars accomplished over the next three days.

The opening game was played before a packed house on Monday afternoon, October 8. A wall of noise surrounded the Stars' William Force as he fanned two of the first three major leaguers he faced. However, the Browns knocked Force out of the box with two runs in the second and four more in the third. St. Louis seemed on its way to a romp, leading 6–0 after three innings and with Dave Danforth, a sixteen-game winner, on the mound.

Ed Wesley cut into the lead when he hit a solo home run to center in the bottom of the fifth. The Stars then erupted for five more runs in the sixth. Stearnes, who had struck out in his first two at-bats against Danforth, this time hung in against the southpaw and slapped a two-out, two-run double to left. Charleston followed with a single to right, plating Stearnes. This brought up Beckwith, who poled a long fly ball over the center-field fence to tie the score. There was bedlam in Mack Park as Wesley stepped to the plate, but he ended the rally by flying out to right.

The game remained tied until the bottom of the ninth. With the park growing cool and dark, lead-off batter Wesley got a chance to redeem himself. He wasted little time. Wesley turned on Danforth's second pitch, walloping it over the right-field fence for his second home run of the day and giving the Detroit Stars a dramatic comeback victory, 7 to 6. "Some folks said it couldn't be done," reported the *Detroit Times,* "but now they are really convinced."[11]

The Stars proved they were no fluke by repeating their remarkable feat the following afternoon. Once again the Browns broke out to a big lead, this time entering the sixth inning ahead by a score of 6 to 1. And once again the Stars fought back gamely, Stearnes and Charleston hitting home runs to draw within two runs of St. Louis entering the bottom of the ninth.

Elam Vangilder, a sixteen-game winner for the Browns, surrendered a lead-off single to the Stars' second baseman, Anderson Pryor. Right fielder Clarence Smith's single sent Pryor to third, and Bruce Petway's infield out scored Pryor. Then pitcher William Force, who had taken over from Andy Cooper in the seventh inning, stepped up to the plate and, as the Browns looked on in disbelief and the crowd of 5,000 cheered itself hoarse, smacked the ball out of Mack Park to climax another come-from-behind, 7–6 win for the Stars.

It's not hard to imagine what St. Louis manager Jimmy Austin told his players before they took the field for the third and final game on Wednesday. As freighted with importance as many black players and fans might make these games, the fact remained that they were meaningless exhibitions—at least to the whites. Still, while losing one game to a black team could be viewed as an aberration, losing two was an embarrassment. To be swept would make for an especially long winter and some vicious bench jockeying come the spring. Their pride pricked, the Browns went on to defeat the Stars, 11 to 8, in the finale, reversing the tables by scoring five times in the ninth to erase an 8–6 Detroit lead.[12] But the damage had been done.[13] Soon afterwards, Judge Kennesaw Mountain Landis, the commissioner of baseball, moved to dilute the meaning of these exhibitions. He ruled that major leaguers would no longer be allowed to barnstorm as intact teams. Henceforth, individual players from different clubs would have to band together and bill themselves as "all-star" squads when arranging exhibitions. When Rube Foster asked Landis about this, the judge reportedly replied, "Mr. Foster, when you beat our teams, it gives us a black eye."[14]

As the Stars-Browns series of 1923 so convincingly revealed, the myth of white superiority was just that—a myth. Jim Crow cast a long, imperious shadow over most aspects of American life. But on the diamond, its pseudoscientific underpinnings were being dismantled, sometimes with embarrassing ease.

John Holway has researched the history of black-white competition and unearthed some interesting figures. Of the 445 games barnstorming Negro leaguers and white major leaguers are known to have played against each between 1886 and 1948, black teams won 269, lost 172, and tied four. That's a winning percentage of .601, or victories in three out of every five games.[15]

"Here's the thing," explained Cool Papa Bell. "In a short series we could beat these guys. In a whole summer, with the team we had, we couldn't. We only had fourteen or fifteen men to a team."[16] George Giles, a first baseman who played with Bell in St. Louis and Detroit, agreed. "The thing the big leaguers had on us: They had more good pitchers. We had two pretty good pitchers, two fair. But the big leaguers carried more ball players, guys who could fill in. It made a difference."[17]

Of course, not every black ballplayer was legitimate major-league material, a reality that often gets overlooked in the rush to state the Negro leaguers' case. For every Turkey Stearnes and Oscar Charleston and Bullet Joe Rogan who would surely have reached stardom in the white leagues if given the chance, there were probably a couple who would have been quite ordinary players or reserves and another five or six borderline players who may have risen no higher than Double-A or Triple-A ball. In other words, they may have been good, but not quite good enough. In terms of all-around ability, the average major leaguer of the 1920s was better than the average Negro leaguer, but this had nothing to do with genetics. Rather, it was the result of superior training, equipment, and diet. Most Negro leaguers admitted as much. The tendency by some revisionists to imply that all or most blacks would have automatically entered the major leagues simply ignores the Darwinian nature of competition in those days. There were no other major professional sports to siphon off the talent pool. The best athletes, black and white, grew up playing baseball, which made even a professional career in the high minors an achievement to be proud of.

On the other hand, had blacks been allowed to field a major-league team composed wholly of Negro leaguers—well, that would have been a horse of a different color. A *thoroughbred,* insisted Dave Malarcher of the Chicago American Giants, who played with and managed a generation of black stars. "Now, if we had picked a Negro team for the major leagues in those days," said Malarcher, "we wouldn't have had weaklings, we would have had the stars because we would have had all the Negro stars to pick from. Just like when you picked the major league team, you picked the best from all the race . . . we could have a ball club that probably could have won the pennant in the major league. All Negroes." [18]

According to George Giles, the idea made economic sense. "I used to be out at Sportsman's Park in St. Louis when they wouldn't have 500 people there [to watch the Browns]. I told guys then that they ought to put one solid colored team into the National or American League. There were enough Negroes in towns like Detroit and Chicago to fill a ball park, but a lot of white people want to see a good ball game, they don't care who's playing." [19]

Examining organized baseball's historic racism through the perspective of the owners, it's maddening to realize that any one of them with the courage of his convictions could have stepped in and broken the game's color bar, long before Branch Rickey signed Jackie Robinson to a Brooklyn Dodgers' minor-league contract in 1946. By the 1920s the reasons not to do so were slowly being chipped away by the public's growing acceptance of blacks in such entertainment industries as music and vaudeville. Certainly, baseball qualified as entertainment.

Why, then, with whites' growing fascination with black culture during the 1920s, and the mounting evidence of Negro leaguers' playing ability, didn't the game desegregate sooner than it did? After all, no written rule kept the doors closed to blacks. There were several reasons, none of them very satisfactory to the socially progressive. One was the presence of so many southern whites in the game; roughly one-third of all players hailed from the former Confederacy. Owners assumed that many would simply refuse to share a locker room or a ball field with blacks. This seemed a legitimate concern, especially with Detroit owner Frank Navin, whose manager and star attraction had a long history of violent anti-social behavior towards blacks.

Ty Cobb has come down through the years as perhaps the game's consummate bigot, a characterization that's hard to dispute. Cobb was a native of Georgia whose ancestors included Confederate officers and the treasurer of "the Lost Cause." After joining the Tigers in 1905 he was involved in numerous racial incidents, including an assault on a black woman in spring training in 1907 that had prompted Navin to shop him around the league. Bill Moore, a Tiger farmhand in the early 1920s, witnessed Cobb's irrational prejudice:

> Cobb hated a colored person worse than anything. I remember once when I was with Rochester, we were barnstorming north, zigzagging across the countryside, playing games with Detroit. I can't remember exactly where it was—some small town in Georgia—but

▲ Ty Cobb, the Detroit Tigers' manager and center fielder for most
of the 1920s, confers with owner Frank Navin before a game at
Navin Field. Except for a series of exhibitions in Cuba in 1910,
Cobb refused to take the field against blacks. When the Tigers were
getting ready to play a three-game postseason series against the Chicago American Giants in 1922, a black weekly noted: "Of course
old Ty Cobb of Georgia won't show up."

I remember the incident. We were in a restaurant after the game
when Cobb asked this black waiter something. I don't know what
was said, but the waiter said, "No." God almighty, you would've
thought a bomb exploded in there! Cobb jumped out of his chair and
grabbed the waiter by the lapels and told him, "You so-and-so nigger,
it's 'No, sir' and 'Yes, sir' when you talk to a white man!" And then
he went on a tirade about the blacks.[20]

Cobb was raised in an environment where the social inferiority of
blacks was a given and their occasional lynchings went largely unpunished. Fred Lieb, a New York sportswriter, maintained that during the
1920s, Cobb, Tris Speaker, and Rogers Hornsby—three of the game's

biggest stars—were members of the Ku Klux Klan, the extremist group that experienced a resurgence of popularity during the decade.[21] If Cobb was indeed a member, he was too smart to involve himself in cross-burnings. Instead, he registered his distaste for "darkies" in other ways. When a group of Tigers played a postseason series against the Chicago American Giants in 1922—winning one game, losing another, and tying a third—the Detroit manager was conspicuous by his absence. He undoubtedly remembered the series in Cuba, when Bruce Petway had gunned him down trying to steal a base and Jose Mendez had struck him out. Cobb wasn't about to embarrass himself again, this time in front of an American audience, for any amount of money.[22]

While Cobb was an exceptionally violent bigot, a large share of the prejudice exhibited around the diamond was more a reflection of ignorance than outright malice. White ballplayers with Negroid features—full lips, say, or dark skin—were routinely dubbed "Nig," including that most American of icons, Babe Ruth. The Tigers fielded a pair of southern outfielders in the early '30s, Joyner "Jo-Jo" White and Gerald "Gee" Walker, whose pet name for each other was "nigger." Billy Rogell, who broke in with the Boston Red Sox in 1925, recalled that he could get under the skin of Ben Chapman—a product of the Deep South—by calling him "a nigger ballplayer."[23]

The era's lack of ethnic sensibilities created a flood of players nicknamed "Dutch," "Mick," "Wop," and "Irish." The Tigers' star relief pitcher from 1929 to 1936 was Elon Hogsett, who had perhaps three drops of Cherokee Indian blood in his veins. Nonetheless, like all Native Americans in the game, he was predictably dubbed "Chief" Hogsett. Whenever he would take the mound at Navin Field, fans would break into war whoops and Ty Tyson, the Tigers' radio broadcaster, would mention something about Chief "coming in to put down an uprising on the reservation."[24] It's well known that Hogsett's teammate, first baseman Hank Greenberg, took considerable abuse for being Jewish.[25]

The art of bench jockeying was alive and well then, recalled Art Herring, who came up to the Tigers in 1929. "Man, them bench jockeys," he said. "We had Jews, Polacks. . . . You'd have two teams going at each other all afternoon." Recalled Herman "Flea" Clifton, a hard-nosed Tiger infielder in the 1930s: "That agitating went on all the time. You didn't pay no mind to that. If you did, you were dead. . . . Anything they thought could get you riled up, they'd try. They'd talk about your mother, your father, your sister. But they rode everybody. Oh, sure. Shit, these bench jockeys, they'd call their friends from down south 'nigger lovers.' Tried to get them stirred up."[26]

In 1938, the Yankees' Jake Powell innocently told a radio audience

◀ Southern ballparks had segregated seating, but it was no inconvenience for those black fans hoping to catch a glimpse of national hero Babe Ruth during one of his frequent postseason barnstorming tours. Unlike Ty Cobb, Lefty Grove, and several other major league stars of the 1920s and 1930s, Ruth demonstrated no racial bias on or off the field, which helped make him a favorite of black players and fans. (Courtesy of the Library of Congress.)

that he kept in shape in the off-season "by cracking niggers over the head" as a policeman in Dayton, Ohio. For the sake of appearance, Powell was suspended for ten days by Judge Landis, but it's telling that few in organized baseball saw anything unusual in his remarks. "In ordering the suspension, Landis charged that Powell made disparaging reference to Negroes in the broadcast," reported the Associated Press, "but added that he believed the remark was due more to carelessness than intent."[27]

For all the owners' worries, very little racial animosity bubbled up when major leaguers and Negro leaguers faced each other. Once, after suffering a tough loss in a California exhibition, Bobo Newsom mumbled, "I'm not going back to the major leagues 'til I beat these niggers." That remark was overheard by Cool Papa Bell, who responded, "We're gonna keep you out here 'bout two more years."[28] Perhaps the biggest crime was one of omission—that is, the selective memory of some white stars. Robert "Lefty" Grove of Philadelphia, the top pitcher in the American League for much of the twenties and thirties, was beaten on more than one occasion by black nines. However, years later Grove's bruised ego wouldn't allow him to admit to an interviewer that he had even played, much less lost to, blacks.

Much more often than white owners supposed, there was mutual respect between professionals, the kind of admiration for another's talent that typically binds people of the same occupation. Babe Ruth, affable to

▲ Two of a kind: the Tigers' Charlie Gehringer and Negro leaguer
James "Cool Papa" Bell.

a fault, was adored by Negro leaguers. When Christobel Torriente, a Cuban star often referred to as "the black Babe Ruth," slammed three home runs to Ruth's none in a 1920 exhibition, Ruth was understandably piqued—not at Torriente, but at his own failure as a professional to deliver.[29] The buffoonish Jay Hanna "Dizzy" Dean, who grew up with country blacks in Arkansas, was another white star who got along famously with his rivals, even when they managed to solve his storied fastball for a victory.

Charlie Gehringer and Cool Papa Bell, who first faced each other during a 1929 barnstorming tour, formed a mutual admiration society of sorts that reached an appropriate climax, some forty years later, when Bell was inducted into the Hall of Fame in Cooperstown. In the fall of 1929 Gehringer's squad of big leaguers, lured by the prospect of making two or three hundred dollars a game, played an all-star congregation of blacks in Chicago. Gehringer's team lost six of eight games, several by one run.[30] "Gehringer was the only one who looked good," remembered Bell. "He was some ballplayer."[31] Gehringer recalled Bell and his teammates hitting proven pitchers like Willis "Ace" Hudlin, George Uhle, and Earl Whitehill with ease. "They had some great players," he said. "It's a shame they couldn't have played in the major leagues."[32]

In terms of talent and temperament, the two men—born just six days apart in May of 1903—were very much alike. Gentle, keen-witted, and meticulous in their dress and work habits, both were universally respected by their peers. Each could be considered a "momma's boy." Gehringer, who was raised on a small farm near Lansing, Michigan, attended Catholic mass every morning, even as a player on the road, and put off marriage until he was forty-six in order to care for his ailing mother. Bell had grown up poor in Starkville, Mississippi. "My mother always told me that it didn't make any difference about the color of my skin, or how much money I had," Bell said. "The only thing that counted was to be an honest, clean livin' man who cared about other people. I've always tried to live up to those words."[33] If there was hope for Rube Foster's dream of a truly national pastime, it could be found in these two ambassadors of the game.

Because of attitudes like Bell's and Gehringer's, incidents on the field were rare.[34] Those major leaguers who had a problem with competing against blacks simply didn't participate in interracial games, greatly reducing the chances for trouble. Had big-league owners in the 1920s wanted to desegregate, they could have taken a lesson from this and threatened potential troublemakers with suspension or dismissal. This tactic quieted would-be strikers when Jackie Robinson came up to the Brooklyn Dodgers in 1947. The prospect of a lost payday usually works wonders on misguided principle.

Another of the owners' concerns was the possibility of fan riots and boycotts. Actually, fan violence was not an uncommon occurrence in the early decades of the century, a tumultuous era in American history. Urbanization, immigration, the labor movement, and prohibition had all been accompanied by (and frequently fostered) great leaps of violence and criminal behavior among ordinary citizens. As in most parks, the operators of Navin Field naively provided patrons with potential missiles in the form of pop bottles and seat cushions. These were hurled with abandon during a 1923 game between the Tigers and the Yankees, when one thousand fans joined both clubs in a wild, ninth-inning melee that prompted the umpire to forfeit the game to New York. A decade earlier, a crowd of Detroit fans had rushed onto the field after a home-plate collision had precipitated a free-for-all brawl between Detroit and Boston players. Brandishing clubs and rope, the angry mob had milled outside the Boston dressing room for more than an hour, threatening to lynch one of the Boston players.[35]

In 1934 Navin Field became the site of the worst World Series riot in history. In the deciding seventh game, some 15,000 fans in the temporary bleachers in left field held up play for twenty minutes as they hurled fruit, bottles, and sandwiches at St. Louis outfielder Joe Medwick, who had angered the crowd with a hard slide into the Tigers' third baseman. A "terrifying sight," is the way a sportswriter on the scene described it. "Every face in the crowd, women and men, was distorted with rage.

Mouths were torn wide, open eyes glistened and shone in the sun. All fists were clenched."[36] If the crowd could vent their frustration at a white man, owners undoubtedly reasoned, imagine if the offending party were *black.*

At best (this line of thinking continued), white fans would simply boycott any team that signed a black player. The argument that white patrons would be turned off by the presence of large numbers of black fans flew in the face of evidence, at least in Detroit. Frank Navin had rented out his park to Negro leaguers as early as 1916. That summer the Chicago American Giants and the Indianapolis ABCs played a game so exciting, recalled participant Dave Malarcher, the next day's *Free Press* "said that if the National and American leagues could play this kind of baseball that we saw today, they would have to enlarge their seating capacity."[37] Blacks had long attended games at Navin Field without incident. Charles "Red" House, a young black fan of the period, recalled that the worst things got was when someone let slip the word "nigger" while jostling for a seat, a hot dog, or a foul ball.[38]

A final reason for the majors' color bar was the most prosaic, but also the most compelling: tradition. Blacks had not been allowed to play during any of the owners' lifetimes, so why should they now? This mindless intransigence unfortunately characterizes most private clubs of conservative, middle-aged white businessmen, which is precisely what the American and National leagues were. Those owners who for either moral or economic reasons harbored secret desires to desegregate—Philadelphia's Connie Mack, for example—were not about to go against the unspoken will of the majority.

All of these excuses, taken individually, were rather weak explanations for organized baseball's uncompromising stand. Collectively, however, they built a barrier that no owner felt brave enough to attempt to hurdle.

Meanwhile, Negro leaguers continued to showcase their brilliance against all comers. Unfortunately, Detroiters were never treated to a series between the city's black and white pro teams similar to those that had taken place in St. Louis, Chicago, and Philadelphia before Judge Landis's ban. Imagine the spectacle of the Detroit Tigers and Detroit Stars facing off at Mack Park or Navin Field. Ty Cobb wouldn't have played, of course, but that would still have left room for Harry Heilmann to dig in against Bill Holland or Turkey Stearnes to test Earl Whitehill. There certainly was a tremendous curiosity among the players. Several, including Heilmann, Stearnes, and the Tigers' Bobby Veach, Johnny Neun, and Donie Bush, occasionally visited each other's parks when both teams were in town and one had the afternoon off.

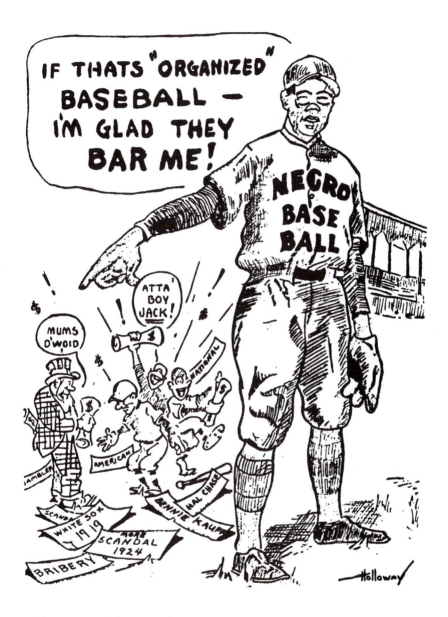

▲ This cartoon, which appeared in the black *Pittsburgh Courier* in 1924, made reference to several gambling scandals that rocked the major leagues in the years immediately following the First World War. The black press came down just as hard on the open betting among fans that was a staple of Negro-league games.

Eddie Batchelor, Jr., often accompanied his father to Mack Park and Navin Field, where the sportswriter expertly evaluated the teams' comparative strengths and weaknesses. "I remember my father saying several times that there were some years when the Stars could've beaten the Tigers," said Batchelor.[39] One of those years was 1930, when the Stars fielded perhaps their best team ever, coming within one game of capturing the NNL pennant. That season the Stars' management, including manager Elwood "Bingo" DeMoss, spoke with Frank Navin about a city series. With both teams hurting financially in the first full year of the depression, such a series was a cinch to put a few thousand much-needed dollars into each team's coffers. From the fans' point of view, the games promised to be as exciting and evenly played as the Stars-Browns series of 1923, when all three games were decided in the ninth inning. The games could even have been broadcast over WWJ, which like most radio stations was always looking for fresh programming of a local origin. While Ty Tyson had been covering the Tigers over the station since 1927, a radio broadcast would have been a first for the Stars. But all of this was a pipe dream. The owner of the fifth-place Tigers wouldn't consider it. According to Stars third baseman Bobbie Robinson, "Navin told Bingo that we had a very good ball club and that if we won, it would hurt his prestige."[40]

By the early 1930s the entrance of black ballplayers into the major leagues was considered inevitable by such respected members of the press as Westbrook Pegler and the *Detroit News'* Harry Salsinger. The key question, as posed by one black newspaperman in 1930, was: "What loop club owner will have the courage and the wisdom to see the handwriting on the wall?"[41] Most Negro leaguers of the time were realistic while waiting for the answer.

"In those days we never talked about a black player going to the majors," George Giles reflected in his old age. "But," he admitted, "there was a lot of wishing."[42]

Chapter Seven

FROM VALLEY TO MOUNTAINTOP

No matter how one views it—socially, culturally, economically, politically—the Roaring Twenties represented the turning of a corner, especially in the wild-west environs of the Motor City. The 1920 census showed for the first time more Americans living in the cities than in the country. "Living it up" would be the more precise term. In an America stuck at the confluence of postwar disillusionment and incredible technological progress, morals loosened, hemlines were raised, and even movies talked. Most people thought of little else but having a good time in what promised to be a new age of permanent prosperity.

Nowhere were the good and evil of the modern urban society more intricately intertwined than in Detroit. In newspapers and magazines around the world, "Dynamic Detroit" was held up as the symbol of modern times, a badge which city fathers wore proudly. "We have the biggest of nearly everything," bragged the 1925–26 edition of the *Detroit City Directory*, "the tallest building, the biggest electric sign, the longest bridge, the most money. . . ." There was no need to state the obvious: the biggest industry. By 1929 more than five million cars were being built annually, with the Ford Rouge plant alone employing 120,000 workers. Fifty years earlier that had constituted the entire population of Detroit.

By the middle of the 1920s, Detroit was edging towards two million people and threatening to overtake Philadelphia as the country's third-largest city. The congestion, the frenzied building, the babble of foreign languages—all added up to a super-charged pace of life that at times threatened to overwhelm sophisticated urbanites and freshly arrived sharecroppers alike.

During the 1920s Black Bottom took in another 70,000 southern blacks, bringing their number in the ghetto to 120,000 by the end of the decade. These included many whose names would grow into greatness. Up from Sandersville, Georgia, for example, came Berry Gordy, who opened the Booker T. Washington Grocery and Meat Market at the corner of St. Antoine and Theodore; thirty years later his son, Berry, Jr., would turn a small frame house into the headquarters of Motown Records.[1] Walker Smith was two years old when his family left Georgia for the promise of the assembly line; after spending his formative years in Black Bottom, Walker left for New York to ply his trade as prizefighter "Sugar Ray" Robinson. Disembarking a train from Tuscaloosa, Alabama, in 1923 was Coleman S. Young, a barber and tailor by trade and an alcoholic gambler by nature; some fifty years later, his then five-year-old son, Coleman, Jr., would be elected Detroit's first black mayor.

Perhaps the most famous transplant was a twelve-year-old boy whose sharecropper family exchanged their dilapidated, gray cabin near Lafayette, Alabama, for a dilapidated, gray frame house on Macomb Street in 1926. "You can't imagine the impact that city had," recalled Joe Louis Barrow, who dropped his surname and a good many opponents on his way to becoming the heavyweight champion and world's most famous athlete in the 1930s. "I never saw so many people in one place, so many cars at one time; I had never even seen a trolley car before. There were other things that I had never heard of—parks, libraries, brick schoolhouses, movie theaters. People dressed different, and then I realized that even with those brand-new overalls and country shoes, I wasn't dressed right. But one thing I knew, Detroit looked awfully good to me."[2] Louis would later have occasion to change his mind, after he heard the word "nigger" directed at him for the first times in his life. For Detroit also had something the city directory neatly sidestepped: world-class prejudice.

Racial bias manifested itself in a variety of ways. By law, blacks were allowed into theaters and restaurants. By custom, they were placed in the worst seats—the balcony, for instance, or by the swinging kitchen door. Many entertainment venues, such as the Graystone Ballroom on Woodward, deflected criticism and lawsuits by setting aside a certain day of the week (usually Monday) for their "colored customers." Theoretically, blacks and whites enjoyed equal protection under the law. In practice, blacks were many times more likely to be stopped, slapped around, arrested, convicted, and jailed than whites. And that was if they were lucky. In one eighteen-month period in 1925–26, twenty-five blacks were shot dead by Detroit police. New York, whose black population was twice as large, recorded just three such deaths during the same period.[3]

During the 1920s blacks were moving north to Grand Boulevard and east to Dequindre, generally taking over the rundown, turn-of-the-century housing that ethnic whites abandoned as they moved into middle-class neighborhoods west and north of the core city. Although the ghetto's boundaries were expanding, Black Bottom still was stretched as thin as an overinflated balloon. The housing shortage affected everyone, but at least whites didn't have to contend with the violence and housing covenants realtors and homeowners employed to keep certain neighborhoods "clean."

On the sweltering afternoon of September 8, 1925, the Detroit Stars were getting ready for the fourth game of a five-game set with the Cuban Stars. At the same time, in the same neighborhood, a thirty-year-old black dentist, Dr. Ossian Sweet, was moving his wife and infant daughter into a brick house at 2905 Garland. The house, about seven blocks south of Mack Park, had cost Sweet $18,500. But the price, and the less-than-friendly reception the family had been warned to expect from neighbors, were deemed to be worth it by Sweet, who wanted—and could afford—something better than a cramped apartment in Black Bottom.

The neighborhood, which newspapers later described as "declining," was still largely populated by working-class families of German, Polish, and Swedish extraction. Although a sprinkling of blacks had moved into the area without incident over the past several years, a recently organized group of homeowners called the Waterworks Improvement Association looked to check any further encroachment. The homeowners, who reportedly boasted, "We'll load this nigger's goods on the same van that brings them out and send them back where they came from," looked to recent events for encouragement. On at least four previous occasions that year, white mobs had succeeded in driving black families from white neighborhoods. The most notorious episode occurred in June, when 3,000 whites had practically dismantled a house that a black physician, Dr. Alexander L. Turner, had moved into on Spokane Avenue on the west side. After just one day, Turner sold the property and fled.[4]

Sweet, a cosmopolitan, educated man, liked to think that he was made of sterner stuff. Among the furnishings he moved into his corner house at Garland and Charlevoix was a small arsenal of weapons. As Sweet later explained, "I felt that I could never respect myself if I allowed a gang of hoodlums to keep me out of it."[5]

▲ The murder trial of Detroit dentist Ossian Sweet in 1925 drew national attention. The verdict helped establish the principle that a man's home was his castle—even if the homeowner happened to be black.

▲ The Sweet home at 2905 Garland, just a few blocks from Mack Park.

The first night in the new house was ominous. A large crowd gathered around the property, jeering and throwing rocks. Eleven policemen ringed the house to keep the hoodlums at bay. The following evening, however, more and more people were attracted to the scene. The rumblings grew louder as the muggy night unfolded. A passing automobile with two blacks inside was stopped. "There goes a Negro!" some in the crowd yelled. "Catch him. Stop him!" The windshield was shattered by stones, but the car sped away. The crowd continued to direct a hail of rocks at the Sweets' home, breaking windows and terrorizing the occupants. A taxi pulled up, and several members of the mob attempted to seize the two men who got out. "They're niggers," someone cried, "get them!" Despite the police detail on hand, it looked as if the mob were preparing to storm the house. Suddenly, a volley of shots erupted from inside. Across the street, one man fell dead and another crumpled to the ground with a bullet in the thigh.[6]

"Dear God! Must we not live?" declared W. E. B. DuBois, after Sweet and ten other family members and friends inside the house at the time of the shooting were jailed and arraigned on murder charges. "And if we live may we not live somewhere? And when a whole city of white folk led and helped by banks, Chambers of Commerce, mortgage companies and 'realtors' are combing the earth for every decent bit of residential property for whites, where in the name of God can we live and live decently if not by these same whites?"[7]

The two Sweet trials of 1925–26 were landmark cases, involving two white men—one at the end of a brilliant career, the other just starting his—who intentionally used them as headline material to educate the public to their liberal and civil-libertarian viewpoints. Clarence Darrow, at sixty-eight the most famous defense attorney in the country, agreed to take on the case for the National Association for the Advancement of Colored People. The NAACP decided to muster all of its national resources, realizing, as did Darrow, that its outcome would set a precedent for other cases of violence arising from racial segregation. The Detroit Recorder's Court judge who eagerly assigned himself the case was young, ambitious Frank Murphy. His sympathetic but fair handling of the proceedings would propel him into the national spotlight and on to a long political career, including stints as mayor of Detroit, governor of Michigan, U.S. attorney general under Franklin D. Roosevelt, and Supreme Court justice.

The trial played out against a backdrop of heightened racial tension, much of it brought on by the reemergence of the Ku Klux Klan in the early 1920s. The Klan boasted several thousand members in Detroit (including many policemen); they had grown so bold as to burn crosses in front of City Hall and the Wayne County Building in late 1923. Railing against blacks, Jews, and Catholics, the Klan was a political force in the city, backing Charles Bowles in the 1925 mayoral race. On November 3, two days before testimony in the Sweet trial began, Bowles barely lost the election to incumbent John W. Smith.

Nearly seventy witnesses were called by the prosecution, which attempted to discredit the defendants' contention that their lives were in immediate danger. Darrow skillfully poked holes in their testimony and, despite the prosecutor's adamant objections that he was turning the case into a "sociological clinic," helped win over the twelve white male jurors by introducing Sweet's experiences as a black man into evidence.

Sweet, the only defendant to take the stand, was nearly as eloquent as Darrow. He described the many racist incidents he had encountered while growing up in Florida, including a lynching. He recalled the postwar riot in Washington, D.C., when he saw a black man pulled off a streetcar and stomped. He couldn't even escape racism while studying in Europe: His pregnant wife was turned away from an American hospital.

When asked to describe his state of mind on the night of the shooting, Sweet replied: "When I opened the door and saw the mob, I realized I was facing the same mob that had hounded my people through its entire history. In my mind I was pretty confident of what I was up against, with my back against the wall. I was filled with a peculiar fear, the kind no one could feel unless they had known the history of our race. I knew what mobs had done to my people before."[8]

After deliberating for forty-six hours, the jurists could not reach a decision. Murphy declared a hung jury. The prosecutor immediately announced that the case would be retried. This time the prosecution tried only Henry Sweet, Ossian's brother and the only defendant to have admitted firing a gun. The evidence and testimony was much the same. Darrow rested the defense's case with a stirring summation that lasted seven and a half hours. The performance deeply affected everyone in the courtroom, including Judge Murphy. "This is the greatest experience of my life," Murphy later said. "That was Clarence Darrow at his best. I will never hear anything like it again."[9] On May 19, 1926, the same day the Stars dropped a 17–16 slugfest to St. Louis, the jury reached a verdict: not guilty.

No Detroit Stars from the 1925–26 teams survive to describe their thoughts on the famous Sweet trials, although there was a casual but interesting link. In 1925 Moses L. Walker, a black customs inspector, had been named an officer of the Stars by new club owner John Roesink. Walker also was vice president of the Detroit chapter of the NAACP. In the hectic weeks following the shooting, he worked with the national office in securing counsel and donations. As a liaison between Roesink and the team, Walker undoubtedly had occasion to discuss the trials with the players. Since the Stars were among the best-paid and most accessible blacks he knew, it can be assumed that Walker approached them for contributions to the NAACP's new Legal Defense Fund. The fund, which by the spring of 1926 totaled some $75,000, was a milestone in the history of the organization, as it created among blacks "the habit of giving and of giving systematically for definite objects," said W. E. B. DuBois.[10] The Sweet case proved that the young organization could be an effective force for justice.

Whatever the ballplayers' thoughts, Detroit's blacks—who daily packed the courtroom, even as the trials dragged on—realized the case's impact on future housing forays into transitional neighborhoods. One boiled Ossian Sweet's significance down to its purest essence. "Sweet stood up," said John Glover. "He wasn't going to give up his home. It was a landmark for all of us. It meant we didn't have to stand for that shit anymore."[11]

☆

For all the negative symbolism that the Sweet case and Ku Klux Klan created for the city during the mid-1920s, Detroit was still considered "a good town then," insisted Ted "Double Duty" Radcliffe, a native of Mobile, Alabama, who joined the Stars as a twenty-six-year-old pitcher-catcher in 1928.[12]

Unlike Ossian Sweet, ballplayers encountered little trouble finding a place to park their pillow. The club usually found them a bachelor apartment a short trolley ride from the park, or else introduced them to a family thrilled to have a ballplayer under their roof. As a rule, a player's salary and status allowed him to live in the more fashionable, less congested sections of black Detroit. Mule Riggins, for instance, roomed with a West Indian sport named Doc Moses on Mullett Street, close to what is now the Wayne State campus, while Turkey Stearnes rented apartments at various times on Canfield Avenue and on Illinois Street in the Kentucky district north of Gratiot. These were always furnished rooms, since, during the season, most ballplayers' possessions were limited to a suitcase of clothes, a bat bag with three or four bats, and a suit roll, which contained two uniforms, a glove, and shoes.

Because of their vagabond lifestyle (not to mention the opportunities to be found on the road), most ballplayers waited until they were at the end of their careers or retired to marry. Some, like Radcliffe, set up "light housekeeping," a street term for living with a woman outside of marriage. "But her mother interfered and I left," Radcliffe said of a nice girl he was living with in Detroit. "I couldn't live with both of them."[13]

Visiting teams usually stayed at Black Bottom's more fashionable hotels, which typically were grand, nineteenth-century brick homes converted to commercial use. During the 1920s, the choice of accommodations included the Biltmore on St. Antoine, owned by O. H. Banks and featuring a popular cafe; the Tanzy ("owned by one of our race," B. W. Tanzy), which was an old brick rooming house, also on St. Antoine; and the ghetto's largest, the Norwood, located on Adams between Beaubien and St. Antoine. The "luxury" New Oceola Hotel at the southwest corner of Catherine and Hastings offered rooms at $2.50 a night and up, while the Hotel LeGrande at 1365–83 E. Lafayette featured fish and chicken dinners in its dining room. The eighty-eight-room Hotel Williams ("Finest and best race hotel in Michigan") at 550 E. Adams offered running water and a phone in each room—luxuries that thousands of Black Bottom residents still lacked. A player didn't necessarily have to stay at a hotel; with the manager's blessing, he could spend an evening or the entire series at the home of a friend while in Detroit. Unlike the major leagues, which had strict rules regarding fraternization, the Negro leagues took a more tolerant view of friendships between members of opposing teams.

In the basement of the Norwood was the Club Plantation, where bands like the McKinney Cotton Pickers and Chocolate Dandies per-

While organized ball remained closed to blacks, America's postwar entertainment boom created opportunities in other fields, especially for musical artists such as King Oliver's Creole Jazz Band (featuring Louis Armstrong, center, on trumpet) and Bessie Smith, the wildly popular "Empress of the Blues." Musicians and Negro leaguers tended to be especially close, frequently turning out to watch each other perform and, in several cases, marrying.

formed. The Buckner brothers, Ted on sax and Milt on the organ, also played there, as did clarinetist Fred Kewley and comedian Johnny Hudgins. The postwar boom in the entertainment industries had created opportunities for blacks and helped form a lively subculture in practically every American city. Even white theaters like the Gayety in Cadillac Square featured *Lucky Sambo—A Flash of Black Lightening,* a production advertised as "The Largest and Best Colored Show the World Has Ever Known." Similar acts were featured at the old vaudeville houses on Gratiot: Joel Goldberg's "Water Melons" burlesque act with Jack Snowball and "25 singing and dancing demons" at the Koppin, or Mamie Smith and Her Jazz Hounds at the Dudley.

"To be sure, blacks in movies, in cabarets, and on the stage were not playing *Hamlet,*" observed jazz historian James Lincoln Collier. "They were supposed, instead, to perform the blues, the jazz dances, and the stereotypical slapstick comedy, replete with references to watermelons, stolen chickens, and razors, that it was assumed they had a natural aptitude for. But at least the doors to careers in entertainment were open to blacks." [14]

Most Detroiters associate the golden era of black nightlife with Paradise Valley, an entertainment and commercial district that developed along Hastings Street after the First World War. The area around lower Hastings had been referred to by that name at least as early as the 1890s, when it was populated by many Italian and Jewish immigrants. The black ghetto started forming in the early years of the century. Although many white merchants remained in the area, by the mid-1920s Hastings and adjoining streets had lost much of their Jewish population. "If you wanted authentic bagel or lox or cottage cheese," remembered one Jew, "you took a streetcar back there. But almost nobody was left there by 1930." [15]

Paradise Valley would reach its stride in the 1930s and 1940s, after the repeal of prohibition allowed many of the clandestine drinking spots to operate in the open and whites started flocking to the popular "black-and-tans" that catered to both races. Like Black Bottom, whose name came to encompass a geographical region much larger than its original boundaries, the name Paradise Valley grew to include the entire area bounded by Vernor to the north, Gratiot/Madison to the south, Hastings to the east, and John R to the west. Within were grocery stories, pool halls, bowling alleys, hotels, restaurants, music stores, and a score of nightclubs. According to Al Stark, during its heyday the Valley was alive with "dandies and their dollies," as well as "hustlers, gamblers, street corner preachers, ladies of the night, peddlers, swells and would-be swells. . . . Everyone was welcome in the Valley, whites as well as blacks, as long as they brought the right tolerance of human nature. Everyone

▲ A favorite venue for black acts during the Roaring Twenties was the Koppin Theatre on Gratiot Avenue. On this particular day in 1929, the "Twenty Dark Spots of Joy" were in town to perform. (Courtesy of Manning Brothers, Photographers.)

dressed up. Even if you had to borrow the stuff, you dressed up for a night in Paradise Valley."[16]

Wherever the action was, the social lubricant was booze—illegal, and all the more tasty for it. It's an odd fact that the lifespan of the Detroit Stars coincided almost exactly with the era of prohibition in the city. Michigan's 1918 prohibition act preceded the Eighteenth Amendment—national prohibition—by almost two years. By the time both acts were repealed in 1933, the Stars were on their last legs—a wobbly condition that hundreds of thousands of pickled scofflaws understood all too well.

Estimates of the number of speakeasies in the city ranged between 15,000 and 25,000 (including a popular spot right across the street from police headquarters). By the middle of the decade the manufacturing, transportation, protection, and sale of booze was determined to be Detroit's second largest industry. Only automaking had greater revenues and employed more people.

"In the downtown section every manner of store-front is used to disguise the 'blind pigs,'" observed one out-of-town journalist in 1925. "I went to a radio sales store which seemed well equipped and had several salesmen and clerks in attendance. A very suave, respectable-looking gentleman nodded recognition to my companion, and we walked through the railing gate, back through the stockroom, into a completely furnished

▲ Detroit was riddled with vice, with such criminal activities as boot-legging and prostitution rivaling automaking as major growth indus-tries. In the 1920s the city had an estimated 20,000 speakeasies and thousands of whorehouses, including several in the Erskine-Rivard section of Black Bottom, pictured here in 1929. (Courtesy of Manning Brothers, Photographers.)

barroom with easy-chairs, a white-coated bartender, and several people sitting around nonchalantly sipping their drinks. This same experience was repeated in a trunk store and a laundry. I was told of an undertaker's shop which served as a 'blind pig' and stored its liquor in caskets."[17]

That same year, the city recorded 232 murders, including seven police officers slain in the line of duty. Fifty-three bodies were pulled from the Detroit River, and there were ten gangland murders and disappear-ances. Extortions and kidnappings were popular money-making activi-ties. The entire city was riddled with vice, but downtown and the near east side were particularly notorious. One reporter described these areas as swarming with prostitutes and "underworld small fry."[18]

At the top of the criminal ladder was the Purple Gang, an infamous collection of young Jewish thugs who grew up together in the working-class neighborhoods around lower Gratiot. By 1925 they were involved in a number of illegal activities, including extortion, kidnapping, contract murders, and bootlegging. The gang evaporated in the early thirties, but in their prime they supplied Chicago gangster Al Capone with cases of Old Log Cabin, his favorite whiskey. They also employed many street-corner blacks to do their dirty work. "They operated from the Detroit River," said Joe Louis, who ran errands in the Valley with his schoolyard pal, Fred Guinyard. "We'd see the police stop trucks—bootleg liquor and stolen goods. Sometimes we saw the police take bodies away after a murder. Hastings Street was a bad street."[19]

One activity the Purples and seemingly everyone else with a spare mattress were involved in was prostitution, which was a major growth industry in a blue-collar town where the number of young, unattached males far outstripped the number of single women. In 1926 a survey by the American Social Hygiene Association found 711 "disorderly houses" within a one-mile radius of City Hall. Most of them were operating in the open. On Catherine near Rivard "were 'the best little whorehouses in Detroit,'" one Black Bottom resident remembered fondly, "with *les girls* sitting demurely in the front windows, ostensibly reading books but really waiting for customers."[20] As with blind pigs, it didn't take much to open up a brothel: a couple of "hot beds" set up in a back room and perhaps some complimentary rotgut. In the late twenties, Stars pitcher Jack Marshall had a place around lower Gratiot, said Ted Radcliffe. "He had a couple good girls. He was what we called a 'player.' It was raided two or three times. I was in it one time, but the policeman recognized me and let me go."[21]

Like all teams, the Detroit Stars had its share of rounders. The fair-skinned catcher, Leon "Pepper" Daniels, took full advantage of his popularity with Mack Park fans after games. "He was a really good-looking guy," said Lou Dials, who joined the team in 1930. "The women were right after him." As members of the Detroit Stars and Chicago American Giants during their careers, Floyd "Jelly" Gardner and Christobel Torrienti sampled the best of two of the country's most notorious sin cities. "Always at the nightclubs," is how Webster McDonald, another Detroit-Chicago veteran, remembered them.[22]

John Jones, who enjoyed seven productive seasons as a right fielder at Mack Park, "was a great athlete," said teammate Bobbie Robinson. "But he'd drink. There were a few on that club—Nelson Dean was another—who drank heavy. I'd tell them, 'After night falls, you don't even look at your watch.'"[23] Shortstop Frank Warfield, who played in the city for four years in the early 1920s before jumping to Hilldale, had a reputation as "a crazy man" who packed a knife while making his nocturnal rounds. While any incidents involving Warfield that might have occurred in Detroit have gone unrecorded, it's known that in a fight during a crap game in Cuba in 1929, he permanently disfigured the handsome face of teammate Oliver Marcelle by biting off the end of his nose.[24]

Detroit, while a popular destination of many ballplayers, wasn't the only city on the NNL circuit that was hopping. The South Side of Chicago was an all-black enclave of speakeasies, soul food restaurants, and twenty-four-hour dice games. And any player lucky enough to have his team schedule exhibition games back East usually made it a point to visit New York's Harlem. There, vaudeville houses like the Lincoln, Lafayette, and Alhambra featured Bessie Smith belting out "Down-Hearted Blues," or Gertrude "Ma" Rainey singing "Slow Driving Moan," "Oh Papa Blues," and other simple but powerful songs of everyday life. The center of Kansas City's wide-open nightlife was 18th and Vine, famous for Bennie Moten's and other jazz orchestras. The Detroiters and Monarchs roomed at the elegant Street's Hotel in Kansas City, and many were the times when that afternoon's heated opponents headed out, arm-in-arm, into the sweet summer evening. "Wasn't nothing but vice in this town back in them days," said bartender Jesse "Kingfish" Fisher. The ballplayers were "in between vice and what we called Society. Society on one side, vice on the other. Sometimes they would come together."[25]

These types of environments exacted occasional human costs. St. Louis pitcher "Steel Arm" Dickey was stabbed to death by bootleggers during the winter of 1922–23 in his home town of Etowah, Tennessee, while the Monarchs' married shortstop, Dobie Moore, had his brilliant career ended when his girlfriend shot him outside her Kansas City apartment. Dave Brown, bailed out of a Texas jail by Rube Foster to pitch for the Chicago American Giants, killed a Harlem man over a cocaine dispute. According to some accounts, Brown fled out West and was later found with his throat slit. Birmingham pitcher Robert Poindexter, who never had much luck against Detroit, had even less luck with Memphis first baseman J. C. McHaskell. One day in 1929 the two players got into an off-field fight and Poindexter wound up shooting McHaskell in the foot, ending his career. Not long afterwards, Poindexter was found murdered. Several other Negro leaguers, including a couple of Detroit Stars, also checked out of this world in episodes tinged with mystery.

Taken as a whole, however, the number of tragedies affecting Negro leaguers during this period was no greater or less than that of any other group of men arranged by occupation. The one that hit closest to home for some Detroit Stars involved Christobel Torriente, a handsome, reckless Cuban who joined the team prior to the 1927 season.

The "black Babe Ruth," whose most productive years were with Chicago earlier in the decade, certainly lived like the Bambino. Mack Park fans, including more than a few women, were attracted by his flam-

▲ Turkey Stearnes (third from left) "wasn't a good mixer," admitted a fellow ballplayer. Unlike many Negro leaguers, the Detroit outfielder neither smoked, drank, nor kept late hours. The taciturn Stearnes usually kept his mouth shut and his coat on, as this off-the-field shot of him and several Kansas City Monarchs attests.

boyance, which included wearing a red bandanna around his neck. A fixture at after-hour spots in every league city, Torrienti spent his winters in his native Cuba, where he had been born in 1895. He led the Cuban league in steals and home runs several times. For Chicago, Torrienti hit .400 twice and in 1923 led the NNL in batting with a .389 mark.

Life was already changing for the worse when the thirty-two-year-old was traded to Detroit for outfielder Charles Blackwell. Torrienti continued to star, hitting .326 in 1927 and .333 in 1928 for Detroit. He also took an occasional turn on the mound, compiling a 9–4 won-lost record in two seasons. But the easy availability of booze, and the unsavory characters usually associated with it, finally caught up with Torrienti.

"Instead of going back to Cuba to manage, he stayed in Chicago and made his own booze," recalled one teammate. "The winter was cold, and he drank, drank, drank. His face swelled up from the booze. At spring training he couldn't stand up in the batter's box without falling. He was in such bad condition, no team wanted him." Torrienti drifted into the lower-level black leagues, then on to New York and Chicago. Old friends discovered him living in poverty, and in about 1938 he died, an alcoholic. According to one player, "the only friend he had was liquor."[26]

These kinds of cases, and numerous less sensational ones, prompted the *Chicago Defender* to complain: "No one wants to pay to see a ball game and know that the star was out getting brimful of synthetic gin or . . . any other kind of poison the night previous to the big game."[27]

Most players tried to live right, not so much to set an example, perhaps, but to prolong their career. "I didn't drink, smoke, or keep late hours," claimed Bobbie Robinson. "I was in bed every night between 10:30 and 11, no matter where I was."[28] Despite that incident in Jack Marshall's whorehouse, Ted Radcliffe maintained a low profile. "I was kind of a quiet fella," he said. "I didn't drink. Never went to nightclubs. I'm over 90 years old today. I never would've lived that long if I had."[29]

Stars managers such as Bruce Petway and Elwood "Bingo" De-Moss regularly spoke to church groups. Usually they had a player or two in tow. On one typical occasion in 1927, DeMoss and pitcher Harold "Yellowhorse" Morris lectured members of the YMCA's sixteen-team Sunday School League "on [the] fine points of baseball," reported the *Detroit Independent.* "A great deal of interest was evidenced and many questions were shot at these experts."[30] Community relations didn't end there. Bill Hines, whose family came up from Georgia in 1919 when he was five years old, remembered playing third base on a team called the Junior Stars, which was composed of Black Bottom youths and several players' sons. Sponsored by the Detroit Stars, the Junior Stars played their games prior to regularly scheduled Negro league contests.[31]

Turkey Stearnes, one of the few ballplayers to live year-round in the city, brooked absolutely no nonsense on or off the field. John Glover once tried sneaking into Mack Park through a hole in the center-field fence. Stearnes immediately called time, grabbed the young man, and escorted him back out the same hole, "all the while saying some uncomplimentary things about me," said Glover.[32] Stearnes remained true to his character, even when noticed on the sidewalk by admiring fans. "Turkey wasn't a good mixer," said one player. "After he left the ball field, that was it. You have to get out and meet the public. He wasn't that type."[33]

Stearnes's demeanor notwithstanding, the Stars inspired considerable hero worship in many Black Bottom residents—everyone from barefoot boys begging to carry their bat bag to the dugout to merchants anxious to rub shoulders with some of the few black professional athletes

▲ Bobbie Robinson wore the uniform of the Indianapolis ABCs when he broke into the Negro National League in 1925. The Alabama native also played for the Cleveland Elites, Memphis Red Sox, Detroit Stars, Cleveland Stars, and Cleveland Red Sox during his career. (Courtesy of Dick Clark.)

in the country. Ballplayers always got a good seat and suffocating attention at favorite eateries like the St. Louis Lunch at 1723 St. Antoine, or the 250-seat Crisis Cafe on Clinton, where Homer Ferguson operated "Detroit's most fashionable colored restaurant." John Brosher, whose restaurant was just three storefronts over from the Detroit Urban League on St. Antoine, whipped up a plate of his biscuits and sausage gravy for any player on demand. Unlike personnel at the Urban League, he also knew exactly where to steer interested newcomers to the best in women, booze, and gambling. Herman Stark, a men's furnishings store at 636 Gratiot, always gave away a free shirt to the first Star to hit a home run in Sunday's game. The prize, Bobbie Robinson ruefully noted, usually went to Turkey Stearnes.[34]

Robinson, who spent his occasional day off strolling around Belle Isle or simply fanning the breeze, once toured Black Bottom with a celebrated opponent in tow. They walked into one store. "Do you know who this fella is?" Robinson asked the merchant.

▲ Black Bottom's population increased by 70,000 during the 1920s. These southern transplants included family names destined to become famous a generation later. Coleman Young, Jr., shown here at about age thirteen, arrived in 1923 as a five-year-old child from Tuscaloosa, Alabama.

"He looks familiar," the storeowner admitted. Once Robinson pointed out that it was Satchel Paige, in town with Birmingham to play the Stars, a crowd quickly gathered, shaking hands and asking for autographs. The owner, anxious to make a good impression, opened his shop to whatever the famous pitcher wanted. Satch, evidently enjoying a successful road trip, opted for two boxes of ladies' panties.[35]

Perhaps the Stars' biggest fan—literally and figuratively—was a shaved-headed bear of a man named Henderson "Ben" Turpin, who was a fixture around the park when he wasn't busy manhandling criminals and ordinary citizens. "Ben Turpin? You didn't have no run-ins with that guy," said Saul Davis, who played for several NNL teams, including the Stars. "You gave him all the respect in the world. He was a character. He was jolly, though. And he really liked his sports."[36]

Long after his death, Turpin remains one of the ghetto's true legendary figures, so its forgivable to digress a little to explore his life.[37] He came to Detroit in early 1925 as a twenty-seven-year-old former shoe-

▲ A bear of a man and a baseball fanatic, patrolman Henderson
"Ben" Turpin (standing at far left) was a familiar and imposing sight
around Black Bottom.

shine boy from Kentucky. After eighteen months as a train porter at
Union Station (where he regularly caught glimpses of Negro leaguers
stylishly arriving in Pullmans on road trips to Detroit), he was appointed
a police officer on August 1, 1927, and assigned to the Third Precinct on
Gratiot Avenue. There was no police academy then and Turpin "didn't
have to pass any kind of test to get on the force," remarked one contemporary. "He was hired for just one reason: to kick ass."

Which he did. Using his fists, nightstick, or the two pearl-handled
revolvers he kept strapped around his considerable waist, Turpin liber-
ally administered hands-on civics lessons throughout Black Bottom. No
one was immune to this kind of treatment, as Coleman S. Young found
out in the early morning hours of August 5, 1928. As recorded in a complaint to the police department, Young was making his way home a bit
unsteadily down St. Aubin when he was arrested "without cause" by
Patrolman Turpin, who "struck the said Coleman Young in the mouth
with his fist and without provocation, and told the said Coleman Young
that if he opened his mouth he would beat his brains out with his club."
The father of the future mayor added in his complaint that, "since the

above attack, the said police officer has threatened the said Coleman Young and told him to keep off his beat." Turpin was reprimanded for this incident by his white superior officers, who privately considered the swashbuckling bully a perfect detriment to crime in the ghetto.

Late in the evening of October 14, 1929, Turpin strolled into a drugstore on St. Antoine to buy a newspaper, undoubtedly anxious to read of that afternoon's thrilling World Series contest between Chicago and Philadelphia. Glancing around, he saw a face he thought he recognized.

"What the hell are you looking at?" the man snarled.

"At you, motherfucker," replied Turpin.

With that, the two pulled out pistols. Louis P. Bryant, a Purple Gang henchman with a lengthy police record, fell dead. Turpin was charged with first-degree murder, but a Recorder's Court jury deliberated just twenty minutes before acquitting him.

On another occasion, Turpin spotted a moonshiner named Charles Jackson unloading two cans of hooch from his car. Turpin made the arrest.

"I'll carry the cans," suggested Jackson, "and put them in the back of the car for you. Then we can go to police headquarters." Turpin was agreeable. Jackson bowed, got into the car, and then fled out the opposite door, Turpin in pursuit. After an extended chase, Turpin fired three shots, the third of which hit Jackson in the leg. While all this was taking place, a third character drove away with the car and the evidence.

Bouncing erratically between bravery, buffoonery, and bullying, Turpin earned a notoriety that quickly spread throughout Black Bottom. One of only a handful of blacks on the force, and an absolute nut about baseball, he often managed to get himself assigned to duty at the Stars' home games. There, displaying his customary belligerence, he managed to keep an eye on the fans and the game.

Turpin also kept an eye out for youths who displayed some athletic ability, aware that sports could keep a good kid from going bad. Better, it offered the gifted a way out of the ghetto. Joe Louis, for one, credited Turpin with saving him from the clutches of the neighborhood gang.[38] Sometime in the 1930s, Turpin organized a squad of Black Bottom boys, which he grandly labeled "Turpin's Athletic Club." They played church teams, semipro nines, and barnstorming pros, occasionally taking to the road as far west as Grand Rapids and Chicago. Turpin fancied himself a catcher, so he often poured his massive body into chest protector and shin guards for important games. And, just to make sure that his team got an even break from the ump, he occasionally kept his revolvers strapped on during play. Despite his good intentions, Turpin could not always escape his true personality. Once, upset over his team's dismal

▲ The semipro Detroit Cubs, seen here in 1935, played their games at Dequindre Park on the east side. Otis Johnson (standing, fourth from right) was an original member of the team when it was organized in 1928. Catcher-manager Barney Jenkins (standing, third from left) enjoyed a certain cachet, having played briefly for the Detroit Stars in 1929. (Courtesy of the National Baseball Library, Cooperstown, New York.)

performance, Turpin abandoned them in Chicago and drove the bus into the countryside in search of superior talent.

Inspired in part by the Stars, other young blacks formed their own nines. The most popular semipro squad of the era was the Detroit Cubs, which was organized as a neighborhood team in 1928. Otis Johnson played center field when he wasn't working at the Ford Rouge plant. "Back then one street would form a team and play the others," he recalled. "We'd play Saturdays and Sundays, raking and scraping a field where we could. We got organized from there."[39] The Cubs were a competitive nine throughout the 1930s, due in large part to the field leadership of catcher-manager Barney Jenkins. The speedy, fiery backstop enjoyed a certain cachet among his teammates, having played briefly with the Detroit Stars in 1929. He was often compared to his white counterpart on the Tigers, Mickey Cochrane, who turned the town on its ear when he delivered a pair of pennants in 1934–35. Ironically, Cochrane was nicknamed "Black Mike" by the white press.

When their work schedules allowed it, the Cubs barnstormed

against teams in Grand Rapids, Bad Axe, and Canada, although they usually confined themselves to weekend games at Dequindre Park, at Modern and Dequindre. Fred Williams, who grew up in the neighborhood, recalled the scene: "I can see it in my mind so clear. You'd go there on Sunday and see at least a doubleheader. Cost maybe a buck to get in. It was mostly black crowds, because in those days the whites would go to Navin Field to watch the Tigers. That park would always be full, too. The park would hold a few thousand. It had those old wooden bleachers. Nothing fancy.

"One of the teams would be the local guys, who couldn't travel because they had to raise families or there wasn't enough money in it to make a living. There was no fighting or anything like that at those games. It was like a big family picnic. You had people walking around with coolers, selling hot dogs, beer, pop, ice cream. A lot of people would bring a shoe box, lined with wax paper and filled with fried chicken and biscuits. Oh, that was quite an era."[40]

No matter how differently fans expressed their affection for baseball in general and the Stars in particular, it was clear that Negro leaguers were celebrities in the black community. They had money, they had talent, and they traveled to places and saw and did things that few members of their race would ever experience. As in the white community, those rooted to the routine of everyday life lived vicariously through their diamond heroes. Unlike their major-league counterparts, however, the exploits of Turkey Stearnes and Andy Cooper and Edgar Wesley were not broadcast on radio or described at length in large-circulation dailies. They did not endorse Wheaties on billboards or Camel cigarettes in magazine ads. Their very existence, much less their achievements, remained unknown to most whites. But in the city within a city that was Black Bottom, Negro leaguers were regarded as something special, and ballplayers like Bobbie Robinson knew and appreciated it.

"I was always highly respected," said Robinson. "Everyone in the neighborhood would say that they were coming to see me play. And they would."[41]

Chapter Eight

OF SATCH AND OSCAR AND OTHERS PASSING THROUGH

The stream of talented black ballplayers that passed through Detroit during baseball's apartheid era was truly remarkable. During these years Detroiters had the opportunity to watch the likes of Satchel Paige, Oscar Charleston, Martin Dihigo, Josh Gibson, Judy Johnson, and Cool Papa Bell square off against the home team. All of these Negro leaguers have since been elected by a special committee to the National Baseball Hall of Fame in Cooperstown. An excellent case can be made that several other regular visitors to Mack Park, including Mule Suttles, Willie Wells, Biz Mackey, John Beckwith, and Christobel Torrienti, belong there as well.

Just how often teams from within and without the Negro National League visited the city depended on several variables, including economics, logistics, and box office appeal. Generally speaking, each year NNL clubs scheduled one or two road trips to each city, where they played at least four games and usually five. Independent clubs and members of rival circuits, such as the Bacharach Giants, New York Black Yankees, and Homestead Grays, might swing through town once a year on a barnstorming tour. Ultimately, everything revolved around money. A team in financial difficulties felt little obligation to undertake a money-losing road trip just to complete its NNL schedule.

Undoubtedly the greatest single drawing card in the history of the Negro leagues was Leroy "Satchel" Paige, who was once described by *Detroit News* sports editor Harry Salsinger as "a first-class throwing man."[1] That was in 1941, after Paige had helped attract 35,000 fans to Briggs Stadium as the star attraction of the Kansas City Monarchs. By then, the lanky, rubber-armed pitcher's reputation as a showman and his prowess on the mound had both reached mythic proportions. Yes, Paige once intentionally walked the bases loaded in an important game so he could strike out the powerful Josh Gibson. But no, Satch didn't call in the outfield and strike out the side, or throw a no-hitter, *every* time he pitched. Yet the chance that he just might do something dramatic or bizarre created the same rare sense of anticipation and excitement that characterized America's other larger-than-life hero, Babe Ruth.

Records indicate that Paige was born on July 7, 1906, in Mobile, Alabama, although some suspect the ageless wonder was born a year or two earlier. Satchel, who earned his nickname while carrying baggage as a porter at the Mobile railroad station, spent several years in a reformatory before signing his first professional contract in 1926 with the Chattanooga Black Lookouts of the Negro Southern League. His manager was William Lowe, a member of Tennessee State University's first graduating class in 1924, and the Detroit Stars' starting third baseman (at $180 a month) before jumping leagues. Paige first appeared in Detroit the following year as a member of the Birmingham Black Barons, for whom he pitched four seasons (1927 to 1930).

What Mack Park fans saw resembled a buzzsaw on stilts. The comically proportioned Paige was nearly 6 feet, 4 inches tall, and weighed about 150 pounds. His long, skinny feet were poured into size-12 shoes. His arms, legs, and feet all flapped like fan blades as he went through his windmill windup, but the result more often than not was a fastball at the knees that even eagle-eyed batters had a hard time following. "That last one sounded a little low, didn't it, ump?" questioned one strikeout victim. Adding to Satchel's effectiveness was his pinpoint control; as a stunt during warmups he sometimes substituted a postage stamp for home plate.

Over the span of several decades Detroiters would pay to see Paige pitch at a variety of venues and in a wide array of uniforms. First it was

◀ Leroy "Satchel" Paige at Briggs Stadium, Detroit, in 1941. This time the peripatetic pitcher is wearing the uniform of the Kansas City Monarchs, the team with which he is most closely associated. (Courtesy of the National Baseball Library, Cooperstown, New York.)

at Mack Park in the 1920s as a member of the Black Barons. In the early 1930s he appeared at Hamtramck Stadium with the Pittsburgh Crawfords. Later he toed the slab at Briggs Stadium for the touring Kansas City Monarchs. And, once the American League finally desegregated after World War II, he dazzled Tiger batters as a reliever and occasional starter for the Cleveland Indians and St. Louis Browns.

Paige was a natural self-promoter. Part of his genius was in intuitively knowing how to please both races. His ambling gait, eccentric mannerisms, and colorful speech comforted whites by reinforcing the racial stereotypes of the time, while his extraordinary athletic ability lifted the spirits of blacks, who saw in his consistently overpowering performances irrefutable evidence that men of color could compete on an equal basis with whites. On one occasion Paige racked up twenty-two strikeouts against an all-star team of white professionals.

Paige's cross-country tours with Dizzy Dean in the 1930s and Bob Feller in the 1940s were wildly popular and helped make him the best-paid Negro leaguer ever: an estimated $35,000 to $40,000 in his peak years. Promoters regularly hired him to pitch on a one-time basis; by Paige's own estimation, he free-lanced for 250 or so different teams in his lifetime.

Satchel had a carefully cultivated public persona, but in private the crowd-pleasing showman disdained close friendships and remained very much his own man. "Off the field," wrote Robert Peterson in his groundbreaking study of the Negro leagues, *Only the Ball Was White,* "Satchel Paige went his own way, unfettered by the calendar and clock of lesser mortals." Jimmy Crutchfield, who had played with Paige in Birmingham, told Peterson that "Satchel was always a restless guy":

> He would pitch for us on Sunday—he'd shut some team out in Yankee Stadium, and we wouldn't see Satchel maybe until the following Sunday. Maybe we'd be playing in Cleveland or some other big city. We'd leave the hotel, go to the ballpark—no Satchel. Fifteen minutes before gametime, somebody would say, "Hey, Satchel just came in the dressing room." He was always full of life. You'd forgive him for everything because he was like a great big boy. He could walk in the room and have you in stitches in ten minutes' time. He'd warm up by playing third base or clowning with somebody and then he'd go out and pitch a shutout. How could you get mad at a guy like that?[2]

Paige's talent and drawing power made him irresistible to maverick owner Bill Veeck of the Cleveland Indians when the majors finally opened the door to black athletes. Satch made his major-league debut on July 9, 1948, two days after his forty-second birthday. In half a season the oldest rookie in big-league history compiled a 6–1 record, helping the Indians capture their first world's championship in twenty-eight years. Just as important, the large crowds that flocked to see this living legend in action helped Cleveland set an all-time, single-season attendance record. In 1951 Veeck brought Paige to the St. Louis Browns, where he was given his own rocking chair in the bullpen. The following season Satch was good enough to win twelve games and save ten others for the lowly Browns.

After leaving the majors in 1953, Paige continued to barnstorm throughout the sixties, enduring the same exhausting bus rides of his youth. He came back into the big leagues briefly as a coach. In 1965, looking to qualify for a major-league pension, he took the mound for the Kansas City Athletics. Although he was now fifty-nine years old, Paige pitched three scoreless innings against the Boston Red Sox, giving up but one hit. Fans serenaded him with a rendition of "The Old Gray Mare."

No one knows how many games Paige pitched or how many he won during his forty-some years of barnstorming and professional play throughout the U.S., Canada, Mexico, and the Caribbean. Some researchers estimate he pitched 2,500 games against sandlot, semipro, Negro-league, Latin-league, major-league, and white all-star teams and won 2,000 of them, including about 100 no-hitters. Such numbers are impossible to verify. In the end, it really doesn't matter. His reputation alone made him an obvious choice for the first class of Negro leaguers inducted into the Hall of Fame in 1971.

In his latter years Paige made ends meet by working in promotions and as a deputy sheriff in Kansas City, Missouri. Suffering from heart disease and emphysema, he passed away on June 8, 1982. As someone who had always considered himself to be in a form of entertainment, Paige had a keen sense of how baseball history might have been rewritten had he and other black players been allowed to compete in "the big show."

"If I'd been pitching to people like Babe Ruth and Lou Gehrig," he said a couple of years before he died, "they would have hit fewer homers and those lifetime batting averages might not be so impressive."[3]

While Satchel Paige may be the most fondly remembered Negro leaguer ever to step onto a diamond in Detroit, he wasn't the only rival ballplayer to enjoy a wide following. Crowd favorites such as Oscar Charleston were regularly showered with applause and coins from Mack Park fans, who were unquestionably more boisterous in their praise of the visiting team's efforts than their Navin Field counterparts.

The following profiles include some of the more popular or notable black ballplayers who regularly competed against the Detroit Stars between 1919 and 1933. Each is identified by the position and the team he was most closely associated with during these years. An asterisk indicates that the player spent part of his career with the Stars. These standouts are just a sampling of talent, not a conclusive all-star team. There could just as easily be another fifty to one hundred names added.[4]

Oscar Charleston
Center fielder, Indianapolis ABCs

Who was the greatest Negro leaguer of all-time? That question can spark an entertaining debate, although the vote often comes down to one of two men. The first is John Henry "Pop" Lloyd, a shovel-handed shortstop who was referred to as the "black Honus Wagner." The other is Oscar Charleston, a man some liked to call the "black Ty Cobb." Those who saw the multi-talented black outfielder play, including Cobb's teammate George Moriarty, loved to reverse the image. "Ty Cobb," they insisted, "was the white Oscar Charleston."

Charleston was born October 14, 1896, in Indianapolis, where he launched his pro career in 1915. He subsequently played on or managed a host of teams, although in the early days of the Negro National League he was best known as the temperamental but brilliant long-ball-hitting center fielder for his hometown ABCs. Dave Malarcher described the 6-foot-1, 185-pound lefthander: "He was all muscle and bone, no fat, no stomach, perfect broad shoulders, fine strong legs, strong muscular arms, and powerful hands and fingers. He was fast and he was strong."[5] One Negro leaguer remembered Charleston flagging down a deep outfield drive with his bare hand. Admiring major leaguers once saw him smash a 450-foot home run over the center-field fence at Pittsburgh's Forbes Field, a spot then untouched by any white hitter.

Charleston played the 1921 season with the St. Louis Giants, batting .434 and leading the league with fifteen home runs and thirty-four stolen bases. The following summer he was back in Indianapolis, where he continued to display his versatility by once again winning the home-run and stolen-base titles. He won a third straight stolen-base crown in 1923 before jumping to Harrisburg in the Eastern Colored League, where he topped the circuit in round-trippers three times in four years. He then played two seasons with Hilldale (where he concluded one argument with owner Ed Bolden by punching him in the nose) before moving onto the Homestead Grays in 1930. Two years later he became the playing manager of the mightiest black nine ever assembled, the Pittsburgh

Crawfords, who were bankrolled by a local black racketeer, Gus Greenlee. Charleston stayed six seasons.

By now considerably heavier and stationed at first base, Charleston still "loved to play baseball," recalled outfielder Ted Page. "There was nothing he liked to do better, unless it was fight. He didn't smoke, he didn't drink, but he enjoyed a good fight—with the opposition."[6]

Charleston also had several superb seasons in Cuba and was dynamite against major-league pitching. In a 1922 series against the Detroit Tigers, he collected three singles, a double, and a home run in nine at-bats. In a 1930 series, he pounded the Tigers' Earl Whitehill for four hits in seven at-bats. All told, in fifty-three exhibitions he solved major-league pitching for a .318 average.

In the late 1930s Charleston moved on to manage black clubs in Toledo and Philadelphia, where he frequently took his turn in the field and at bat. When he was fifty-three years old he found a job in the baggage department of the Pennsylvania Railroad Station. There, wrote James Bankes, the man who was arguably the greatest Negro leaguer of all time "became an object of ridicule as the typical old man who fantasized about his athletic past."[7] On October 5, 1954, a week before his fifty-eighth birthday, Charleston suffered a fatal heart attack at his Philadelphia home. His death and subsequent burial in Indianapolis went largely unnoticed by the white press. However, as the story of the Negro leagues began to unfold, Charleston's accomplishments underwent a scrutiny they never did during his playing days. In 1976 the "black Ty Cobb" posthumously joined the "white Oscar Charleston" and other baseball greats at the Baseball Hall of Fame in Cooperstown.

Josh Gibson
Catcher, Homestead Grays

Coleman A. Young, Detroit's longtime black mayor, once recalled for sportswriters his youth in Black Bottom. Among his favorite memories of the 1920s and 1930s were listening to Ty Tyson's radio broadcasts of Tiger games and sneaking into Navin Field. Did he ever dream of one day playing for the Tigers, one writer innocently asked. No, replied the mayor, who also closely followed the Negro leagues. "I would have been more likely to dream about playing for the Homestead Grays."[8]

The circuit clouts of Josh Gibson, the Negro leagues' Bunyonesque slugger, had that effect on starry-eyed youngsters. Gibson, who started his career with the independent Homestead Grays in 1930, made several cameo appearances in Detroit during his career. Other fans remember

▲ Josh Gibson at bat for the Homestead Grays, circa 1932.

him from later in the decade, by which time he was playing for the powerful Pittsburgh Crawfords. The Crawfords, like the Grays, usually found their way to the Motor City at least once a summer on western tours. If they didn't actually play the Stars (who had since passed from the scene), they caused considerable excitement barnstorming against local semipro nines or other top Negro-league clubs. At any rate, it would be unforgivable not to include Gibson in this roundup of Detroit favorites. Outside of Satchel Paige (whose fastballs he caught for several years in Pittsburgh), his name remains the most recognizable in black baseball history.

Born Joshua Gibson on December 21, 1911, in Buena Vista, Georgia, the heavily muscled righthander got as far as ninth grade before surrendering to the siren call of the diamond. To be precise, it was more of an emergency call. Sitting in the stands during a night game between the Kansas City Monarchs and the Grays, Gibson—then a teenager playing for a local semipro team—was pressed into duty by Grays' owner Cum Posey when his regular catcher lost a ball in the lights and split his finger. Gibson didn't collect any base hits in his debut, but he stayed with the team for the rest of the summer, often playing the outfield just so the Grays could make use of his volatile bat.

Gibson had three separate tours of duty with the Grays, which originally was an independent club based in a smokestack suburb of Pittsburgh. He played there from 1930 through 1933, then signed with the Crawfords, helping them to a pair of pennants in the reorganized Negro National League. In 1937 he returned to the Grays, playing through 1940. After spending the 1941 season in Mexico, he returned to the Grays in 1942, where he spent the final five years of his brilliant, abbreviated career. The Grays had become a member of the Negro National League upon Gibson's first homecoming in 1937; thanks in large part to his slugging, they would win the pennant nine straight seasons.

As a receiver, Gibson was more than adequate, but not in the same class as Bruce Petway or Biz Mackey. Although he had a strong arm, he was weak chasing pop flies. It hardly mattered, since he clearly was hired for his hitting. Standing 6-foot-1 and weighing about 220 pounds in his prime, he could knock balls over—and sometimes almost through—any ballpark in the land.

"The center-field fence at Comiskey Park was 435 feet from home plate," recalled Jack Marshall of the Chicago American Giants. "The wall was low and on top of it was a loudspeaker about 20 inches in diameter. Josh hit a line drive to center field that didn't seem to rise. It went like a frozen rope right smack into the middle of the loudspeaker. It stuck there and a groundskeeper had to pry it out."[9]

No one knows how many home runs Gibson actually hit during his lifetime. One number that was used for many years—962, or more than Babe Ruth, Hank Aaron, or anyone else has ever hit—included hundreds against semipro creampuffs as well as those hit against the cream of Negro-league, Latin-league, and major-league pitching. According to one source, Gibson hit .354 in sixteen Negro-league seasons, including 141 home runs in 439 recorded games. That works out to roughly one home run for every three games played, about fifty-one homers projected over the 154-game major-league schedule of his era.

On the basis of contemporary observations, there can be little doubt that, had he been given the chance, Gibson would have approached similar numbers batting against big-leaguers. As an eighteen-year-old, he smashed a ball over the center-field fence at Forbes Field, the first person of any color to do so. (Over the next forty years, only Oscar Charleston, Dick Stuart, and Mickey Mantle would duplicate this prodigious feat.) In 1943 the Grays rented Washington's Griffith Stadium for games. That summer Gibson slammed eleven home runs to distant left field, reportedly surpassing the number hit by all American League teams combined.

During this time there were persistent rumors that Gibson would be signed by Washington owner Clark Griffith, making Josh the majors' first twentieth-century black. Because of Griffith's cold feet, that dream never materialized. It was just one of many heartbreaks the gregarious Gibson suffered during his life. In 1931 his wife had died delivering twins, and possibly as a result the young ballplayer fought a long battle with the bottle. Then, during his prime, he was diagnosed with a brain tumor, which produced mind-numbing headaches and blackouts.

Gibson died of a stroke at his home on January 20, 1947. He was only thirty-five. Many years later, the commissioner's office paid for a proper headstone to replace the numbered metal cap that had marked Gibson's simple pauper's grave. The stone gave Gibson his due, stating that here rested a great ballplayer. There was no room on the tablet for the many stories describing Gibson's extraordinary strength, including a favorite that has him walloping a game-winning home run one day in Pittsburgh. The jubilant Crawfords then embarked on a road trip. Midway through the following day's game in Philadelphia, the ball finally came to earth, plopping into a startled outfielder's glove.

The umpire turned to Gibson, who was standing in the batter's box. "Yerrr-r-r out!" the ump declared. "Yesterday, in Pittsburgh!"

Judy Johnson
Third baseman, Hilldale

Johnson is best remembered as the heady third baseman of the great Pittsburgh clubs of the 1930s, but he first made his reputation playing for Hilldale, whom he helped lead to three consecutive ECL pennants in the 1920s.

Born William Julius Johnson on October 26, 1899, in Snow Hill, Maryland, "Judy" got his moniker from his resemblance to an outfielder on Hilldale who had the same nickname. Based in the Philadelphia suburb of Darby, the Hilldales had started as a neighborhood nine in 1912. The club grew into a powerhouse starring the formidable battery of spitballer Phil Cockrell and slugging backstop Louis Santop. At 5–11 and 155 pounds, Johnson wasn't a long-ball threat, but he was a scientific hitter and a terror in the clutch. "I was no great hitter, but I would try almost anything to get on base," he once said. "Me being a right-handed batter, I would have the left sleeve a little baggier than my right, and then I'd lean and just let the ball hit my sleeve, or I'd puff up my shirt in the front and let the ball tick me there."[10]

Johnson joined the Pittsburgh Crawfords in 1932 and played five seasons. The Crawfords' lineup, which included future Hall-of-Famers Satchel Paige, first baseman Oscar Charleston, catcher Josh Gibson, and outfielder Cool Papa Bell, is generally considered the most powerful in Negro-league history.

Johnson retired from the Crawfords in 1936 and later became a scout for both the Philadelphia Phillies and Athletics. He made history as the majors' first black coach in 1954, a year after his son-in-law, Billy Bruton, broke in with the Milwaukee Braves.

Until his death on June 15, 1989, in Wilmington, Delaware, Johnson was affectionately known as "Mr. Sunshine," a tribute to his serene and positive disposition. Newt Allen of Kansas City called him "a gentleman all through those years when baseball was just as rough as could be. He was the type of fellow that didn't try to hurt anyone. He just went along and played the game."[11] Judy Johnson played it well enough to get elected to the Hall of Fame in 1975.

Biz Mackey
Catcher, Indianapolis ABCs

Detroit fans were treated to a relatively brief look at Raleigh "Biz" Mackey, but it was enough to convince many that they were watching the

▲ Judy Johnson, "Mr. Sunshine," starred at third base for Hilldale in the 1920s and for the Pittsburgh Crawfords in the 1930s.

best catcher in the Negro National League. As members of the Indianapolis ABCs from 1920 to 1922, he and Oscar Charleston packed a wallop in the middle of the lineup, Mackey finishing runnerup to Charleston in the home run department in 1921.

More impressive than the switch-hitter's .318 lifetime average, though, were his masterful handling of pitchers and his overall defensive play. A lifetime of foul tips turned the receiver's large fingers into pretzels, but he could knit them around a ball and fire it faster and more accurately to the bag than any other backstop. "He could squat on his honkers [haunches] and throw you out," marveled "Crush" Holloway, who played the outfield for the Detroit Stars and several other teams in the 1920s and 1930s. "The ball would pass the pitcher about belt-high and still reach second right on the dot." [12]

Mackey was born in 1897 in Seguin, Texas, and grew into a cheerful giant of a man with a weakness for the bottle. He was twenty years old when he started his professional career with the San Antonio Black Aces. After three years in Indianapolis, Mackey jumped to the Eastern Colored League, depriving the Mack Park faithful of one of their favorites. In all, Mackey wound up spending half of his twenty-four-year Negro-league career in Philadelphia with the Hilldales (1923–32) and the Philadelphia Stars, where he was often compared with his white counterpart on Connie Mack's great Athletics team.

"When I was a kid in Philadelphia I saw both Mackey and Mickey Cochrane in their primes, but for real catching skills, I didn't think Cochrane was the master of defense that Mackey was," recalled Hall-of-Fame backstop Roy Campanella, who owed his career to the catcher's paternal guidance and patient instruction. "I gathered quite a bit from Mackey, watching how he did things, how he blocked low pitches, how he shifted his feet for an outside pitch, how he threw with a short, quick, accurate throw without drawing back." [13]

In 1936 Mackey moved on to the Baltimore Elite Giants, where he shaped Campanella into a virtual clone of himself, then closed out his career as player-manager of the Newark Eagles from 1939 to 1947. There he helped develop Monte Irvin, Don Newcombe, and Larry Doby for the majors. Despite his contributions to the game, Mackey spent the remainder of his life driving a forklift in Los Angeles. He died there in 1959.

Martin Dihigo
Infielder, Cuban Stars

For sheer versatility, few players in the history of the game can match Martin Dihigo. John McGraw, the manager of the New York

Giants, called the tall, good-humored gazelle one of the greatest natural ballplayers he had ever seen. Others have called him the greatest utility player of all time.

Born May 24, 1905, in Matanzas, Cuba, Dihigo came to the United States as an eighteen-year-old first baseman and pitcher for the Cuban Stars, which operated as a permanent road club in the Negro National League. During the 1920s, visitors to Mack Park may have seen the 6-foot-1, 190-pound righthander play every position except catcher. As a fielder he was stylish and exhibited great range; as a hitter he racked up batting averages of .421 in 1926 and .370 in 1927 for the Cuban Stars; as a pitcher he relied on a strong arm to win a handful of games. But these partial statistics do him a disservice. Spending most of his career in Latin American leagues, he won in the neighborhood of 250 games and batted over .300 lifetime.

Dihigo died May 20, 1971, in Cienfuegos, Cuba, where fans like dictator Fidel Castro (himself a former semipro pitcher) had long considered *El Maestro* a national hero. That summer, Satchell Paige was inducted into Cooperstown. "I'm not number one," Paige said in a rare moment of humility. "Martin Dihigo is."[14] Six years later, Dihigo joined Paige in the Hall of Fame.

Cool Papa Bell*
Outfielder, St. Louis Stars

The oft-told story is that James "Cool Papa" Bell was so fast that he could turn off the light switch and jump into bed before the room got dark. Such tales emphasized the slender center fielder's flying feet, which he employed to steal bases, leg out triples, score from second on groundouts, and chase down long pokes to the outfield during nearly three full decades of Negro-league play.

Bell was born May 17, 1903, in Starksville, Mississippi. When he was sixteen he moved to St. Louis, working in a packinghouse for fifty-three cents an hour while playing semipro ball on the weekends. In 1922 the lefthanded pitcher caught the eye of the St. Louis Stars of the Negro National League, which signed him up for $90 a month. Bell's first start was against the powerful Chicago American Giants, whom he beat, 4 to 3. After the game he was challenged to a foot race with the Giants' Jimmie Lyons, reputedly the fastest man in the league. Bell, who had played for years barefoot in Mississippi, beat Lyons wearing a pair of dilapidated $1 shoes.

Bell, who in 1924 was timed circling the bases at an almost unbelievable twelve seconds (the major-league record is 13.3 seconds by Evar Swanson of the Cincinnati Reds), was soon converted into a switch-hitting outfielder by St. Louis. He helped the Stars to three NNL pennants before splitting the abbreviated 1932 season with Kansas City and Detroit. He later was a member of the famed Pittsburgh Crawfords of the mid-1930s.

In addition to the summer Negro leagues, Bell played winter ball throughout the tropics. No matter where the gentle, soft-spoken Bell flashed his smile, the story was the same: a batting average in the .320-to-.400 range, a bushelful of stolen bases, and an army of admirers. Teammate Ted Page remembered Bell as "an even better man off the field than he was on it. He was honest. He was kind. He was a clean liver. In fact, in all of the years I've known him, I've never seen him smoke, take a drink, or say even one cuss word."[15]

In 1974 Bell was working as a night watchman in St. Louis when he learned that he had been elected to the Hall of Fame. He passed away March 7, 1991.

Mule Suttles*
First baseman, St. Louis Stars

George "Mule" Suttles, born in Brockton, Alabama, on March 31, 1901, began his Negro-league career with the Birmingham Black Barons in 1923. Detroiters got their first glimpse of the powerfully built outfielder the following year, when the Barons began play in the Negro National League. In 1926, now playing first base for the St. Louis Stars, Suttles hit .418 and pounded out twenty-five doubles, nineteen triples and twenty-seven home runs. All were league highs. The following year he was hitting .456 and slugging the ball at an impossible .937 clip when a broken ankle sidelined him after thirty games.

Few players of his era, black or white, hit the ball as hard and long as Suttles. All told, in a Negro-league career that stretched from 1923 to 1944, Suttles hit 183 known home runs for several teams, including a couple for Detroit in 1932. According to researchers, that ranks him just behind Turkey Stearnes as the all-time home run champion of the Negro leagues. As more scoresheets are unearthed, it's possible he may pass Stearnes.

The 6-foot-1, 215-pound righthander wasn't choosy about who he hit against. In exhibitions against white major leaguers, he hit .374 and cracked eleven home runs in ninety-nine at-bats. "Gol, he could hit a ball nine miles," said Hall-of-Famer Charlie Gehringer, recalling a 1929 barn-

▲ The St. Louis Stars consistently fielded one of the Negro National League's strongest teams in the late 1920s. In 1930 the Stars defeated Detroit in a seven-game playoff for the NNL pennant. The 1928 roster included (standing, from left) manager "Candy Jim" Taylor, Clarence Palm, Ted Trent, George "Mule" Suttles, J. Williams, "Slap" Hensley, Willie Wells, Henry Williams, and Dewey Creacy. Sitting, from left, are batboy Norman James, John Henry Russell, James "Cool Papa" Bell, Branch Russell, Richard Carron, Roosevelt Davis, Wilson Redus, and Luther "Vet" McDonald. (Courtesy of the National Baseball Library, Cooperstown, New York.)

storming tour between major-league and Negro-league stars. "I remember [Earl] Whitehill was our pitcher, and he couldn't get Suttles out. And Whitehill was a good pitcher. Suttles wore poor ol' Whitehill out." [16]

Suttles played his last several years for the Newark Eagles and New York Black Yankees. He died in Newark in 1968, his once massive body wasted away to nearly nothing by cancer.

Willie Wells*
Shortstop, St. Louis Stars

Many observers have made the case that the best black shortstop of the 1920s was this stocky, bowlegged native of Austin, Texas. Favorably compared to Negro-league pioneer John Henry Lloyd, Wells didn't possess Lloyd's cannon arm, but he compensated with a range and accuracy that was second to no one.

Born October 10, 1904, Wells started his career at seventeen with

San Antonio. He moved to St. Louis in 1924 to play with the Stars. At 5-foot-9 and 165 pounds, Wells was a compact dynamo from the right side of the plate, compiling a batting mark of about .330 during his quarter-century of Negro-league play. This included seasons of .382 in 1927 and .403 in 1930, the latter leading the Negro National League. That year he and Ted Trent, Mule Suttles, and Cool Papa Bell helped St. Louis defeat Detroit in a thrilling seven-game playoff for the NNL pennant. While he didn't normally hit for distance, his speed and power made him a constant extra-base threat and resulted in a league-high twenty-seven home runs in 1929.

Wells played with Detroit in 1932, batting .296 in sixteen known games and fielding his position flawlessly. He went on to play for a succession of black clubs on the East Coast and in Mexico before calling it quits in 1948.

Wells, who was nicknamed "Devil," was anything but. Proud and competitive but always modest of his considerable achievements, he was well-liked by fans and opponents. After leaving baseball he worked at a delicatessen in Austin, where he died January 22, 1989.

Ted Trent*
Pitcher, St. Louis Stars

Judging by his performances against barnstorming white major-leaguers, particularly against a pair of proven .400 hitters, Ted Trent would surely have been a force in the big leagues. He reportedly struck out Rogers Hornsby three times in one game and Bill Terry four times in another. As it was, the rawboned righthander had to settle for being one of the premier moundsmen of the Negro leagues for thirteen years. During his career he racked up a 94–49 won-lost record, including a 21–2 mark in 1928.

Trent was born December 17, 1903, in Jacksonville, Florida. Filling out to a 6-foot-3, 185-pound frame, he joined St. Louis in 1927 and over the next five seasons pitched them to two NNL pennants. According to James Bankes, Trent "owned an assortment of wicked curves." He played briefly for Detroit in 1932, winning four of his six starts, before latching on with the Washington Pilots and New York Black Yankees.

Trent went on to pitch six seasons for the Chicago American Giants, becoming the anchor of their mound staff in the 1930s. He settled in the Windy City upon his retirement in 1939, dying there January 10, 1944.

Dave Malarcher*
Third baseman, Chicago
American Giants

"Gentleman Dave" was a mainstay of Rube Foster's great Chicago American Giants, playing a spiffy third base between 1920 and 1934 and succeeding Foster as manager in 1926. A switch-hitter, the slightly built (5–7, 147 pounds) Malarcher wasn't much of a threat at the plate, generally hitting in the .270 range, but he was a fine clutch performer and an outstanding glove man.

Possessed of an even temperament and superior intelligence, the hard-working Malarcher was a favorite of players and fans. The secret to his work ethic can be found in his upbringing. He was born October 18, 1894, in Whitehall, Louisiana, the youngest of eleven children. His mother, a former slave, pushed her children to get an education. Malarcher labored in the cane and cotton fields when he wasn't studying or playing ball. His performance in a 1916 game against the barnstorming Indianapolis ABCs prompted the team to offer him a spot on their roster for $50 a month; Malarcher, making $10 a month as a house boy while attending New Orleans University, readily accepted. Two years later, while serving with the 309th Pioneer Infantry Unit in France, he received a letter from Rube Foster inviting him to join the Chicago American Giants upon his return home.

Foster first sent Malarcher to Detroit when he opened a satellite operation there in 1919, but by the following season he was back with the Giants for good. Between 1920 and 1927 he helped Chicago cop five NNL pennants. It wasn't the opposition but the insufferably long road trips, including one memorable 1,700-mile bus trip from Louisiana to Winnipeg, that finally drove Malarcher from the game. "They were conditions which I could not continue to bear," he told Robert Peterson many years later.[17]

As an old man, Malarcher was once asked why he had developed into such a fine athlete. He replied, "Because I led a good clean life, because I swam the Mississippi, ran through the woods looking for rattlesnakes, worked in the cotton fields, and I was really strong."[18] Malarcher sold real estate in Chicago until his death on May 11, 1982.

◄ "Gentleman Dave" Malarcher, who enjoyed success as a player, manager, and poet. (Courtesy of Dick Clark.)

Willie Foster
Pitcher, Chicago American Giants

Although Willie Foster was Rube Foster's younger brother, it wasn't nepotism that made the solidly built lefthander the ace of the Chicago American Giants' mound staff. An overwhelming arsenal of pitches did. "Willie Foster's greatness was that he had this terrific speed and a great, fast-breaking curve ball and a drop ball, and he was really a master of the change-of-pace," said his manager, Dave Malarcher. "He could throw you a real fast one and then use the same motion and bring it up a little slower, and then a little slower yet. And then he'd use the same motion again, and Z-zzzz! He was really a great pitcher."[19]

Foster came into the world on June 12, 1904, in Calvert, Texas. He

159

▲ Willie Foster's Negro-league career was nearly as distinguished as that of his much older brother, Rube. Between 1923 and 1937, Willie won 137 games and lost only 62.

entered the NNL as a member of the Memphis Red Sox, then switched to his brother's club. In the 1926 playoffs against the powerful Kansas City Monarchs, he won both ends of a doubleheader against Bullet Joe Rogan, giving Chicago their fourth Negro National League pennant in seven seasons. He then went on to win two games in the Colored World Series against the Eastern Colored League's representative, the Bacharach Giants, including a 1–0 shutout in the finale.

The following season Foster compiled a sparkling 21–3 record, the best of his fifteen Negro-league seasons. As of this writing, nobody has won more games in the Negro leagues than Foster, who between 1923 and 1937 won 137 games and lost only sixty-two for Memphis, Chicago, the Homestead Grays, Kansas City Monarchs, and Pittsburgh Crawfords.

Foster went on to become dean of men and baseball coach at Alcorn College in Lorman, Mississippi. He died in Lorman on September 16, 1978.

Jelly Gardner*
Outfielder, Chicago
American Giants

Detroit served as a pair of bookends for the career of Floyd "Jelly" Gardner, who played for the Stars in 1919 and again in 1931. In between were eleven years of brilliance for the Chicago American Giants, for whom the 5-foot-7, 160-pounder batted leadoff and patrolled the outfield for five pennant-winning teams.

Gardner, who was born September 27, 1896, in Russellville, Arkansas, had a reputation as a fun-loving playboy, someone who thoroughly enjoyed the Roaring Twenties at jazz joints in Detroit and elsewhere. The partying might account for his wildly fluctuating batting averages. A line-drive hitter who swung lefthanded, his averages ranged from a low of .182 in 1920 to a high of .357 in 1924. He hit .286 lifetime with just one known home run. However, his speed made him a valuable commodity in the outfield and on the bases even in his final season; batting .193 for Detroit in 1931, he still managed to lead the short-lived league in stolen bases.

Gardner worked for the railroad after his baseball days. He died in Chicago in 1977.

Bullet Joe Rogan
Pitcher, Kansas City Monarchs

A compact, powerfully built righthander, Joe Wilbur Rogan was a fixture with the Kansas City Monarchs for nearly two decades, from 1920 to 1938. His greatest seasons were 1924, when he won sixteen games and lost five, and 1925, when he won fifteen and lost but two. Both years he led the league in wins and, most important, the Kansas City Monarchs to NNL pennants and a victory over Hilldale in the first Colored World Series.

Born July 28, 1889, in Oklahoma City, Rogan grew up in Kansas City. His prime years were spent in the largely unrecorded leagues of the Southwest, where he played for the Army's 25th Infantry team. It was Casey Stengel who discovered Rogan while on an exhibition tour in the fall of 1919. Stengel recommended Rogan and several of his Army teammates to J. L. Wilkinson, then forming the Kansas City Monarchs for the inaugural Negro National League season. The following spring Bullet Joe joined Rube Foster's circuit as a thirty-year-old rookie.

As his nickname suggests, the 5-foot-6, 155-pounder had a crackling fastball, as good as Satchel Paige's in many players' eyes. What set him apart was a devastating curve that "broke straight down," said Babe Herman, the Brooklyn outfielder who played against Rogan in California and Canada.

And his hitting. Outside of Babe Ruth, no ballplayer of any color surpassed Rogan as a pitcher and slugger. When he wasn't taking his turn on the mound, Rogan played the outfield or occasionally second base for the Monarchs. In 1922, for example, he won thirteen games, lost six, and walloped a league-leading sixteen home runs. The following year he hit .416 and was 11–7 on the mound. In 1929, at the age of forty, Bullet Joe was back in the outfield full-time, hitting .341 and stealing twenty-three bases in seventy-six games. All told, Rogan hit .343 and compiled a 113–45 pitching record in Negro-league play. In sixteen games against barnstorming white major leaguers, he hit .389 off the likes of Charlie Root, Dizzy Dean and Bob Feller.

After many years of managing the Monarchs, Rogan spent several more working for the post office in Kansas City. He passed away on his farm on March 4, 1967. Three decades later, he has still not received his proper due. "The guys they put in the Hall of Fame are a joke," Babe Herman once told Casey Stengel. "Rogan's the guy ought to go in."[20]

Chet Brewer
Pitcher, Kansas City Monarchs

Chet Brewer, who was born January 14, 1907, in Leavenworth, Kansas, couldn't match teammate Bullet Joe Rogan at the plate, but for a time in the mid-1920s he was more than his equal on the slab. In 1926, his first full season with the Kansas City Monarchs, Brewer had a 12–1 record; three years later he was 17–3. Both years he led the Negro National League in winning percentage. The 6-foot-4, 180-pound righty often "cut" or sandpapered the ball, earning him the nickname of "The Crook," but he had masterful control of his pitches, illegal and otherwise.

Although he is most closely identified with the Monarchs, Brewer also played for the Washington Pilots and New York Cubans in the 1930s and the Philadelphia Stars and Chicago American Giants in the forties. He finished his long stint in the Negro leagues in 1948 with the Cleveland Buckeyes, but he never really left the game, spending the balance of his life coaching youth baseball in Los Angeles and scouting for the Pittsburgh Pirates.

Brewer's final tally in the Negro leagues was an unremarkable eighty-nine wins and sixty-three losses. However, throw in several barnstorming seasons and others spent in the competitive Latin American leagues during the 1930s and 1940s, and Brewer emerges as one of the game's finest pitchers of color in the years before integration. He died March 26, 1990.

Newt Allen*
Second baseman, Kansas
City Monarchs

The diminutive second baseman's nickname was an abbreviation of his proper name, Newton, not a comment on his size. Born May 19, 1901, in Austin, Texas, Allen played twenty-one seasons with the Kansas City Monarchs between 1922 and 1944, an unusually long association with one club, particularly by Negro-league standards. Outside of the usual winter ball in Mexico and the Caribbean, his only time spent away from the Monarchs were brief stays with the St. Louis Stars in 1931 and the Detroit Wolves in 1932.

Five-foot-eight inches tall and weighing but 158 pounds, Allen—together with shortstop Dobie Moore—formed one of baseball's greatest double-play combinations during the 1920s. "When you see Newt Allen and Moore, you could take Charlie Gehringer, Frankie Frisch, and any of that bunch," exclaimed teammate Frank Duncan. "Brother, you're talking about a combination!"[21]

Batting from both sides of the plate, Allen compiled a .296 career average. In 1945 he helped groom his successor at second base, Jackie Robinson, who because of injuries wound up playing shortstop for the Monarchs. While Robinson broke the majors' color line two years later and went on to a brilliant big-league career with the Brooklyn Dodgers, his tutor became foreman of a county courthouse.

Newt Allen died June 11, 1988, in Cincinnati, having lived to see Robinson and several Negro-league contemporaries admitted into the Hall of Fame.

Dobie Moore
Shortstop, Kansas City Monarchs

Newt Allen's keystone partner was born Walter Moore in Georgia in about 1893. The stocky (5-foot-11, 230 pounds) righthander first raised eyebrows as a teenaged member of the all-black 25th Infantry Regiment service team, one of the strongest amateur congregations ever assembled. After soldiering for several years in the Pacific and Mexico, the strong-armed shortstop joined Bullet Joe Rogan and other army buddies on the Monarchs in 1920. Over the next seven seasons the notorious bad-ball hitter banged the ball at a .365 clip, including a league-high .453 in 1924. John McGraw reportedly told him, "You'd be worth $50,000—if only you were white."[22]

Boisterous, brash, and illiterate, Moore had a devil-may-care atti-tude that did him in just as the Monarchs were pursuing a fourth straight NNL pennant in 1926. Back home from a lengthy road trip, Moore ducked out on his wife and a team party in Kansas City to visit a girl-friend, with whom he got into an argument as he attempted to get through her door. As the frustrated Moore left through the alley, his angry lady friend leaned out a window and fired several shots from a pistol at him, shattering his leg and ending his career.

Crippled and broke, the person many considered the best black shortstop of all time reportedly drifted to Detroit. As is the case with so many of the Negro leaguers who passed through the game in the 1920s, what happened to him after he left baseball remains a mystery to this day.[23]

Chapter Nine

THE WAY IT WAS: SAUL DAVIS

Few ballplayers personify the quintessential Negro leaguer of the 1920s and 1930s better than Saul Davis, a Louisianian whose wandering nature was evident even before he became a journeyman infielder with several black teams, including brief tours of duty with the Detroit Stars in 1925 and 1931. Davis also played for the Birmingham Black Barons, Chicago American Giants, Cleveland Tigers, and Memphis Red Sox during his Negro National League career. After an additional quarter-century of barnstorming across the United States and Canada, the long, winding road finally stopped for good in Minot, North Dakota, where today Davis lives alone in a small house.

No, traveling wasn't hard on me. I was taking care of myself. I looked out two and three months ahead of time. The thing about it is, I picked my spots. If things got rough, I didn't stay there. I'd just get to traveling. Hop a freight if I didn't have no money. All my life I've been traveling.

You want my life story? Well, I was born on the twenty-second of February, 1901, in Louisiana, and raised at the Monticello Academy School in Arkansas. My father never played baseball. He was in the horse business. During those days my people didn't have the chance they have now. Back then the Negroes worked for the rich white people. The Wells brothers, they were big horsemen, and my father worked for them all his life.

The Way It Was: Saul Davis

We lived in the backwoods, in cabins on the bayou. Indoor plumbing? Yeah, we had the whole bayou. We didn't know what indoor plumbing was. We didn't have no baseball then. Only thing we had was alligators and snakes.

You know, that bayou was a pretty tough place to live. We only had around seven or eight acres of land to live on. The rest of it, we were living in water. No crops. We had cypress trees. See, a lot of my people were huntsmen and woodsmen and they made all kinds of things out of cypress. That cypress wood is the toughest kind of wood you can get. Back then that part of the country was thick with cypress. You couldn't get through there hardly. No roads. You made your own trail.

I never got bit by a snake. They taught us how to avoid them. How? You step on his head with your foot. With your bare foot. You didn't have shoes half the time. You learn how to charm them, like, and get their attention. When you get them steady, that's the time you take them. A lot of times you use a fork or a stick to catch the head. You don't take many chances jumpin' on the head. That's just the sport you get out of it.

A lot of times it's just how much patience you got. And you gotta have patience if you want to live. If you get caught out in the evening, you climb up in a tree and you don't try to come back home. See, sometimes you're eight, nine years old and you're away from home for two or three days, but they don't worry about you because they can see you floating in that bayou someplace. You're alright. You can come back home and they're glad to see you.

My mother was a Creole. She and her grandfather and all them were swamp people. She liked to travel. I traveled all up and down the Mississippi River during my baby years. I had half-brothers and half-sisters. I don't know how many I had. The onliest one I can remember is my full brother.

My mother could pass for being white. For her having two black kids, she got through life pretty good until we started getting around six, seven years old. Then she couldn't take us different places. She had to leave us here and there. Then I guess she got tired of that so she got on my dad to put us in schools. He paid for that. We didn't see him but once the year, where we was living. He couldn't come out to the swamp. It's all water. There were no roads, so you couldn't bring no horse there.

I ran away when I was around fourteen, fifteen. I wanted to see the world. I wish today I would've stayed in school. The world has been my

◀ Saul Davis as a member of the Birmingham Black Barons, 1923.
(Courtesy of the National Baseball Library, Cooperstown, New York.)

life and my experience. Everything I've got, I got myself. Myself and God, too.

I made myself in Hot Springs, Arkansas. By me being a bellboy and working my way through life, I became acquainted with the Boston Red Sox and the Philadelphia Phillies when they were practicing there in the spring. I got to shaggin' balls out there in the field with some of the ballplayers.

Hot Springs had a Negro league. I got with the Vapor City Tigers in Hot Springs. We played in the old Boston Red Sox field, Whitaker's Park. I started from there. See, the Negroes wasn't playing with the whites then. I was pretty smart, if you want to call it, or clever or something, and I'd taken up a lot of ideas from the white ballplayers on the Red Sox because I could go in the clubhouse. I was pretty clever on racial matters. I mean, I had sense enough to know when you went into those places, whatever was said, I did. Of course, I was jolly with them. I had a few jokes and a few tales to tell them about rattlesnakes and gorillas and things. I'm tellin' you how I got through.

I played shortstop for Vapor City. I was a pretty good glove man and I had a pretty good arm. I got my help from the white ballplayers. The fella who played first base for the Little Rock team—I'm trying to remember his name—he took quite a liking to me and he used to talk to me and tell me a lot of different things. He was a lefthanded first baseman. I don't know what happened to him. I don't think he went into the majors.

That first year after I started playing for the Vapor City Tigers, I got a call from the Negro Texas League. I started down there with the Houston Black Buffaloes in 1918. That was during the World War. I played there until 1923, when I got a call into the Negro National League with the Birmingham Black Barons. We had a lot of boys on that Houston team that came into the league. They all made reputations.

I weighed 165, 170 pounds, and stood five-feet-eleven. I tried to stay in good condition. Never had a sore arm. I'd get a rubdown, all that, about once a month. I'd hit .260, .270. I'd try to lay the ball down or try to place-hit. I didn't care too much for home runs. I didn't try to hit 'em hard, no way, except once in a while trying to show off. Especially if I was playing in St. Louis, with that short left field. I hit one or two in the car barn. That's where they parked the streetcars.

I look at these ballplayers today and it's a shame. Big-league ballplayers and they can't even lay a ball down. If you couldn't lay the ball down in Chicago, you'd be going someplace else. You see, that league wasn't no baby. If you couldn't play ball, you didn't stay long.

I don't know why, but I made friends with the bosses. I tried to stay in good words with those guys in order to stay on the job. You tell me to do something, I'm not gonna tell you to go to hell or something, which some of them did. Some ballplayers get to playing good and think they own the club. That never came into my mind. Ain't no club I want to own. All I want to do is try to make a living and get hold of some money and try to beat that other guy to stay on the ballclub.

My reputation was: no pals. I had good friends, but once you get out on the field, that's it. My home is on that ballfield, 'cause when I leave that ballfield, I got nowhere else in the world to go, except to another ballclub somewhere. See, I was one of those outlaw ballplayers. Didn't have no home to go to. I had to make myself that way because, playing ball, you can't be buddies.

One day in 1925 Rube Roster came down to Birmingham and put me in one of those big old roadsters and took me to Gadsden, Alabama, where we were training. Rube, you know, liked to steal all the ballplayers he could, and he got me traded to the Chicago American Giants.

That was a heck of a ballclub then. We had Steel Arm Davis and Jim Bray and Jim Brown. Sandy Thompson, Jelly Gardner, and Christobel Torriente played the outfield. We called Torriente "the black Babe Ruth." He could hit that ball. We had some heck of a pitching staff: Willie Foster, Webster McDonald, Pat Padrone.... Padrone, he was from Cuba. He's the one that taught Willie Foster to pitch.

I took shortstop away from little Bobby Williams. He was from Pittsburgh. He was a hell of a ballplayer. When I come on the ballclub, Jelly Gardner, he'd been on the team seven, eight years. Him and Bobby Williams were friends, so he'd throw me bad hops from the outfield and try to make me look bad. That was for the manager. See, I done beat his friend out of a job. Well, heck, I don't care nothin' about his friend. Now, if he says anything, that he wants to whup me, then okay, we can go someplace and fight. But if you want to play ball, don't try to show me up on the field. You're trying to make a living and I'm trying to make a living, my friend. I watch all the tricks on the ballfield, and I think I know some pretty good ones. Well, I had a good arm for that infield. I'll walk up on you ten or fifteen feet and shove it at you. Jelly and I were good friends after I got him fixed, after I throwed him one or two bad hops and they knocked him in the mouth.

We had some big crowds in Chicago then. Especially when we played the good clubs. Kansas City had a good one. So did Detroit. Kansas City had that Frank Duncan catchin'. Frank put that uniform on and you'd think it was tailor made. That Dobie Moore at shortstop, he was some ballplayer. I'd take after him. Dobie could get between a runner and the base [in a rundown] and stick his big behind out and you'd have to run all the way 'round him. I was at that dance in Kansas City when he got shot by his girlfriend. He couldn't play ball no more after that.

Detroit had a heck of a ballclub one time with Turkey Stearnes and that outfit. That was back in '25, '26, around through there. That Turkey could hit a ball a thousand miles. You get it into him, you did wrong. Turkey was a homeboy. He didn't get out much. But he was a good fellow. A gentleman. And that Lefty Cooper, he had everything—curveball, fastball, and he'd knock you down too. He was with Detroit a long time.

Ed Wesley? Doggone right he was a pretty good ballplayer. And he was a pretty mean guy. He was a hard guy. You couldn't fool with him. I don't know what happened to him. Didn't he go to Cuba or Japan or someplace? Some of them went down to South America. I just don't know.

I didn't mind the traveling. In the beginning we were riding in Pullman cars, but after a while we started riding in touring cars. Lincolns and Cadillacs. It was rough with nine of us in a car. You had that board running across those two little seats, you know. Six in back and three in the front. You could get from Chicago to Detroit overnight.

On the way to Detroit we'd go to Battle Creek, Kalamazoo, towns like that. Barnstorming. When we went back East we'd play some of those company teams, like Goodyear Rubber or that Buick ballclub in Flint. Those guys were like pro teams. You didn't get paid nothing extra on those barnstorming trips. You were lucky to get your meal.

We played white clubs. How were we received? Good, no trouble at all. Only time I got something was in Niles, Illinois. I'm coming by this one sonofagun in the grandstand and then he hollers about the niggers: "Hey, nigger! You a good ballplayer?" I cussed him out right then and there and kept on walking to the field.

The white teams, we could beat them any time, any way we wanted to. They couldn't play with us. Of course, we couldn't show off too much. We kept the score down 'cause we didn't want to embarrass them. Well, you had to, you know. They taught us that.

Used to love to go to Detroit. Oh, we had a lovely time in Detroit. Stayed at the Biltmore Hotel. Used to eat right in the hotel. We'd get dressed there for games and a bus took us out to Mack Park. I went to a lot of parties and things, but I don't know where they were. I still don't know where they were. The chauffeurs' club was one. There was prohibition, but not in the clubs, not downtown. You got all the drinks you wanted. We didn't have no trouble with the police. The bridge and the tunnel wasn't even built then. We used to catch a boat and go over to Windsor.

Women? Oh God, yeah. They'd meet you at the park, and take you home too. Leon Daniels, now he was a ladies' man. So was Jelly Gardner. So were most of the owners. Myself? Well, I'd wait for 'em. I let them do whatever they want to do. I got married once. She's in New York someplace. I was twenty-three. I met her in Birmingham. I was married six, seven years. Had a daughter. I had another girlfriend. She was out of Chicago.

I played for Rube Foster for a couple of years. He went insane, you know, in 1926, and so the club was kind of shaky. I jumped the club and went to the Memphis Red Sox. I didn't like it there so I went to Ohio and played for the Cleveland Tigers. And I left Cleveland and went to the Detroit Stars. Bingo DeMoss got me to Detroit.

I was rooming with Ed Rile, a big first baseman. His wife had a corner apartment. We was staying out in Hamtramck. That son of a gun, he was a good pitcher, too. Oh God, that Ed was a honey. Anderson Pryor was playing second base and Turkey Stearnes was playing the outfield and that's about as far as I can remember.

Money? I started with the Birmingham Black Barons in 1923 for $125 a month and quit the Chicago American Giants in 1926 for $200 a month. In Detroit I was supposed to get paid $175, but I didn't get paid nothing. This was 1931. It was the depression, all right. A depression for about two months for me. I borrowed ten dollars or five dollars, two dollars, three dollars from the company, whoever it was. I don't even know who the company was.

I left Rile and they got me a room crosstown. I was staying with some fella and his wife. Nice neighborhood. I caught a trolley car out to Hamtramck. That park on Mack had burned down, so we were playing at Hamtramck Stadium. Nice stadium. Had a big field and grandstand. I didn't stay in Detroit long enough to get out on the road, so I don't know how they were booking road trips then.

I played in the Negro National League from 1923 to 1932. After that I started barnstorming. Abe Saperstein—he was the promoter for the Harlem Globetrotters—got me to manage the Zulus, barnstorming the U.S. and Canada. That was a good ballclub. We had a makeup club, you know.

I was pretty silly then, I guess. I wanted more money, so I jumped the ballclub and went to Minot, North Dakota. When I came here they supposedly had the best ballplayers in North Dakota, so I asked if I could come play on their ballclub. They said come on. They didn't have no

▲ Ed "Huck" Rile: "Oh God, that Ed was a honey." At six-foot-six, Rile (far left) not only was an effective pitcher and power-hitting first baseman, he also was the tallest player ever to appear in the Negro leagues. In this photo, taken in about 1928, Rile towers over three Detroit teammates, including outfielder Wade Johnston (far right), a former prizefighter from Steubenville, Ohio. (Courtesy of Minnie Johnston Martin.)

other black boys out here. So I got in there with the Minot Merchants. I could've played with the New York Black Yankees and a couple other clubs back East in the '30s, but I didn't want to play in the eastern part of the states. They played too much ball there, see. I started playing tournaments in Iowa and Wyoming and places out west, following up Grover Cleveland Alexander and Babe Didrikson. They was pitching for the House of David team. Oh God, Babe Didrikson was a hell of a pitcher. She was athletic before she got into movies. She beat us out of a $1,500 tournament in Council Bluffs once.[1]

I quit baseball here in North Dakota in 1955. I could beat them pretty regular. I was going along fine until Satchel and his gang came out here and started tearing me up. I was playing with Pocatello [Idaho] then. One day I want out to the ballfield. I was playing a traveling club, that's all they told me. Then I looked out there and saw all these Negroes and good God almighty, I thought, where'd they get these guys from? Turned out to be Satchel's All-Stars. So I didn't have no job no more.

Me and Satchel were pretty good friends. I remember my first spring training in Birmingham, we swung by Satchel's house and picked him up. He was seventeen years old. The only stories I got about Satchel was he was a home boy, he loved his grandmother, and he played the jew's harp with his nose.

I batted against Satchel. How'd I do? Well, once in a while you'd hit him and sometimes you couldn't. Times he would walk the bases loaded and call in his outfielders and then strike out the side. He only did that when he was barnstorming.

Satchel was a heck of a nice kid. Down there in Birmingham, he was living with his grandmother and he was a water boy at the steel mill, so you know what kind of chance he had of seeing things. Of course, the world changed after he got with Gus Greenlee and the Pittsburgh Crawfords. Gus got him that Cadillac. I don't think he ever seen a Cadillac before then.

You know, a lot of those owners would get you good jobs after the season, like down in the Palmer House and places like that. I worked as a waiter in the winters. Worked in dining cars on the railroad, too. Go to Grand Rapids, South Bend, Grand Forks. You didn't make any money waiting tables. You made your money on tips, all that you couldn't steal. Of course, the captain, you had to feed his mitts. I made all the way to a hundred-fifty, two hundred on holidays.

I've been a chauffeur, I've been a first-class waiter, I'm a machinist, I'm mostly anything you can ask for. Now I just got through putting out time with the Green Thumbs. I put in twenty-two years. The Green Thumbs is getting jobs for the elderly people in the state of North Dakota. I helped them find jobs. I had five counties here. I done retired on Social Security. I get $570 a month. That'll hold me for a while. Then I got some pretty good friends. I go out maybe once the week and they buy me a meal or two.

I got a little house here. I've been lucky enough to hold onto it. I was doing pretty good for a while, then things got kind of bad. I had to pay out quite a bit. My health has been pretty fair. Only thing I gotta take are those pills every once in a while, for my heart. I had a pacemaker. But that's about all.

This summer I was in New Jersey for five days for the New York Mets. They sent for me. Had a reunion of all these Negro league ballplayers. Monte Irvin was there, and Josh Gibson's boy. Oh God, I met all those guys, some I hadn't seen since '25 or '26. Ted Radcliffe, Bobby Robinson, all of them was there. I still get around, sure. Ninety-one years don't make no difference. I'm only twenty-one years old.

173

You know, going through life, you gotta take it. It ain't gonna be no roses for you. I was coming into Memphis out of Natchez one time. The train stopped there. Old man Joe Rush, who owned the Memphis ballclub, saw the restaurant.

"Come on, Saul," he said. "We'll get us something to eat."

We went into the restaurant, and the man made Mr. Rush pull his hat off. I said, "What the heck," and walked on out. Well now, I know better. That sign said, "Colored not allowed," but old man Rush walks in there with that big old cowboy hat on and he's gonna buy himself a sandwich. I know better than that.

I tried to stay out of situations, but you get foolish a little bit sometimes. I remember one time in Hot Springs I was trying to follow up a white woman. I got in bad a little bit, but I shouldn't have put myself in those places. You can't do those things.

Once I was barnstorming with Oscar Charleston and that outfit. I was in Chicago and they picked me up on the bus. We had a white driver driving the bus. We stopped in Decatur, Illinois. While the driver got out to fill up, Steel Arm Davis got out and said, "Come on, Saul, let's get a drink of water." And I *was* thirsty.

The station had one of those big jugs of water sitting there where you drive in. Steel Arm got the top off the jug and started to draining the water. This white guy saw us. He stopped putting gas into his truck, took the glass out of Steel's hand and throwed it down on the ground.

Steel got hot. "Leave it alone," I said. Then I looked up and there's all of 'em coming out of the bus with bats. Well, you know I didn't want to be in that mess. Man, that was the wrong crew to be messing with. You know, those guys, they'll fight, those sonofaguns didn't care about nothin.'

Man, the chauffeur, he puts us all in the bus, jumped in his seat, and drove away. He pulled the hose right off the gas pump and headed for the highway. And there's three white guys standing in the middle of the bridge! He didn't stop for them. He would've killed all of them. I said, "Oh, God," but I'm tellin' you, we were looking for it, but no one followed us.

No, I never been beaten up by a white man. Never in my life. But I've beaten up quite a few. I practiced boxing a little, so you ain't gonna hit me for nothin'. I'll take care of myself a little while.

Here's the thing: if you do me wrong, I won't say nothing to you. I've had 'em in the crowd, trying to do or say something. I'd take a little side look. I wouldn't say nothing, but don't think I'm not coming back.

A white fella in Benton, Arkansas, did something once. Now, I had to stay in that town for two or three days until I caught him where he's going. I caught that one going around the corner right on Main Street in Benton. I walked up behind him and said, "Say, mister, you remember me?" Bam! Well, that's enough. He's gonna remember me for the rest of his life.

Me? Well, I took off, and ain't seen that town no more since.

Chapter Ten

THE END OF SOMETHING

In a perfect world, the league that Rube Foster so lovingly and expertly nurtured would have blossomed and reached full maturity during his lifetime. His vision of blacks and whites harmoniously sharing a diamond on the major-league level—a grand, giant step towards uniting the races—would have been realized. And, of course, he would have made his fortune. But life rarely follows such golden plot lines.

One night in 1926, Rube Foster stepped out of this world and never fully returned. That evening, George Sweatt, a ballplayer living above Foster's Michigan Avenue apartment in Chicago, was relaxing with his wife when they suddenly heard Mrs. Foster yell at her husband, "Oh no, don't do that!"

Rushing downstairs, Sweatt banged on the door and said, "Mrs. Foster, is there anything wrong?"

"There's something wrong with Rube," she replied, "he's just going crazy down here. I'm going to have to call the law." The police came, but it took five or six men to wrestle the 300-pound Foster into submission. He was hustled away to the state insane asylum in Kankakee, Illinois, where he wound up spending the last four years of his life.[1]

Sweatt and others had seen it coming. There were occasions when, walking home after a game, Foster would suddenly break into a dead

◀ Rube Foster in 1924, a couple of years before his collapse. (Courtesy of the National Baseball Library, Cooperstown, New York.)

run, leaving a puzzled Sweatt behind on the sidewalk. One player remembered Foster racing after imaginary fly balls in front of his Chicago home. In Indianapolis one day, Foster locked himself into a washroom and refused to leave. For a man widely respected for his business acumen, reality had become a funhouse mirror, full of distorted shapes and frightening images.

There has always been speculation over the cause of Foster's insanity. It has most often been described as a nervous breakdown caused by overwork. Foster typically was in his office from 8:30 in the morning until midnight, directing the affairs of the NNL, the Chicago American Giants, and several outside business interests, such as an auto service shop and a barber shop. His only breaks came when he went home for lunch and dinner. "The strain placed upon me has proved great almost beyond endurance," he wrote in the *Chicago Defender* in 1923.[2]

However, there are other theories. One involves an incident that reportedly happened in a hotel room sometime before his crack-up. While stepping out of his bath, Foster slipped on the wet floor, falling heavily and knocking himself out. It being a cold day, the windows were shut and the gas stove was on. Someone finally broke into the room, but not before the unconscious Foster had inhaled a toxic amount of carbon monoxide. A variation on the story has Foster falling asleep on his bed with an open stove jet left on.

The symptoms of Foster's illness—increasingly erratic behavior, vivid hallucinations, gradual insanity—suggest another possible cause. While this is purely speculative, Foster may have been in the advanced stages of syphilis, the scourge of many men of the period, especially blacks. Venereal disease, which generations of unlucky men have known as "a dose of clap," has always been an occupational hazard for ballplayers, soldiers, salesmen, and others whose livelihood puts them on the road for long periods of time. It was particularly troublesome earlier in the century, when public health practices were primitive compared to today. Black urban communities were especially vulnerable.[3]

The year before, Babe Ruth had made headlines around the country when he collapsed during the Yankees' train trip north from spring training and was hospitalized, missing several weeks of the season. What an obliging press corps made out to be abdominal pains brought on by eating too many hot dogs—"the bellyache heard round the world"—was secretly acknowledged by the Yankees' general manager to be an untreated case of venereal disease.[4] If Foster did indeed have syphilis—which, when left untreated, leads to insanity and then death in about one in twenty cases—it typically would have taken several years to run its course. There was no cure for the disease in the 1920s. Foster was one of the best-known men in Chicago, but stature is no defense against a murderous spirochete. When Foster died on December 9, 1930, babbling to the end about his American Giants winning another pennant, syphilis was already well on its way to claiming another famous Chicagoan, Al Capone.[5]

Foster's death certificate listed no cause of death. Whatever the truth, some 3,000 people attended his funeral. Cool Papa Bell and Newt Joseph traveled from St. Louis by train to stand outside in the falling snow and cry. The marbled sky could have been taken as an omen. Less than a year later, the Negro National League would collapse utterly, destroyed by a depression and the absence of a true father figure.

☆

At the time that Foster went insane, his league was still very much a work-in-progress. In 1926 the Dayton and Cleveland franchises failed to play the second half of the split season. The following year, Indianapolis dropped out. In their stead, the Birmingham Black Barons and Memphis Red Sox of the Southern Negro League were admitted as full-fledged members of the NNL, but the high cost of travel to these southern cities practically guaranteed that the Detroit Stars and other northern teams would lose money. It also meant lengthy road trips, sometimes as long as three weeks, in a part of the country where Jim Crow prevented the scheduling of profitable black-white exhibitions. In 1927 only 50 percent of the teams completed the second half.

Both seasons, however, ended with the Chicago American Giants winning the NNL pennant playoff and the Colored World Series against the Eastern Colored League's representative. In 1926 Chicago defeated Kansas City, five games to four, as Rube Foster's younger brother, Willie Foster, won both games of a doubleheader on the final day of the NNL playoff. In the 1927 playoff, Chicago swept Birmingham in four straight games. In the Colored World Series that followed each season, the American Giants defeated the Bacharach Giants, five games to three. Dave Malarcher, who had taken over as field manager with Foster's illness, remained humble as the Chicagoans rolled over the competition. "I'm just doing what the master taught me," he said.[6] Any thoughts of a third straight championship, however, evaporated when the Eastern Colored League broke up in the spring of 1928.

During this period ownership of the Detroit Stars changed hands, and this time they were white. In 1925, forty-five-year-old clothier John Roesink became the second nonblack to own a franchise in the NNL. (Kansas City's J. Leslie Wilkinson was the first.) Particulars of the ar-

179

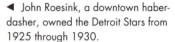

◄ John Roesink, a downtown haberdasher, owned the Detroit Stars from
1925 through 1930.

rangements have been lost to time. Roesink, who already owned Mack Park, had made enough money during Detroit's boom decade to now operate three successful downtown stores: at 13 Campus Martius, 58 Monroe, and 648 Woodward. Blount was kept on as business manager until Roesink hired Moses L. Walker as his assistant. William Mosley, who in the early thirties owned a billiard hall at 2452 St. Antoine, also served the club in some capacity, possibly as a promoter.

Although Roesink would later inspire the wrath of many Black Bottom fans, players generally considered the haberdasher a first-class owner. They were well-paid and continued to travel by train, even as some NNL teams made the switch to more cost-effective touring cars and buses. With unstable franchises a fact of life in the NNL, Roesink had talked seriously of bringing his hometown of Grand Rapids into the league. Detroit and several other NNL teams played exhibitions there in 1928, but nothing else came of it.

After their meaningless third-place playoff with Chicago in Roesink's first season, the Stars shot out of the gate in 1926 under Candy Jim Taylor, a veteran Negro leaguer who had replaced the retired Bruce Petway as manager. After dropping a one-run decision to Dayton on May 25, the Stars didn't lose again until Kansas City demolished them, 19 to 4, on June 19. The Stars' seventeen-game win streak went for naught, as they finished runner-up to the Monarchs for the first-half pennant. A terrible second half, which included just one win in ten outings against Kansas City, placed Detroit fourth in the overall league standings. Wesley slumped to a .300 average and fifteen home runs, while Stearnes batted .375 with twenty home runs and a league-leading twenty-four doubles. Mule Riggins was the only other regular to top .300, although Fred Bell,

Cool Papa's brother, won seven games and hit .299 with nine home runs as he moved between the mound and the outfield.

In 1927 Roesink acquired Elwood "Bingo" DeMoss as manager from Cleveland, which had absorbed players from the failed Indianapolis franchise. Born September 5, 1889, in Topeka, Kansas, the peppery DeMoss had switched from shortstop to second base after throwing out his arm pitching in a pinch for the Topeka Giants. A solid, line-drive hitting righthander with little power but great bat control and tremendous speed, the 6-foot-2, 175-pounder had been an integral member of Foster's great Chicago teams of the early 1920s. DeMoss left Chicago to manage Indianapolis in 1926; although he turned thirty-seven during the season, the aging second sacker still stole twenty-six bases—tops in the NNL— in sixty-seven games.[7] His coming to Detroit was considered a coup, at least by Roesink.

Bill "Plunk" Drake, a free-spirited righthanded pitcher, also came over from Cleveland. He'd already had a taste of DeMoss's managerial style during their brief time together in Indianapolis:

> We had been out all night long, got in about six o'clock that morning. But I knew it was all right, 'cause I was out with the manager all night. So one o'clock came along, time for the ball game, I'll be doggone, that son of a bitch tossed the ball to me, said "You're going."
> "What!"
> Well, we were playing the Cubans. They score four runs off me first inning. I met him at the coach's box coming in from the pitcher's mound. He said, "Nine innings, win or lose." After that I never let DeMoss know nothing about me. He went his way and I went mine. That taught me not to fool with the boss.[8]

The Detroit-Cleveland connection didn't end there. Ed Wesley, just two years removed from his fantastic 1925 season, was part of a trade that sent another seven-year veteran, Mule Riggins, to Cleveland for shortstop Hallie Harding, utility man Stack Martin, and pitcher-first baseman Ed Rile.

Rile stood 6-foot-6 and weighed about 230 pounds. Although he had impressed few people while bouncing from Indianapolis to Chicago to Columbus, he came into his own at Mack Park. Pitching every fourth day, Rile compiled a 14–6 record in 1927. Between starts he anchored first base and, batting from both sides of the plate, hit .406. The great Willie Foster tried to slow Rile down by hiding his favorite bat when the Stars came to Chicago. Once a sympathetic American Giant restored

Rile's war club; Rile responded by hitting Foster's first pitch over the fence.[9]

The 1927 edition of the Stars once again raced out to an impressive start, winning thirteen of fourteen games between May 11 and June 5. Their only loss was a 5–3 setback to St. Louis on May 24. And once again the Stars cooled off, finishing in the middle of the pack in both halves of the season. Christobel Torrienti, acquired from Kansas City, batted .326, second on the team to Stearnes, who hit .339 and also claimed his fourth home-run crown in five years, with twenty.

A disciplinary problem might have cost the Stars a notch or two in the standings. In March 1927, their top pitcher, Andy Cooper, had joined a congregation of NNL and ECL players on a trip to Japan. Playing together as the Philadelphia Royal Giants, the black team visited Japan, China, Australia, Hawaii, and the Philippines before returning to the states in June, well into the NNL season. Some league officials wanted to slap a five-year suspension on the offending players, but cooler heads (who correctly reasoned that the offenders would simply jump to the ECL) decided a thirty-day suspension and $200 fine would suffice.[10] Cooper finished 7–3 in his abbreviated season, but the following year he was traded to Kansas City for five players.

Cooper's Pacific trip underscored the constant struggle for Negro leaguers to make a year-round living. In 1929, for instance, a veteran third baseman such as the Stars' Bobbie Robinson was being paid a monthly salary of $210. Teammate Ted Radcliffe was making $175. To make up for the financial shortfall, the most talented Negro leaguers usually played winter ball in California, Cuba, and Mexico, which featured very competitive leagues and monthly salaries in the range of $100 to $200. Those players who didn't care to travel or who had families went back home to the South or stuck out winter in the North. No matter what direction one faced, off-season employment was a necessity.

Several Detroit players (although not nearly as many as Turkey Stearnes liked to recall) worked at area factories, which continued to boom throughout the 1920s. The Detroit Urban League, which had an arrangement with Henry Ford and other industrial employers, had little difficulty placing young, athletic black men in the disagreeable foundries and paint shops. In fact, at the same time Andy Cooper was posing for photographs with Tokyo's Mayor Nishikubo, Tenny Blount, Turkey Stearnes, and several other Stars were laboring in grimy, sweat-soaked coveralls for the half-owner of the Detroit Tigers, Walter O. Briggs.[11]

Briggs, a tough, self-made millionaire who at one time had sixteen plants and 40,000 employees manufacturing car bodies, used some of his wealth to buy quarter-shares of the Tigers in 1920 and 1927. Although

▲ During the boom decade of the 1920s, Detroit's auto plants provided off-season employment of those ballplayers who desired it. However, the Stars' celebrity status in Black Bottom didn't prevent them from being assigned to such traditional "Negro jobs" as wet sanding and spray painting. (Courtesy of Manning Brothers, Photographers.)

he was a rabid baseball fan, he probably was unaware that the solutions to his team's perennial also-ran status were wet sanding, spray painting, and baking auto bodies right in his plants. Not that it would have mattered, of course; the ballplayers' celebrity status in Black Bottom wouldn't have kept them from being assigned to the usual "Negro jobs" at Briggs's unsafe factories, which justifiably had the worst reputation in the city. Streetcar operators, when calling out destinations, often announced factory stops as, "Briggs slaughterhouse, all off, Mack Avenue."[12]

"We worked in the paint shop in the winter and played ball in the summer," Stearnes recalled. "All that gang, about 19 of us, with the secretary and manager and all, about 22 or 23 of us." In 1927, the Stars left their factory jobs for spring training in the South. Not long afterwards, "the Briggs plant blew up," said Stearnes.[13] On April 23, an explosion inside the third-floor paint shop caused the block-long Briggs plant at Harper and Russell to burn to the ground in a spectacular, two-day fire. The city's first two-million-dollar blaze killed twenty-one workers. Dozens more were horribly burned. The labor press charged Briggs with being negligent, publishing a bitter, ironic poem called "Bodies by Briggs."[14]

"That shows how lucky we were," said Stearnes. "As soon as we hit the street in New Orleans it was in the paper."[15] As it turned out, another fire would soon hit the Stars much closer to home.

On July 7, 1929, the Stars were preparing for a lucrative Sunday doubleheader with the popular Kansas City Monarchs when catastrophe hit Mack Park. Early that afternoon, both teams had arrived at the ballpark to discover that the rain that had cancelled Saturday's contest had made the field a soggy mess. The standard procedure in these cases was to try to dry out the infield and base paths by pouring gasoline over the dirt and then lighting it. Shortly before two o'clock, John Roesink had just finished spreading the second of two five-gallon cans of gas over the infield when a sudden commotion from under the right-field stands, where several hundred early arrivals were sitting out a brief rain shower, caught everybody's attention.

"We were sitting in the dugout while Kansas City was taking batting practice," said Bobbie Robinson. "We heard all this screaming, all this noise, and we thought maybe a fight was going on in the stands. We jumped out and looked and the stands were in a blaze. Man, I never will forget that."[16]

Apparently a carelessly tossed cigarette had ignited the debris beneath the grandstand. Most people on the scene later reported hearing a tremendous explosion, followed by a long plume of black smoke and flames that climbed quickly up the dry wooden support posts. Fire investigators concluded that park employees had left a trail of flammable liquid while carrying the cans of gas onto the field.

"The fire, a burst of flame that flashed through the floor of the stand, reached the seats with a suddenness that caused the people in the stands to scramble in all directions," reported the next day's *Detroit News*. "Some, mostly men, leaped from the back of the stands to the ground, more than 30 feet below, and many were injured. Others making a hurried exit below the stands were struck by whose who leaped from above. In the meantime, the fire spread so rapidly that the roof of the stand fell in and the stand collapsed, injuring many who still were attempting to escape through the exits below. That none was killed in the collapse was considered remarkable by investigators."[17]

Walter O. Briggs. The millionaire industrialist was part-owner of the Detroit Tigers from 1920 until 1935, after which he assumed full ownership until his death in 1952. His reputation for operating the most unsafe factories in the city was enhanced in April 1927, when the block-long Briggs plant at Harper and Russell burned to the ground, killing twenty-one workers and horribly burning many others. The disaster occurred shortly after Turkey Stearnes and several teammates had quit their jobs at the plant and left for spring training.

Quick thinking by the ballplayers saved many lives. Members of both teams rushed to the protective chicken-wire screen enclosing the grandstand and, with a mighty effort, pulled down the two-by-four timbers holding it in place, releasing the flood of men, women, and children piled up behind it. Due to the crowded, narrow streets, firemen were delayed nearly thirty minutes. By that time the central stands, clubhouses, five parked cars, and the caretaker's home had been destroyed. Several hundred terror-stricken fans milled around the park, screaming for lost family members or waiting for transportation home or to a hospital. Some later traveled to Roesink's home at 2075 Taylor Avenue, about five miles west of the park, to express their anger and demand compensation.

As police gathered up bushel baskets full of pocketbooks, coats, shoes, and other articles left behind in the panic, and firemen poked through the ruins looking for any youngsters who may have been sitting on the roof of the grandstand when it collapsed, Roesink estimated his damage for reporters: $12,000 to the stands, and an additional $3,000 in lost revenue now that several games had to be cancelled.[18]

The real damage turned out to be Roesink's reputation. All told, the disaster at Mack Park had injured about 220 people, half of whom were rushed to drug stores and doctors' offices by sympathetic passersby. The rest, including seventy-one men, thirty-three women, and five children, were treated at the emergency room of Receiving Hospital. All but one of the victims were black. Although no one had died, injuries ranged from severe skull and spinal fractures to broken limbs and serious burns.[19]

The dailies, which rarely covered a Detroit Stars game, fell all over themselves in describing the details of the Mack Park disaster. There was the woman whose male friend "fought his way back to her, caught her by the hair and dragged her limp body down the grandstand steps." And a woman who "threw her baby from the top row of the stands into the mass of humanity below just as flames swept over her." And thirty-four-year-old Cleveland Trone, who was "pushed from the top of the grandstand by the mob, landed on the top of a parked automobile and rolled to the ground."[20]

The fire was officially ruled an accident, but many Black Bottom residents blamed the tragedy on Roesink, who they suspected was lying when he insisted that no full cans of gas had been stored carelessly under the stands. Adding to their anger was an incident shortly before the fire broke out. Scores of fans, convinced that the intermittent rain would cancel the game, had descended on the box office to demand refunds. Roesink refused, and then put in a riot call to the police. They were on hand when the fire started.

▲ Mack Park after its disastrous fire of July 7, 1929. Miraculously, no one was killed, although more than two hundred panic-stricken spectators were injured. Quick thinking by players undoubtedly saved several lives. (Courtesy of *The Detroit News*.)

The ballplayers, who had lost everything when the clubhouses were destroyed, were fully compensated by Roesink. But his apparent lack of concern about the many victims left a lingering bitterness among fans and would wind up costing him—not in court (where no ordinary black had the money to pursue a civil case), but at the box office.

Playing the balance of their home schedule at Dequindre Park, the Stars had a second half as disastrous as the first, at one point losing fourteen of sixteen games. Stearnes, who had captured his fifth home-run crown in 1928 with twenty-four roundtrippers, followed up with a .375 average and nineteen home runs in 1929. Outfielders Wade Johnston and John Jones hit .357 and .341, respectively, while Bobbie Robinson kicked in with a .309 mark and Ted Radcliffe batted .310. Despite batting .315 as a team, easily their best ever, the Stars had their first losing season. Given the chaos, controversy, and recriminations surrounding the season, and the fact that no ballplayer had the money or inclination to play the stock market, probably no one on the Stars' roster noticed when Wall Street crashed in October.

The effects of what was to become the longest and most severe depression in the country's history were to become particularly pronounced in a one-industry town like Detroit. Between 1929 and 1932 car production would drop from a record 5.3 million to just over one million, putting thousands of shame-faced but hungry families on the dole. Oth-

ers would resort to selling pencils and apples on street corners or stealing dog biscuits from the city pound. The shocking transformation of
what had been the auto age's golden city would prompt Edmund Wilson
to write: "The enormous organism of Detroit is now seen, for all its
Middle Western vigor, to have become atrophied. It is clogged with dead
tissue now and its life is bleeding away."[21]

But over the winter of 1929–30, few were thinking in such cata-
strophic terms, especially in Black Bottom, where citizens were accustomed to marginal living even in the best of times. Until Detroiters
caught on that the swelling number of factory layoffs was permanent, not
cyclical, many thought the economic downturn would turn out no worse
than the recession of 1921–22.

John Roesink, for one, was bullish enough on the future to build a
brand new ballpark, this time in the ethnic enclave of Hamtramck. In
1930 the 2.1-square-mile village, located completely within Detroit's city
limits, was home to more than 56,000 hard-working, hard-drinking Poles,
most of them foreign-born, and nearly all of whom owed their livelihood
to Dodge Main, the sprawling, soot-stained factory on Joseph Campau.
Undoubtedly looking to attract both spectators and factory teams from
Dodge Main's huge workforce, Roesink wedged his park onto a parcel
of land six blocks north of the plant.

Although the Stars were once again plunked down in an overwhelmingly white neighborhood, they experienced little if any racial animosity. Poles and blacks, who occupied the two lowest rungs on the
socio-economic ladder, had long been working and living side-by-side.
Unlike Detroit's, Hamtramck's public and private facilities were fully integrated. "If you were black in Hamtramck, you were accepted by the Polish people," recalled Bill Hines. "We were called 'black Polacks,' that's
all. All that anti-black sentiment that came later, that was put there by
rednecks. There was always Polish jokes. They were dumber than the
Negro jokes."[22]

According to some estimates, Roesink spent in the vicinity of
$30,000 to build his park on the site of an old Detroit Lumber Company
yard bounded by Gallagher, Roosevelt, Jacob, and Conant. The Calvert
Coal Company bordered the north wall of the stadium, while tracks of
the Grand Trunk Railroad, which daily delivered tons of parts to Dodge
Main, ran between the south end of the park and the factory. Gene Berlin,
a white fan who grew up a mile away on Belmont Avenue, remembered
the tops of boxcars serving as depression-style sky boxes for neighborhood kids and idle adults. "Sometimes there were more people on the
boxcars than in the stadium," he said.[23]

The configuration of the concrete football-style stadium gave a new look to the Stars. Righthanded hitters had no complaints about the 315-foot left-field fence. But lefthanded sluggers, once the team's strong suit, frowned at the 407-foot distance to right field and the ten-foot-high corrugated steel fence that ringed the stadium. The cavernous center-field pasture and finely graded infield greatly aided fielders and the pitching staff, which saw its runs-per-game average drop by almost two runs from 1929's figure. But it also influenced Turkey Stearnes's decision to jump to the New York Lincoln Giants before the 1930 campaign began. He returned in mid-season, but most of his power now translated into triples instead of home runs.

To fill Stearnes's spot in center field, the Stars signed Crush Holloway, a solidly built switch-hitter formerly with Hilldale. Holloway had acquired his unusual first name because his father had witnessed a train wreck the day he was born, September 16, 1896, in Hillsboro, Texas. Ironically, Holloway's idol while growing up was Ty Cobb. "That's why I ran bases like I did," Holloway once said. "His picture used to come in Bull Durham tobacco. Showed the way he'd slide. That was my hero. I said, 'I want to slide like Ty Cobb. I want to run bases like him.'" And he did. Holloway is regarded by old-timers as the roughest baserunner the Negro leagues ever produced.[24]

The Stars, minus Stearnes and Ted Radcliffe, who had jumped to the St. Louis Stars, opened the season with five-game sets in Chicago and St. Louis before returning home to their new park. The first game played at Hamtramck Stadium—which for many years was more commonly referred to as Roesink Stadium—was Saturday, May 10, as the Cuban Stars squeaked out a thirteen-inning, 6–4 win. The official opening was the following day, when 10,000 curious black and white fans packed the grounds to watch Andy Cooper, recently reacquired after two years in Kansas City, best the Cubans' Edolfo "Yoyo" Diaz, 7 to 4. Roesink prevailed upon an old friend, Ty Cobb, to throw out the ceremonial first pitch—an irony that probably wasn't lost on the Negro leaguers.

Stearnes returned on June 21, just in time for a doubleheader with the powerful St. Louis Stars, who would edge Kansas City for the first-half pennant. St. Louis won both ends of the twinbill, and left town with four wins in five outings. Kansas City visited next, and they pounded the Stars four straight. Mercifully a fifth game was rained out.

Despite the whipping, the Monarchs' series was notable in that it marked the first time professional baseball in Detroit was played under artificial lights. The Monarchs, who were spending what would prove to be their last season in the NNL, had gotten a jump on hard times by investing in a portable lighting system that was the talk of baseball. Five years before the Cincinnati Reds hosted the major leagues' first night

COMING!   COMING!   COMING!
KANSAS CITY MONARCHS
NIGHT BASEBALL

We have successfully lighted every kind of a ball park in the country, including both Major Leagues, AND CAN REPEAT IN ALL OF THEM.

The Greatest Drawing Card Outside the Major Leagues

Headquarters 420 East Ninth St., Kansas City, Mo.

Actual Photograph of One of the Many Towers Supporting Our Flood Lights

Actual Photograph of Trucks Used to Transport the Monarch Lighting Plant and Towers

game, and eighteen years before the Detroit Tigers inaugurated their lighting system, the Monarchs were drawing large crowds by taking their novelty on the road.

When the Monarchs visited Detroit on June 28, posters announcing "The Greatest Drawing Card Outside the Major Leagues" had already been slapped up all over Black Bottom. A large crowd estimated at 10,000 people arrived that evening in a festive mood, fans joining players in gawking at the six telescoping poles whose floodlights towered fifty feet over the playing field. Other lights were placed on the grandstand roof. The 100-kilowatt generator, which provided the electricity, was powered by a huge 250-horsepower motor that sucked up fifteen gallons of gas each hour. The generator was placed in center field, and the noise it made not only drowned out Turkey Stearnes's customary monologue, it vied with the chatter of the infielders. On top of that, outfielders had to be careful not to trip over the wires that snaked through the grass from the generator to the light poles.[25]

"It was very exciting," said Bobbie Robinson. "It was the first time I'd played under the lights. But it was kind of rough. The generators would go down and the lights would start to dim, and then they'd start back up and the lights would get bright again."[26]

Crush Holloway recalled difficulty tracking balls hit high above the top of the towers. "You had to guess where they were coming down. The infield was good. But very seldom you hit a fastball with those lights. I called them candle lights."[27]

Andy Cooper went the distance, giving up twenty-two hits—including three home runs by Goo Goo Livingston over the left-field fence—as the Monarchs blew past the Stars, 17 to 4.[28] The only incident involving light occurred when a photographer's flashbulb temporarily blinded Ed Rile on a play at first base; as Rile chased after the ball even Cooper had to stand there and laugh. The two teams played a second night game on Sunday. By this time the Stars were more comfortable—and competitive—under the lights, losing 5 to 4 in eleven innings.[29]

The Stars finished the first half in fourth place, winning half of their fifty-two games. After starting the second half slowly, splitting the first six games of a southern road trip, they suddenly caught fire. On July 16 in Birmingham, Andy Cooper shut out the Black Barons, 3 to 0, kicking off a twenty-one-game winning streak (which included seven exhibi-

◀ In June 1930, the Stars hosted the first night baseball games ever played in Detroit. Posters were distributed throughout Black Bottom, announcing the Kansas City Monarchs' portable lighting system. (Courtesy of Gladys Wilkinson Catron.)

tions). The Stars didn't lose again until August 17, when they dropped an 8–7 decision to the Cuban Stars in the second game of a doubleheader at Hamtramck Stadium. The solid frontline pitching of Cooper, Ted Shaw, and Nelson Dean, who combined for thirty-six victories, and the reliable bats of Stearnes (.339), Rile (.323), and Wade Johnston (.322, with a team-record thirteen triples), gave the Stars the second-half pennant and the right to face Ted Trent, Mule Suttles, Willie Wells, Ted Radcliffe, Cool Papa Bell, and the rest of the talented St. Louis Stars for the championship of the Negro National League.

Unfortunately, not many people in Detroit cared. Although the major leagues drew more than 10.1 million fans in 1930—a single-season attendance record that would last until 1946—baseball owners John Roesink and Frank Navin, along with everyone else in Detroit, felt the first effects of the depression. When the Stars and Tigers started their seasons in April, the local unemployment rate had reached 13.3 percent, double the national figure. That summer the Tigers suffered a 25-percent loss in attendance, while the Stars, who depended heavily on the discretionary dollars of local factory workers, also played before large expanses of empty seats.

Compounding the problem for Roesink was a three-week-long boycott in August, which seemed to be the work of a small but effective group of disgruntled black fans led by sportswriter Russell Cowans. According to a wire service story in the black press (probably placed there by Cowans), it "grew out of Roesink's failure to advertise in 'shine' newspapers, his arrogant, insulting attitude towards patrons of the game, his failure to compensate, or to visit or even speak kindly to any of the many persons injured in the catastrophe at Mack Park last summer, and the alleged unfair treatment of his players."[30]

None of the players alive today can recall the boycott or Roesink's alleged mistreatment. Most, according to Lou Dials, considered him a fair man. "We got along fine with him," he said. "He paid right on time. You didn't have to wait for your pay."[31] Whatever the problem was, the boycott "brought Roesink down from his 'high horse,'" the report continued. "He has turned the park over to Moses L. Walker, his colored lieutenant, has signed an agreement that he will stay away from the park himself, and his advertisements in the Negro newspapers are asking the fans to again support the team."[32]

Detroit and St. Louis opened their seven-game playoff on September 13 with a night game in St. Louis. Ted Radcliffe started for the home team, and Stearnes nicked him for a two-run homer in the first. But St. Louis, behind their ace pitcher, Ted Trent, stormed back to take a 5–4 decision over Nelson Dean.

▲ The 1930 Detroit Stars, who would come within a game of winning the NNL pennant, posed in St. Louis for this team photograph at the start of the season. Standing, from left: Crush Holloway, Albert Davis, Ed Rile, Andy Cooper, William Love, unknown, Leon "Pepper" Daniels, and manager Bingo DeMoss. Kneeling, from left: Nelson Dean, Clarence "Spoony" Palm, Ted Shaw, Grady Orange, Willie Powell, Wade Johnston, Jake Dunn, and Bobbie Robinson. Missing is Turkey Stearnes, who started the season with the Lincoln Giants but rejoined the Stars several weeks later.

After a one-day rain delay, the Detroiters evened the series with an 11–7 win, as Stearnes pounded out five hits, including another home run and a double. Detroit was clinging to the lead in the bottom of the eighth when Cool Papa Bell and John Henry Russell got on base. With runners on second and third and nobody out, Andy Cooper trotted out to relieve Willie Powell. Cooper's second pitch was lined over the bag at third. Bobbie Robinson flung himself to his right, snaring the ball in the short-fingered glove he preferred using. He touched the bag to force Bell for the second out, then fired to second baseman Grady Orange for the force on Russell. Before the stunned St. Louis fans had a chance to react, the Detroit Stars trotted off the field with a game-saving triple play.

Several New York Giants, in town to play the Cardinals, were in the stands, and they asked Robinson to come over and shake hands all around. After the game the still-beaming third baseman asked the ump for the ball, which he had all of his teammates sign. More than sixty years later, the yellowed ball is happily brought out whenever visitors

Detroit Stars vs. St. Louis Stars
1930 Playoff

St. Louis won series, 4 games to 3

DETROIT PITCHING

Player	GP	GS	CG	Won	Lost	IP	H	R	BB	SO	RPG	ShO
Dean	3	3	2	1	2	25	29	19	9	9	6.84	0
Davis	2	2	2	0	2	17	24	11	7	7	5.82	0
Powell	2	1	0	2	0	10.1	10	8	0	0	6.97	0
Shaw	1	1	0	0	0	5	6	3	3	3	5.40	0
Cooper	2	0	0	0	0	3.2	7	4	0	0	10.81	0
Totals	7	4	3	4		61	76	45	19	19	6.64	0

SAVE: Cooper

DETROIT BATTING

Player	Pos	Games	AB	H	Avg.	2B	3B	HR	SB
Johnston	LF	7	30	6	.200	2	0	0	0
Holloway	2B-RF	7	29	11	.379	0	0	0	1
Stearnes	CF	6	27	13	.481	4	1	3	1
Dunn	SS	7	26	8	.308	1	1	0	0
Palm	C	6	25	8	.320	1	0	0	0
Rile	1B-2B	6	23	8	.348	1	0	1	2
Orange	2B-3B	6	18	5	.278	1	0	0	0
Dials	1B-RF	5	14	3	.214	0	1	0	0
Robinson	3B	4	12	3	.250	0	0	0	0
Davis	P-PH	4	10	1	.100	0	0	0	0
Daniels	C-1B	4	9	3	.333	1	0	0	0
Dean	P	2	6	0	.000	0	0	0	0
Love	RF	1	5	1	.200	0	0	0	0
DeMoss	2B	1	4	0	.000	0	0	0	0
Powell	P	1	2	0	.000	0	0	0	0
Shaw	P	1	2	1	.500	0	0	0	0
Cooper	P	2	1	0	.000	0	0	0	0
Totals		7	243	71	.292	11	3	4	4

to Robinson's Chicago home ask him about his greatest moment in baseball.[33]

The two teams split the next two games. Game three, another night contest, saw Ted Trent win for the second time, 7 to 2. The following day, Nelson Dean edged Slap Hensley, 5 to 4.

The balance of the series was scheduled for Detroit. On September 20 Stearnes broke a fifth-inning tie with a two-run double off Ted Trent. Behind the slants of Willie Powell, the Detroiters won, 7 to 5, putting them just one game away from the championship.

The next afternoon Stearnes knocked in all three of Detroit's runs in a 4–3 loss. The hit that had everybody buzzing was a mammoth fourth-inning blast over the right-field fence, the first time anyone had hit a home run to that part of Hamtramck Stadium. "He hit it to right-center," recalled Ted Radcliffe, "and it cleared the fence with room to spare."[34]

At this point Stearnes had simply overwhelmed St. Louis' finest pitchers, batting .591 with eight extra-base hits and eleven runs batted in with just twenty-two at-bats. His slugging percentage stood at an unbelievable 1.273! The following afternoon, however, with the championship on the line, Stearnes went hitless in five at-bats as the St. Louis Stars trampled Detroit, 13 to 7, in the decisive seventh game. Nelson Dean took the brunt of the beating. The disappointing loss ended the Detroit Stars' best chance in eleven NNL seasons for a championship.

It also ended John Roesink's six-season stint as owner. No financial data are available, but it's doubtful that, on the whole, the beleaguered haberdasher did better than break even, especially in the light of the Mack Park fire, construction costs for Hamtramck Stadium, and the boycott. The aggravation of dealing with the fans surely helped make up his mind, as did the death of Rube Foster two months after the playoff. But overriding everything had to be the deepening depression, which would eventually force Roesink to close two of his stores, and which was threatening to snuff out the already precarious existence of Black Bottom residents.

There were 120,000 blacks squeezed into Detroit in 1930, and by the following year it must have seemed that every one of them had had a personal experience with either a layoff slip or eviction notice. Often one quickly followed the other. Blacks had always been the last hired and the first fired. By early 1931, with Detroit hopelessly "out of gear" and nearly 192,000 of its citizens receiving some form of welfare—as little as two dollars a week for a family of four—it was virtually impossible for a workingman of any color to find decent employment. Even garbage collecting suddenly looked good: out-of-work white municipal employees demanded that Frank Murphy, who had been elected mayor in 1930, fire black collectors and give the jobs to them. Murphy refused. While President Herbert Hoover insisted that economic conditions would improve on their own, Murphy could see with his own eyes the suffering all around him. He had three empty Studebaker and General Motors factories converted into hostels for the unemployed, and established tent colonies in Grand Circus Park and other public spaces for families who had been evicted from their homes.[35]

Following a familiar pattern among blacks, John Glover's father first lost his job at McCord's Radiator and then the family home on Cath-

▲ A Monroe Street alley in 1930, just as the depression was taking hold. Residents of Black Bottom, accustomed to being the last hired and first fired even during good times, coped better than many whites. But the drying-up of their already limited discretionary income doomed the Detroit Stars and subsequent attempts to launch a black professional franchise.

erine Street. All things considered, recalled Glover, the family "did pretty good. We ate a lot of biscuits and the cheapest meat. And we stood in line when they gave out milk and flour."[36]

The desperate drive by professional ballplayers to make a living manifested itself in different ways. The year before, Turkey Stearnes had impulsively joined the financially ailing Lincoln Giants on the promise of a few more dollars a month, while teammate Albert Davis had been jailed for purse snatching. Salaries, by and large, had dropped between the late 1920s and 1931. But at least owner Roesink had met his payroll obligations the first and fifteenth of every month. He'd even given each player two dollars a day for meals, an uncommonly generous amount in the NNL in 1930.

Such examples of fiscal responsibility stopped with the Stars' new owner, numbers kingpin Everitt Watson, a forty-six-year-old former train porter who generally was thought to be one of the few men in Black Bottom weathering the depression. Not so, grumbled Virginia Powell, remembering the 1931 season many years later. "We like to starve to death over there in Detroit," she said. Her husband, pitcher Willie Powell, agreed. "The Stars went broke—they were broke to start with. They never did pay off."[37]

That flew in the face of Watson's reputation, which in his line of work was his most important asset. In the early 1920s the flamboyantly dressed big spender, a familiar figure at nightspots, race tracks, and other sporting events, operated the Waiters and Bellmen's Club out of his home at 664 Adams. Everyone, including the police who were regularly bribed, knew this was a front for illegal drinking and gambling. In 1927 he and John Roxborough became partners in the Big Four policy house. Two years later Watson created the Yellow Dog policy house, which he operated out of a second-story office at 1904 St. Antoine, home to the Watson Realty Company. Over the years he and Roxborough built their houses into the two largest in Black Bottom on the basis of their demonstrated ability to pay off the occasional big winners.[38]

How Watson, who evidently had no background in baseball, wound up as the Stars' owner can only be guessed at. According to Haywood Henderson, a St. Louis native and former Grand Rapids semipro player who did some promotional work for John Roesink when he wasn't collecting bets for Watson, former Stars owner Tenny Blount was working as a "realtor" for Watson in the late 1920s. Although Roesink himself was involved in no illegal activities, Blount probably brought the two together at the end of the 1930 season. By this time Watson had reportedly left the numbers racket, after a disastrous raid in June 1929 that had netted the police $22,000 in jewelry and cash. When police slapped the handcuffs on Watson that day they found $1,200 cash in his pockets.[39] That was more than enough to buy a NNL franchise in 1931, when only six teams—Detroit, Cleveland, Indianapolis, Louisville, Chicago, and St. Louis—took the field. Odds are that if Watson paid Roesink or the league anything, it was little more than a compliment.

At that, the team was overpriced. The league was falling apart. The Chicago club was embroiled in legal problems resulting from Rube Foster's death, while St. Louis had its park sold out from under it and turned into a municipal playground. And the game's biggest draw, Kansas City, had decided to quit the league to barnstorm exclusively. That was the fatal blow. "Fans knew they were going to see a baseball game when Kansas City came to town," observed the *Kansas City Call.* "Say 'Kansas City Monarchs' and the fans poured through the turnstile. Now there aren't any Monarchs this year."[40]

The league lasted a little more than three months into the season, long enough for Turkey Stearnes to claim his sixth, and final, home run

▲ Numbers racketeer Everitt Watson owned the Stars in 1931, the year Rube Foster's original Negro National League finally died. (Courtesy of *The Detroit News*.)

title in a Detroit uniform. All around him, players were jumping ship, although the team they joined often was no more stable than the one they had left. The Stars continued to play at Hamtramck Stadium, which suggests the possibility that Watson paid for the Stars by guaranteeing Roesink a higher percentage of gate receipts.

Whatever the arrangement, it was clear that the cash flow had dried to a trickle. Willie Powell and other players would go down in the morning to Watson's office, hoping to catch him for a handout. "He'd walk by and reach in his pocket," said Powell, "and whatever he came up with, he'd give you. He came out with a five, he'd give you a five. And he ain't going to stop walking, and he ain't going to talk to you." With no money and nothing better to do, the players would "stand on the corner and chew tobacco and spit."[41]

George B. Key, a physician, co-owner of the St. Louis Stars, and vice president of the NNL, had taken over the administration of the league upon Rube Foster's illness. In 1927, Judge William C. Hueston of Kansas City had been elected president by league owners. Neither gentleman had the old master's skills in remedying the daily crises in scheduling, attendance, financing, promotion, and discipline that had been exacerbated by hard times. It's likely that Foster himself wouldn't have been able to hold things together.

Sometime in the middle of August the Negro National League, Rube Foster's handcrafted creation, unceremoniously halted play after a dozen seasons of continuous operation. The official obituary wouldn't be written until the following March, when Judge Hueston announced that the NNL would not operate in 1932. By that time the circuit was a cold body. At the end, only Detroit, Chicago, and St. Louis remained of the original NNL cities. In fact, if the 1919 trial season is included, Detroit fielded a franchise for thirteen consecutive summers—an impressive achievement, given the circumstances.

Nobody in Black Bottom was applauding. The month the league died, the hourly work force of the Ford Motor Company, the city's largest employer of blacks, had shrunk to one-third of its 1929 size. Half of those lucky enough to have jobs worked only three days a week. One of the victims of the massive layoffs was Bill Hines's father, who never made it back to the Rouge's coke ovens. He died that year of tuberculosis. The family of four went on relief, although Hines today insists that their situation wasn't as bad as it was for others. "My brother worked at the soup kitchen," he said, "so we didn't have to stand in line."[42] Attending a baseball game at Hamtramck Stadium or Navin Field (where the Tigers were averaging less than 6,000 customers a game) was a luxury few could afford during the bleak summer of 1931.[43]

With Everitt Watson pulling a vanishing act, some ex-Stars were stranded in the city, including Willie Powell and his wife. "We couldn't get back home," said Powell. Instead, teammate Jelly Gardner "had to get us back home; he knew someone he could borrow some money from."[44]

☆

Several owners tried to keep Rube Foster's vision alive after his passing. J. L. Wilkinson of Kansas City, the only owner left from the original NNL, seemed to be the obvious choice. In fact, in 1932 Wilkinson talked with several owners about forming a new league around his Monarchs. But his attempts to secure a park in Chicago, where he planned to move the club in order to take advantage of the city's large black population, fell through, and the Monarchs remained a road team.[45]

At about the same time, Cumberland Willis "Cum" Posey organized the East-West League with his Homestead Grays as the centerpiece.

Born into an upper-middle-class family in 1890 in Homestead, Pennsylvania, a suburb southeast of Pittsburgh, the fair-skinned, blue-eyed Posey excelled at baseball and basketball, eventually operating barnstorming teams in both sports. When he was nineteen, he joined the outfield of the Murdock Grays, whose rough-hewn players were drawn mostly from the local brickyards and steel mills. In short order, Posey became business manager and then co-owner of the club, which he renamed the Homestead Grays and stocked with outstanding professionals, many raided from the rosters of the Eastern Colored League. He arranged to rent Forbes Field from the Pirates when the major leaguers were out of town (although, true to form, the blacks weren't allowed to use the clubhouses). Despite overtures to join the ECL, Posey referred to operate as an independent club. By the late 1920s the Grays were the strongest, most profitable team in the east. In 1926, for instance, the Grays recorded a 140–13 mark in all games, then beat an all-star squad of major leaguers three of four games in October. In 1931 the Grays had compiled a 136–17 record, with their young catcher, Josh Gibson, smashing seventy-two home runs against a variety of semipro and independent opponents.[46]

However, the deepening depression was rapidly picking off these traditional opponents, convincing Posey that an organized circuit would be the best bet for his survival. In April 1932, the East-West League started play with eight clubs, most of them eastern teams. Looking to create some geographical balance, Posey installed a franchise in Detroit called the Wolves, which played home games at Hamtramck Stadium.

Unlike previous Detroit owners, Posey was an outsider, so he didn't fully understand what a strange and turbulent time it was to launch a black professional team in the city. While blacks made up less than 8 percent of Detroit's population, they represented one-third of the people on relief. A few weeks earlier in March, police had fired into a large crowd of unemployed workers demonstrating outside the Ford Rouge plant. Five workers were killed in what became widely known as the Ford Hunger March Massacre; while tens of thousands crowded downtown for the burial march and spoke stridently of socialism, the sole black victim was quietly buried in a segregated cemetery. During this period a mysterious "prophet" calling himself Farrad Mohammad—actually a street peddler named W. D. Fard—circulated through Black Bottom, preaching racial pride and denouncing the white man as the devil incarnate. He set up the "University of Islam" in an abandoned school before disappearing; a generation later, his followers would resurface as the Black Muslims.[47]

Admittedly, Farrad Mohammad was a minor figure, but so were the

Wolves, who in this climate of social and economic distress failed to attract any kind of popular support. Managed by veteran Negro-league pitcher William "Dizzy" Dismukes, and fielding several players on loan from the Homestead Grays, the Wolves essentially were the St. Louis Stars, which had folded the year before. Beyond the obvious problem of having little or no money to spend on recreation, it must have been hard for longtime fans of the original Detroit Stars to cozy up to Mule Suttles, Cool Papa Bell, and Ted Trent, all of whom had been instrumental in St. Louis beating Detroit out of the NNL pennant eighteen months earlier.

At any rate, the league didn't last long. As the westernmost cities in the circuit, Detroit and Cleveland represented logistical nightmares for teams bumping along the highway in the dead of night. Remembered George Giles, who split the season between the Wolves and the Grays: "There were nine of us riding in one big Buick. I called 'em 'Hotel Buicks.' We'd have a doubleheader in Pittsburgh, ride all night to Buffalo, play a game there, ride back to Detroit for another doubleheader, and then come back to Pittsburgh the next day. All we took along was a toothbrush. We got so we could sleep on each other's shoulders. Somebody'd say, 'Swing,' during the night, and we'd lean the other way."[48]

"We tried to play every day," said Lou Dials, who had latched on with Hilldale after two seasons with the Detroit Stars. "But cities like Cleveland and Detroit couldn't support that."[49] With two teams, Posey found himself losing money twice as fast. In early June he combined the Grays and Wolves. It was to no avail. Sometime after Independence Day, the league broke up. It was a shame. Behind pitchers Bertrum Hunter and Charles "Lefty" Williams, the Wolves easily had the best record in the league, winning better than two-thirds of their games. The players went their separate ways, some rejoining Homestead for several months of barnstorming.

The short-lived East-West League did introduce one powerful character, William A. "Gus" Greenlee, and one famous team, the Pittsburgh Crawfords, into the game. Greenlee, the flashy, high-living, uncontested king of rackets in black Pittsburgh, already owned one of the city's leading nightspots, Crawford Grille, when he decided to bankroll a baseball team in direct competition with Cum Posey. Throughout 1931 and 1932, Greenlee set about stocking his team with the best players money could buy, including pitchers Satchel Paige and Sam Streeter and outfielder Jimmy Crutchfield. In 1932 he lured several players away from the financially troubled Homestead Grays, including Josh Gibson, third baseman Judy Johnson, outfielder Ted Page, infielder Jud Wilson, second baseman John Henry Russell, and first baseman Oscar Charleston, who also was made manager. Greenlee also spent a reported $100,000 to build his own facility, the 7,500-seat Greenlee Field at 2500 Bedford Avenue. It

Homestead Grays of 1931

▲ For a time in 1932, Cumberland "Cum" Posey (standing at far left) operated two teams in the six-member East-West League. He stocked the Detroit Wolves with several players from his strong Homestead Grays squad, but it was to no avail. The Wolves and the rest of the circuit quickly evaporated. In this photograph are Oscar Charleston (first uniformed player standing at right), Josh Gibson (standing third from right), and Ted "Double Duty" Radcliffe (kneeling third from right). (Courtesy of the National Baseball Library, Cooperstown, New York.)

was the first baseball park ever built by a black. And since every dynasty needs someone to beat up on, Greenlee winked at the odds and created a brand new Negro National League.[50]

The second NNL was organized in January 1933, with Greenlee elected league chairman. Besides the Crawfords, the original six-team circuit included clubs in Chicago, Baltimore, Nashville, Columbus, and Indianapolis.

As they had so many times in the past, the Indianapolis ABCs fell apart soon after the season started, leaving Greenlee scrambling to find a replacement. He found it in a new version of the Detroit Stars, who assumed Indianapolis' won-lost record, player contracts, equipment, and team bus sometime between the ABC's last loss in Pittsburgh on May 8 and the opening of a series in Columbus against the Blue Birds on May 14. Club management included Walter Norwood, owner of the Norwood Hotel, and possibly Everitt Watson. The extent or cost of their involvement is unknown, but it's obvious that neither was willing to throw good money after bad.

Managing the club was Candy Jim Taylor (who had gotten his nickname from the sweets concession he once ran inside the lobby of Chicago's Brookmont Hotel). Taylor, known to be a patient instructor of young talent, had previously managed Detroit in 1926. There were some other former Stars on the team—outfielders Clarence Smith and Wade Johnston, catcher Spoony Palm, and second baseman Anderson Pryor—but the team had little of the old Stars' flash and strut and none of its success. Existing game accounts show that Detroit won thirteen and lost twenty of its league games in 1933, including the 1–6 record inherited from Indianapolis. However, team members could later boast of having broken in a rookie infielder, Ray Dandridge, who in 1987 would become the tenth Negro leaguer (and the only Detroit Star) to be elected to the Hall of Fame.

"Ray Dandridge was fantastic," said Monte Irvin, a Hall-of-Famer who played with and against some of the greatest third basemen in the Negro and major leagues. "Best I've ever seen at third.... He had the best hands. In a season he seldom made more than one or two errors. If the ball took a bad hop, his glove took a bad hop. He came in on swinging bunts, grabbed the ball bare-handed and threw to first base without looking and got his man."[51] Thanks to Taylor's tutelage, Dandridge also developed into a dangerous spray hitter. Wielding a long, heavy bat, the righthanded Dandridge distributed line drives to all parts of the field, making him an effective number-two hitter for most of his career.

Dandridge was spotted during the Stars' swing through Baltimore in late May, when the club detoured through the countryside for a game with the Paramount All-Stars in Richmond, Virginia. Dandridge, who usually played the outfield for Paramount, filled in at shortstop. "That day I had the best day in a long time," he later recalled. "Everything I did was right." Candy Jim Taylor was suitably impressed with the squat, bow-legged nineteen-year-old to immediately ask him if he'd like to play for Detroit.

"Man," said Dandridge, "where is Detroit?"

He soon found out. Taylor spent all night talking with Dandridge's invalid father, ultimately bribing him with twenty-five dollars to convince his son that greener pastures existed in the Motor City. Not terribly thrilled about leaving Richmond, Dandridge nonetheless dutifully packed his straw suitcase. At six o'clock the next morning he boarded the team bus for parts unknown.

"When I went to Detroit," Dandridge later recalled, "I didn't have enough to come back." That surely was the truth. Instead of drawing a regular salary, the Detroiters had to rely on splitting the meager gate receipts. Emulating their mode of transportation, this latest version of the Stars wheezed, coughed, and lurched through the summer on fumes before finally running out of gas sometime in September. While Gus Greenlee and Chicago owner Robert Cole argued over whose team had won the pennant, Candy Jim Taylor fulfilled his promise to Mr. Dandridge to get his son safely back home the only way he could.

He pawned the team bus.

Epilogue

Come in Out of the Dark

The story of America's Negro leagues continued long after Detroit's participation ended. In 1934, Gus Greenlee's Negro National League managed to get through a second season, despite a 50-percent turnover in franchises. One of the casualties was the Detroit Stars, which existed only on paper at this point. Because of the Stars' demonstrated instability, Candy Jim Taylor couldn't secure a lease at Hamtramck Stadium or any other facility. So the franchise—the term is used lightly—wound up in Columbus, Ohio. There Taylor organized a brand new team that played the season as the Nashville Elite Giants. The Elite Giants returned to Columbus for the 1935 season, then collapsed sometime before the 1936 season started.

That January Greenlee talked with John Roxborough about bringing a team back to Detroit. By then Greenlee had stabilized the NNL with massive infusions of gangster capital. Alex Pompez, the Harlem mobster who had set Greenlee up in the numbers racket in the 1920s, owned the New York Cubans. Ed "Soldier Boy" Semler operated the New York Black Yankees. Teams in Baltimore, Newark, and Philadelphia also were financed with laundered money. Even Cum Posey had turned to Homestead racketeer Rufus "Sonnyman" Jackson to save the Grays.[1] So Roxborough, who was using much of his underworld profits and contacts to boost the career of up-and-coming heavyweight Joe Louis, actually fit the profile of the typical NNL owner.

Louis, for one, "loved the idea" of co-owning a team, he later admit-

▲ Joe Louis (in sunglasses) and boyhood pal Freddie Guinyard (left) attend a game at Navin Field in the 1930s. In early 1936 the prizefighter seriously considered buying a franchise in Gus Greenlee's reorganized Negro National League.

ted. He had shagged balls for the Stars as a teenager and was a huge fan of the Detroit Tigers—particularly big Hank Greenberg, whose awkward but earnest attempts to master first base in the early 1930s undoubtedly reminded Louis of himself. If it hadn't been for boxing, Louis said, "I would have loved to have been a baseball player." He was already indulging that fantasy. After knocking out former heavyweight champions Primo Carnera and Max Baer in 1935, Louis had organized a score of his unemployed friends from Black Bottom into the Brown Bombers Softball Team. Louis frequently played first base for the team, which traveled around the country by bus. By the time the Bombers played out the string in 1938, Louis had spent an estimated $50,000 on his hobby.[2]

While Louis's wife, Marva, fretted over the money involved in an NNL franchise, Roxborough was more concerned about his fighter's image. It wouldn't do for the man who was trying to get out from under the shadow of the last black heavyweight champion, the controversial Jack Johnson, to be associated with a league baldly run by gangsters. In fact, Roxborough, who in his own quiet fashion was as much a "race man" as Rube Foster, would gradually retreat into the background as Louis's national stature grew through the decade. So the answer to Greenlee's overture was no.

Although that particular effort failed, in 1937 a wholly new, low-rent version of the Detroit Stars appeared as a charter member of the Negro American League. Organized by Horace G. Hall, president of the Chicago American Giants, the NAL fielded teams in Detroit, Chicago, Kansas City, Cincinnati, Memphis, Birmingham, Indianapolis, and St. Louis.

The Detroit entry was simply the sandlot Titus Stars, owned by Hastings Street meat merchant James Titus, handed a new name. This was as pure a home team as one will ever find in professional sports. Only two former NNL Stars were on the team: Jim "Double Duty" Webster, who, like all of the era's Double Dutys, divided his time between the mound and behind the plate; and Turkey Stearnes, who at thirty-five was still stationed in center field, mumbling under his breath about the pitchers. Both were working at least part-time at area auto plants. Home games were played at Dequindre Park, at Modern and Dequindre on the far east side. At least one game was played at Singer Park, a sandlot field on Linwood near Fenkell. Both sites demonstrated the league's lack of stature.

Representative of the club's personnel was twenty-five-year-old third baseman Charles "Red" House, who had grown up near Hastings Street. As a teenager, he had played sandlot ball and worked out with the Stars at Mack Park, where pitcher Charlie Henry took a liking to him. When the Bacharach Giants came through town in 1929, both joined the eastern club on a three-week barnstorming tour. Only seventeen years old at the time, broke, and a little homesick, House came back to Detroit. For the next several years he alternated between looking for work, playing baseball, and boxing at the Brewster gym with his younger friend, Joe Louis. House was the 1932 Golden Gloves middleweight champion at the same time he was playing weekends fore the Titus Stars at Hamtramck Stadium. "I loved both sports," he recalled. "But baseball was a little better because they didn't hit you back."

House tried boxing professionally, but gave it up. "The money was

KANSAS CITY MONARCHS

BASEBALL CLUB OF KANSAS CITY, MO.

WILL PLAY THE

DETROIT STARS

NEGRO AMERICAN LEAGUE

WORLD COLORED CHAMPIONS

MUEHLEBACH FIELD
KANSAS CITY, MO.

SUN. JULY 18   DOUBLE HEADER 2:00 P. M.

MON. NIGHT 8:30 p.m. JULY 19

Grand Stand 40c   Bleachers 25c

▲ An all-new version of the Detroit Stars emerged in the Negro American League in 1937, but folded after one summer.

too short," he said, "Four dollars for a six-rounder." Instead, he hooked up with the Zulu Giants, traveling as far west as Seattle and Oakland in 1934. "We wore straws skirts and painted our faces. Yeah, that's right. How do you think we drew crowds? Especially whites. They were crazy about it." House was just starting a factory job at Ford in 1937 when he was offered $300 a month to play full-time with the Stars, "which was real good money, I'm tellin' ya."[3]

For House and most of his teammates, 1937 would prove to be their only full season in the Negro leagues, although over the next several years House, feeling the tug of the diamond, would take occasional leaves of absence to barnstorm with various black professional teams. As with so many other talented athletes lost in the neighborhoods, throughout his adult life House would be stretched and pulled like taffy between family obligations—he had a wife and six children—and the gnawing thought that if he just kept trying, he would one day make it big.

To date, few game accounts and boxscores for the Stars' season have been uncovered. Standings published in the black press showed that the Detroiters won twelve of twenty-seven games in the first half of a split schedule before evidently folding sometime late in the summer. Once again, the Stars' rise and fall perfectly mirrored that of the local economy. The league was launched when the country was slowly lifting itself out of the depression. The assembly lines were humming again, people were back at work, and there were dollars to be spent. The Roosevelt administration felt confident enough about the economy to drastically slash the massive federal work programs. To Washington's shock, the fragile recovery collapsed. Auto production fell 48 percent between 1937 and 1938, once again throwing tens of thousands of factory hands, including Red House, out of work.

Despite problems with the economy and unscrupulous white promoters, who controlled access to the white-owned ballparks, the NAL managed to stumble through the rest of the decade, franchises coming and going at a dizzying rate. By 1942 it had solidified to the point that it was holding an annual World Series with the pennant winner from the rival Negro National League. Several of these postseason games were played at Griffith Stadium in Washington and Comiskey Park in Chicago. Just as important for showcasing black talent were the annual East-West Classic all-star games that Gus Greenlee had inaugurated in 1933. By the Second World War these contests were drawing more than 50,000 people, many of whom left the park wondering why these men weren't wearing major-league uniforms.

Strangely, no new Detroit franchise surfaced in either Negro major league during the 1940s, this despite the fact that the city had one of the largest black populations in the country. The chief reason was the lack of financial backing. The standard of living for individual blacks rose as work in defense plants and auto factories boomed throughout the 1940s, but capital for enterprising businessmen remained in the tight fists of conservative white bankers. As James Titus had learned in 1937, operating a ball club on a big-league level required considerably more cash than an ordinary meat merchant was able to provide.

Traditionally, the financial angels of Detroit's black community, particularly its athletes, had been the underworld. By 1940, estimates of their annual take ranged from $2 million to $10 million.[4] Tenny Blount and Everitt Watson had owned the Detroit Stars for much of their history, and black racketeers had also bankrolled many of the city's promising young prizefighters of the 1930s, including heavyweights Roscoe Toles and Joe Louis. Any hope that they might do the same for another Negro-league franchise vanished during the sweeping one-man grand jury investigations of Senator Homer Ferguson. In the early 1940s, Roxborough, Watson, and twenty-five others—including a former mayor, Wayne County prosecutor, and Wayne County sheriff—were sent to prison for their involvement in the city's numbers racket. East side Italian gangsters Joe Bommarito and Pete Licavoli, not exactly known for their support of black athletes, immediately filled the vacuum left by Roxborough's and Watson's imprisonment.

A black semipro team called the Motor City Giants was active dur-

◄ After the original Negro National League dissolved in 1931, Turkey Stearnes went on to play for the Kansas City Monarchs, Chicago American Giants (where he won a batting title and another home run crown), and the Philadelphia Stars. In 1937 he signed on for a tenth season in Detroit with the new Detroit Stars, charter members of the Negro American League. The league lasted, but the team didn't. Stearnes finished out his career in Chicago and Kansas City. He returned to Detroit during the Second World War, got married, and spent the balance of his working life at a Ford factory.

ing the war, playing the likes of Satchel Paige's All-Stars and the St. Louis Stars at Briggs Stadium. In 1945 they were charter members of the United States Baseball League, put together by Brooklyn owner Branch Rickey and Gus Greenlee, who had withdrawn his Pittsburgh Crawfords from the Negro National League in 1939. Also included in the circuit—which the crafty Rickey used as an opportunity to scout prospective players—were Rickey's Brooklyn Brown Dodgers, the Toledo Rays, Hilldale, and the Chicago Brown Bombers, who were managed by former Stars skipper Bingo DeMoss.[5]

The following year, the wartime clamor for civil rights, added to the undeniable brilliance of the Negro leaguers' play, finally opened the door for black ballplayers. There's no need to recount the particulars of Rickey's well-known historic first step of signing Kansas City infielder Jackie Robinson to a minor-league contract except to say that desegregation was a double-edged sword.[6] "I was really happy," said Red House, who played his final Negro-league games in 1946 with the Homestead Grays. "But I didn't feel so good about the black leagues breaking up. There were so many good players."[7]

Most evidently escaped the gaze of Walter O. Briggs, who had assumed full control of the Tigers upon Frank Navin's death in 1935. Throughout his tenure in the front office, Briggs set a standard of excellence for the rest of major-league baseball to follow. He spent $2 million to double-deck Navin Field and rededicated it in 1938 as 52,000-seat Briggs Stadium. It immediately rivaled Yankee Stadium as the country's top all-purpose sporting venue. Players and fans were spoiled by the millionaire industrialist, who considered his ball club a community resource, not a business investment.

The argument quickly arose that, at least in Briggs's eyes, the Tigers were a *white* community resource. The number of Detroit blacks had mushroomed to 300,000 during the 1940s, but the only crumbs Briggs threw to this vast and potentially lucrative audience were occasional Negro-league exhibitions. Even then, the large crowds of blacks were discomfiting enough for Briggs to place guards at the concession stands. When Detroit's racial friction finally exploded in June 1943 in a deadly riot that claimed twenty-three blacks and fifteen whites, the Tigers' owner used his influence to have three hundred armed troops installed throughout his ballpark—a major-league first. Wendall Smith, a native Detroiter and sportswriter for the *Pittsburgh Courier,* described Briggs as "oh, so very prejudiced. He's the major league combination of Simon Legree and Adolf Hitler."[8]

Baseball's desegregation created a fire sale among Negro-league owners, most of whom were financially devastated as black fans quickly shifted their allegiance to the suddenly color-blind majors. Despite their deep pockets, the Tigers refused to seriously consider signing either established Negro leaguers or talented sandlotters. Judy Johnson, then a scout with the Philadelphia Athletics, remembered that anyone could have signed an Indianapolis infielder named Henry Aaron for $3,500.[9] Briggs, who had signed the game's first "bonus baby," outfielder Dick Wakefield, off the University of Michigan campus for $52,000 in 1941, sat on his wallet as Aaron and others were snapped up at bargain-basement prices.

"The saying around the press box was 'No jiggs with Briggs,'" said Edgar Hayes, sports editor of the *Detroit Times* during the 1950s. "Despite the fact that the winning teams in both leagues were those that were signing the good black players, he was dead-set against having blacks play for him."[10]

A variety of civil rights groups besieged the front office during the decade. Briggs died in 1952, but his son, Walter "Spike" Briggs, Jr., repeated his father's contention that the Tigers had not found any young black players with sufficient ability. It was a feeble argument—especially for a club that would finish last in 1952—for there certainly was no shortage of talented sandlotters around town. In 1951–52 alone, the St. Louis Browns, Chicago Cubs, and Chicago White Sox signed seven black Detroit high schoolers.[11] By 1953 every team in the majors except Detroit had blacks in its farm system, and by 1958 every club except Detroit and Boston had integrated its major-league lineup.

The Tigers' intransigence ended when a syndicate headed by Kalamazoo media magnate John Fetzer purchased the team in 1956. Within two years the organization had seventeen blacks signed to minor-league contracts. On June 6, 1958, feeling the pressure from an ad hoc civil rights group called the Briggs Stadium Boycott Commission, the Tigers finally fielded their first black: Ozzie Virgil, a third baseman who had been born in the Dominican Republic.

"Nobody thought Virgil was black," said Willie Horton, who grew up in the city's housing projects in the 1950s, a time when the city's black population reached 450,000. "Larry Doby was the first black. Doby came along the next year, when he was at the end of his career." Second baseman Jake Wood and outfielder Billy Bruton both joined the Tigers in 1961, but Horton became the team's first legitimate black star, wearing the old English D from 1963 through 1977. Now the executive director of the Police Athletic League, he admits that around the sandlots and projects of the inner city, the perception was that blacks "weren't welcome" by the Tigers' organization. Even spring training in Lakeland, Florida, featured segregated hotels. Horton blamed that on Jim Crow ordinances that the ballclub didn't contest.[12]

Whether the Tigers were purposely ignoring blacks or not, Briggs's legacy has been hard to eradicate. Even during the fairy-tale season of 1984, when the Tigers won their last World Series with such black stars as Lou Whitaker, Chet Lemon, and Larry Herndon, black fans were conspicuous by their absence. Said coach William "Gates" Brown, who played thirteen seasons for the Tigers (1963–75): "I've heard a lot of tales that the blacks got turned off a long time ago—back to the days of Walter O. Briggs—and they're still turned off. I'll tell you something: This is 1984, but they're still bitter about the way the black players have been treated in Detroit." Added Al Dunmore, a veteran black sportswriter: "The black community over age 40 believes it's an organization steeped in racism."[13] Judging by the low percentage of blacks in the park in the 1990s, the perception of racism continues to be as costly as any reality.

☆

Turkey Stearnes, who usually kept his own counsel about such matters, regularly attended games at Briggs Stadium (renamed Tiger Stadium in 1961) long after he had finished his diamond career in 1942 in Chicago. Happy to have a wife, a house, and a job at Ford, he spent his

▲ The Negro leagues exhibit at the National Baseball Hall of Fame and Museum in Cooperstown features uniforms, pennants, posters, photographs, and other memorabilia. (Courtesy of the National Baseball Library, Cooperstown, New York.)

summers in the center-field bleachers, a gaunt, deaf pensioner watching a succession of young, black outfielders patrol the thick blue-green grass that, had he been born forty years later, he might very well have been gliding across himself.

In their old age Stearnes and his contemporaries enjoyed the satisfaction that their accomplishments were being revived during their lifetime. A flickering interest in the Negro leagues was fanned by Robert Peterson's 1970 book, then stoked by several other writers, film makers, and historians.

A lot of what first appeared was pure hokum, of course. The movie *Bingo Long and the Traveling All-Stars and Motor Kings,* for example, angered many Negro leaguers by portraying them as unprofessional clowns.[14] And too many of the tall stories told by gregarious old timers happy for the sudden attention were accepted as truth by unquestioning journalists. The formation of the Society for American Baseball Research in 1971 soon provided a skeptical counterweight to every catcher's claim that he had thrown out Ty Cobb twice—no, three times—in a game back in 1915. The fiction had a positive effect, entertaining while informing Americans about a subculture that few knew ever existed. Coupled with the growing scholarship and evidence of their diamond deeds, it helped secure a belated entry for Rube Foster and ten other Negro leaguers into the National Baseball Hall of Fame in Cooperstown between 1971 and 1987: Satchel Paige, Buck Leonard, Josh Gibson, Monte Irvin, Cool Papa

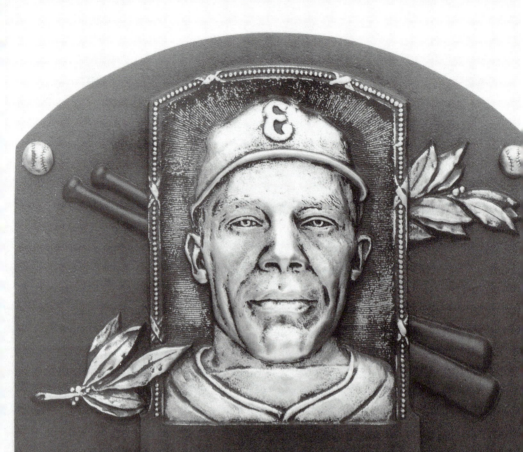

RAYMOND EMMETT DANDRIDGE
NEGRO AND MEXICAN LEAGUES
1933 – 1948

FLASHY BUT SMOOTH THIRD BASEMAN. DEFENSIVELY,
A BRILLIANT FIELDER WITH POWERFUL ARM.
OFFENSIVELY, A SPRAY HITTER WITH OUTSTANDING
BAT CONTROL. PLAYED FOR DETROIT STARS, NEWARK
DODGERS, NEWARK EAGLES AND NEW YORK CUBANS
IN NEGRO LEAGUES AND FOR VERACRUZ AND MEXICO
CITY IN MEXICAN LEAGUES. AMERICAN ASSOCIATION
MVP IN 1950 WITH .311, 11 HOME RUNS AND
80 RBI'S PLAYING FOR MINNEAPOLIS MILLERS.

© 1987 NBHOF

Bell, Judy Johnson, Oscar Charleston, Martin DiHigo, John Henry Lloyd, and Ray Dandridge. Stearnes, who Satchel Paige once declared was "as good as anybody who ever played baseball," belongs there as well. "If they don't put him in the Hall of Fame," said Cool Papa Bell, "they shouldn't put anybody in."[15]

Stearnes died on September 4, 1979, in Detroit of a perforated ulcer. To the last, he refused to complain about being born too soon. "I never heard him say anything about it," said his widow, Nettie. "He was a quiet man, but I guess he felt good that avenues were being opened up for our race."[16]

By the time of Stearnes's passing, most of the other people and places associated with the Detroit Stars were gone, too. Tenny Blount left the city in the 1930s; no one knows what happened to him after that. John Roesink died in 1954, followed by Everitt Watson six years later.[17] About this time Mack Park was torn down to make room for a housing development, while Hastings Street and much of Paradise Valley disappeared under the concrete ribbons of the I-375 (Chrysler) interchange. Hamtramck Stadium still exists as Keywort Stadium, although its symbiotic relationship with nearby Dodge Main ended when the factory was closed and then leveled shortly after Stearnes's death.

Meanwhile, the story of the Negro leagues continues to penetrate popular culture, with reproduction uniforms regularly showing up on network television and theatrical productions running the gamut from *Fences,* by Pulitzer Prize-winning playwright August Wilson, to *If It Ain't Got That Swing,* by Carmen N'Namdi of the Nataki Talibah elementary schoolhouse in Detroit. And, as this is being written, the Negro Baseball Museum is scheduled to open in Kansas City, close to the YMCA where Rube Foster launched his historic league in 1920.[18]

The material gains that black players have achieved since that time are mind-numbing. In 1923, for example, Turkey Stearnes made about $200 a month as one of the finest all-around players in the game. Seventy years later, the Detroit Tigers signed first baseman Cecil Fielder to a six-year contract worth $42 million. That amount could have met the payroll of the entire Negro National League in 1923 for more than two hundred years!

Racially, however, the game rolls along in the worn grooves of the

◀ Ray Dandridge, who started his brilliant diamond career as a Detroit Stars infielder in 1933, is one of eleven Negro leaguers enshrined at Cooperstown. The argument persists that many more black stars, particularly Turkey Stearnes, belong there as well. (Courtesy of the National Baseball Library, Cooperstown, New York.)

past, as demonstrated by the suspension of Cincinnati Reds owner Marge Schott in early 1993 for uttering racial slurs. Major-league baseball, goosed once again by civil rights activists, promised to review its woeful minority hiring record. Whether this will translate into real progress for organized baseball remains to be seen.

Dave Malarcher, the son of a former slave and briefly a member of the Detroit Stars during their inaugural season of 1919, was a sensitive, dignified, educated man who wrote hundreds of poems trying to reconcile America's race question. He, sooner than others, came to appreciate Rube Foster and the Negro National League as being a middle passage of sorts, a bridge between yesterday's Page Fence Giants, who cartwheeled around the bases and bicycled through town to support their livelihood, and the fabulously rich, celebrity ballplayers of today.

"[Rube] knew that all we had to do was to keep on developing Negro baseball, keep it up to a high standard, and the time would come when the white leagues would have to admit us," Malarcher said in his old age. "The thing for us to do, he said, was to keep on developing, so that when that time did come, we would be able to measure up."[19]

Appendix A

Detroit Stars
All-Time Roster

The following is a list of the 206 men who are known to have either played or served as officers for the Detroit Stars between 1919 and 1933. Because newspaper sports pages of the period commonly referred to a player by his last name only, or used a surname in conjunction with an initial or moniker, in several cases a person's proper first name is indeterminable.

Name—Position	Seasons
Grover Cleveland (Buck) Alexander, P	1923–25
Newt Allen, 2B	1932
Herman (Jabo) Andrews, P-OF	1932
——— Armour, P-3B	1933
Percy (Bill) Bailey, P	1933
Robert Baldwin, 2B	1926
Jess Barbour, OF	1922
John (Fat) Barnes, C	1924
Clifford Bell, P	?
Fred Bell, P-OF	1925–27
James (Cool Papa) Bell, OF	1932
Julian Bell, P-OF	1924
William Bell, P	1932
Jerry Benjamin, OF	1933
George (Jew Baby) Bennette, OF	1922

Name—Position	Seasons
Rainey Bibbs, 1B	1933
Jimmy Binder, 3B	1933
Charles Blackwell, OF	1926
John T. (Tenny) Blount, Officer	1919–33
G. Boggs, P	1923
Finis Branahan, P	1925
George (Chippy) Britt, P	1932
Charles Brooks, P	1924
Edward Brown, P	1920
George Brown, OF	1921
Larry Brown, C	1926
Ray Brown, P	1932
(Black Bottom) Buford, 2B-SS-P	1933
—— Busby, 3B-OF	1933
William Carter, C	1920
—— Chase, P	1920
—— Coley, P	1924
Jack Combs, P	1923–26
Andy (Lefty) Cooper, P-OF	1919–27, 1930
Sam Crawford, OF	1919
A. D. (Dewey) Creacy, 3B	1932
Reuben (Rube) Currie, P	1928
Raymond (Hooks) Dandridge, SS	1933
Leon (Pepper) Daniels, C	1921–27, 1930
Albert Davis, P	1927–30
Dwight Davis, P	1930
Saul Davis, SS-3B	1925, 1931
Walter (Steel Arm) Davis, P-OF	1923
Nelson Dean, P	1930–31
Elwood (Bingo) DeMoss, 2B-1B-Manager	1927–31
Alonzo (Lou) Dials, 1B-OF	1930–31
William (Dizzy) Dismukes, P-Manager	1932
John Dixon, P	1926, 1931
John Donaldson, P-OF	1919
William (Plunk) Drake, P	1927
Frank Duncan, OF	1919
Jake Dunn, SS	1930

Name—Position	Seasons
Johnny Edwards, P	1929
Mack Eggleston, C	1920
Lou English, C	1929
Bill (Happy) Evans, OF-SS	1932
Clarence Everett, SS-OF	1927
——— Foote, C	1929
William Force, P	1921–23
——— Gales, 1B	1931
Floyd (Jelly) Gardner, OF	1919, 1931
Bill Gatewood, P	1920–21
George Giles, 1B	1932
William Gill, 1B-3B	1931, 1933
Ernest Gooden, 3B	1923
——— Green, P	1920
Julius Green, OF	1930
——— Haley, P	1923
Perry Hall, 2B	1926
Lewis Hampton, P-OF	1925–27
Hollie Harding, SS-OF	1927–28
Paul Hardy, C-1B	1933
(Chick) Harper, P-OF	1920, 1925
Vic (Moocha) Harris, OF	1932
Arthur (Rats) Henderson, P	1931
Charlie Henry, P	1929
(Slap) Hensley, P	1933
Joe Hewitt, IF	1919–20, 1925–26
Charley Hill, OF	1920–21
Fred Hill, IF-OF	?
Johnson Hill, 3B	1921
J. Preston (Pete) Hill, OF-Manager	1919–22
(Lefty) Hill, OF	?
——— Holcomb, P	1923
Bill Holland, P	1920–22
O. (Crush) Holloway, OF	1930
——— Howard, P	1921
Bertrum Hunter, P	1932

Name—Position	Seasons
Nat Moore, OF	1920–21
Harold (Yellowhorse) Morris, P	1925–27
William Mosley, Officer	1928–33
Everett Nelson, P-OF	1922, 1933
Omer Newsome, P	1925–26
Walter Norwood, Officer	1933
Grady Orange, IF	1928–31
Willie Owens, SS	1931, 1933
Clarence (Spoony) Palm, C-3B	1930–31, 1933
Rufus Peak, Officer	1931
Carl Perry, 2B	1921
Bruce Petway, C-1B-OF-Manager	1919–25
——— Phillips, 2B-3B	1923
William H. (Bill) Pierce, 1B-OF	1924
Cumberland Willis (Cum) Posey, Officer	1932
Willie Powell, P	1930–31
Anderson Pryor, IF	1923–27, 1931, 1933
Bill Pryor, P	1931
Ted (Double Duty) Radcliffe, C-P	1928–29, 1931
Andrew Reed, OF	1919, 1921
John E. Reese, OF	1921
George Richardson, Officer	1925
Orville (Mule) Riggins, SS-P	1920–26
Ed (Big Ed) Rile, P-1B-2B	1927–30
Bill (Bobbie) Robinson, SS-3B	1929–31
Jose Rodriquez, C	1919
John Roesink, Officer	1925–30
——— Rosello, OF	1921
William Ross, P	1927
Herman (Bobby) Roth, C	1924
John Henry Russell, 2B	1932
Harry Salmon, P	1932
Bob Saunders, P-2B	1926, 1931
Carl Sawyer, 2B	1924
——— Scott, C	1920

Name—Position	Seasons
Ted Shaw, P	1928–30
Ray Sheppard, IF	1925–26, 1932
Clarence Smith, OF-1B-3B	1921–25, 1933
James Smith, SS	1925, 1930
——— Snowden, P	1933
Hulan Stamps, P	1933
Norman (Turkey) Stearnes, OF-1B-P	1923–31
——— Stevens, C	1927, 1929
——— Stevenson, C	1929
——— Stokes, P	1933
George (Mule) Suttles, 1B	1932
Jim (Candy Jim) Taylor, 3B-P-Manager	1926, 1933
Leroy R. Taylor, OF	1932–33
Lawrence Terrell, P	1924–25
Clint Thomas, 2B-OF	1922
(Gunboat) Thompson, P	1920
Samuel (Sad Sam) Thompson, P	1933
Levy Tindle, Officer	1933
Christobel Torrienti, OF-P	1927–28
Harold Treadwell, P	1924, 1926
Ted Trent, P	1932
Quincy Trouppe, P-C-OF	1932
Bill (Steel Arm) Tyler, P	1929–30
Columbus Vance, P	1933
(Lefty) Waddy, P	1933
Moses L. Walker, Officer	1925–31
Frank Warfield, 2B-3B-OF	1919–22
Everett Watson, Officer	1931
Johnny Watson, OF	1922–24, 1926
Jim Webster, C	1933
William (Speck) Webster, C	1921
Willie Wells, SS	1932
Edgar Wesley, 1B	1919–23, 1925–27
Frank Wickware, P	1919
Charles (Lefty) Williams, P	1932
Elbert Williams, P	1931

Name—Position	Seasons
Joe (Smokey Joe) Williams, P	1932
John (James) Williams, OF	1933
Poindexter Williams, C-OF	1921–22
Tom Williams, P	1924
Charles Wilson, P-OF	1921–22
E. Wilson, 2B-3B	?
——— Wingfield, OF	1921
James Winston, P	1931
——— Wyatt, C	1929
Tom Young, C	1932
William (Doc) Ziegler, P	1921

Appendix B

Year-by-Year Standings and Statistics

The following standings and statistics for the Detroit Stars and the Negro National League from 1919 through 1933 appear courtesy of the Negro leagues committee of the Society for American Baseball Research. There are, unfortunately, gaps in the data, owing to the haphazard way in which Negro-league games were scored and reported. For instance, such data as runs scored and runs batted in were rarely recorded in box scores then, while other items—at-bats, stolen bases, and pitching breakdowns—also were frequently missing. In many cases this data could be reconstructed from game accounts, but not always. The result is that the information in most categories is underrepresented.

Since Negro-league clubs played against teams of all ability levels, some decisions had to be made concerning what games should be included in the record-keeping. The standings here include only "official" league games played by member clubs, all of which counted towards the pennant race. However, for the sake of compiling individual statistics, the scope was broadened to cover all games played between major black teams, including contests with affiliated members and independent teams. In neither case are the many exhibition games played against white semipro or major-league teams included in the numbers.

Although earned run averages (ERA) for Negro-league pitchers are impossible to ascertain, a somewhat satisfying barometer of a pitcher's performance has been devised. The category of Runs Per Game (RPG) measures how many *total* runs a pitcher surrendered every nine innings. Since this includes unearned as well as earned runs, these figures can appear bloated, especially for such sterling moundsmen as Bill Holland and Andy Cooper. A rule of thumb is to lower a player's RPG by 1.0 to 1.5 to get a rough sense of what his ERA might have been. For instance, Bill Holland's 4.05 RPG in 1921 probably would translate into an

ERA in the range of 2.55 to 3.05 if all the pertinent information were available to researchers.

Those players who led the league in a particular category are identified with an asterisk (*), although some rankings are bound to change as additional figures are unearthed. As of this writing, only the 1921, 1926, 1929, and 1930 seasons are considered to be complete; the rest are still being researched.

1919 Detroit Stars
Manager: Pete Hill

In 1919 there was no Negro National League and no organized schedule. The Stars fielded the following roster in their games against black and white independent teams:

Player	Position
Edgar Wesley	1B
Frank Warfield	2B-3B
Jose Mendez	SS-P
Joe Hewitt	IF
Frank Duncan	OF
Jelly Gardner	OF
Pete Hill	OF
Bruce Petway	C
Frank Wickware	P
Hurley McNair	OF
Sam Crawford	OF
Andrew Reed	OF
Dave Malarcher	3B
Jose Rodriquez	C
Dicta Johnson	P
John Donaldson	P-OF

1920 Negro National League

In 1920 the league did not release any official final standings, although it did declare the Chicago American Giants the pennant winner. The standings below have been reconstructed from surviving boxscores.

	Won	Lost	Pct.
Chicago American Giants	32	13	.711
Detroit Stars	35	22	.614
Kansas City Monarchs	41	29	.586
Indianapolis ABCs	39	35	.527
Cuban Stars	21	24	.467
St. Louis Giants	25	32	.439
Dayton Marcos	8	18	.308
Chicago Giants	4	24	.143

1920 Detroit Stars
Manager: Pete Hill
Individual Statistics

PITCHING

Pitcher	GP	GS	CG	Won	Lost	IP	H	BB	SO	RPG	ShO	SV
Bill Gatewood.............	20	13	9	14*	4	132	109	27	50	3.75	1	0
Bill Holland.................	23	17	12	11	6	154.1	123	29	68	3.32	1	2
Webster McDonald	9	8	4	3	4	49.1	46	21	12	6.39	0	0
——— Thompson........	8	6	2	3	2	37.1	31	22	13	6.03	0	0
Dicta Johnson..............	2	2	2	2	0	18	5	3	3	3.00	0	0
Jimmy Lyons................	5	1	0	1	1	20.1	22	11	6	5.32	0	0
Andy Cooper..............	8	3	1	0	2	36.2	31	19	10	5.15	0	1
George Brown	2	1	0	0	1	5	5	2	0	3.60	0	0
Chick Harper	2	1	1	0	1	11	12	3	2	5.73	0	0
——— Chase	1	1	0	0	0	8	4	—	—	7.88	0	0
——— Green	1	—	—	0	0	—	—	—	—	——	0	0
Totals		53	31	34	21	472	388	137	164	4.33	2	3

BATTING

Position	Player	Games	AB	H	Avg.	2B	3B	HR	SB
1B	Edgar Wesley........	43	158	45	.285	10	1	10*	3
2B-3B	Frank Warfield......	41	170	47	.275	10	4	1	5
SS-3B	Mule Riggins..........	36	125	39	.312	11	2	1	1
INF	Joe Hewitt	31	104	22	.212	3	1	0	6
OF-1B-P	Jimmy Lyons..........	37	136	55	.404*	10	3	8	22*
OF	Pete Hill	28	81	22	.272	4	1	2	4
OF	Nat Moore	17	59	11	.186	4	0	0	2
C	Bruce Petway.........	25	77	14	.182	1	0	0	4
C	Mack Eggleston	24	74	20	.270	7	3	0	0
UT	——— Longware ...	19	62	10	.161	1	0	0	0
OF-P	Chick Harper.........	16	56	14	.250	1	1	2	0
OF	Charley Hill	16	48	13	.271	1	0	0	0
P	Bill Holland............	22	39	4	.103	0	0	0	0
P	Bill Gatewood.......	27	32	13	.406	3	2	0	0
C	——— Scott	6	18	3	.167	0	0	0	0
C	William Carter.......	7	16	1	.063	1	0	0	0
P	——— Thompson...	8	15	3	.200	1	0	0	0
P	Andy Cooper.........	8	12	0	.000	0	0	0	0
OF	——— Long	4	7	2	.286	0	0	0	0
P	Webster McDonald	8	6	0	.000	0	0	0	0
P	Dicta Johnson	1	4	1	.250	0	0	0	0
P	George Brown	2	2	0	.000	0	0	0	0
Totals			1301	339	.261	68	18	24	47

1921 Negro National League

	Won	Lost	Pct.
Chicago American Giants	42	22	.656
Kansas City Monarchs	50	31	.617
St. Louis Giants	40	28	.588
Detroit Stars	32	32	.500
Indianapolis ABCs	35	38	.479
Cincinnati (Cuban Stars)	29	39	.426
Columbus Buckeyes	24	38	.387
Chicago Giants	10	32	.239

1921 Detroit Stars
Manager: Pete Hill

Individual Statistics

PITCHING

Pitcher	GP	GS	CG	Won	Lost	IP	H	BB	SO	RPG	ShO	SV
William Force	27	19	11	13	6	148	127	29	56	4.62	0	1
Bill Holland...........	29	19	18	12	11	173.1	155	35	86	4.05	1	4
Bill Gatewood.......	19	17	7	6	9	115	105	22	43	5.09	1	0
Andy Cooper........	23	16	9	5	8	117	122	13	29	4.46	1	0
Charles Wilson	1	1	1	0	1	9	14	3	1	6.00	0	0
I. S. Lane..............	1	1	—	0	1	—	—	0	0	—	0	0
Doc Ziegler	1	—	—	—	—	2	2	—	—	9.00	0	0
——— Howard.....	1	—	—	—	—	.1	1	0	0	0.00	0	—
Totals		73	46	36	36	564.2	526	102	215	4.54	3	5

BATTING

Position	Player	Games	AB	H	Avg.	2B	3B	HR	SB
1B	Edgar Wesley	33	116	39	.336	7	0	7	3
2B	Carl Perry	22	72	17	.236	2	1	2	0
SS	Mule Riggins	48	189	63	.333	16	2	1	4
3B	Johnson Hill.................	42	153	42	.275	5	5	4	0
OF	Charley Hill.................	30	91	18	.198	3	0	0	6
2B-3B-OF	Frank Warfield	50	180	49	.272	8	4	2	8
OF-1B	Pete Hill	40	134	52	.388	5	5	3	3
C-1B	Bruce Petway...............	40	131	42	.321	5	2	2	9
OF	Andrew Reed	19	80	10	.125	1	0	0	0
OF	——— Wingfield.........	14	56	15	.268	1	0	0	0
C	Speck Webster	20	49	12	.245	1	0	1	0
P-OF	William Force..............	27	42	10	.238	2	1	0	0
OF	——— Long	12	37	11	.297	5	2	3	0
P	Bill Holland	29	37	3	.081	0	0	0	0
OF	John Reese	8	31	7	.226	1	0	0	0
P	Andy Cooper	23	30	7	.238	1	2	0	0
OF	——— Wilson.............	8	28	5	.179	1	0	0	0
P	Bill Gatewood	20	27	12	.444	3	0	1	0
OF	G. Brown.....................	4	15	1	.067	0	0	0	1
OF	N. Moore	4	12	3	.250	2	0	0	1
C	Poindexter Williams	4	12	2	.167	0	0	0	0
P-3B	——— Howard	2	9	3	.333	1	0	0	0
OF	Clarence Smith	1	3	2	.667	0	0	0	0
P	Charles Wilson............	1	3	0	.000	0	0	0	0
C	Pepper Daniels	3	1	1	1.000	0	1	0	0
Totals			1538	426	.277	70	25	26	35

231

1922 Negro National League

	Won	Lost	Pct.
Chicago American Giants	36	23	.610
Indianapolis ABCs	46	33	.582
Kansas City Monarchs	46	33	.582
Detroit Stars	43	32	.573
St. Louis Stars	35	26	.573
Pittsburgh Keystones	16	21	.432
Cuban Stars	19	31	.380
Cleveland Tate Stars	17	29	.370

1922 Detroit Stars
Manager: Bruce Petway
Individual Statistics

PITCHING

Pitcher	GP	GS	CG	Won	Lost	IP	H	BB	SO	RPG	ShO	SV
Bill Holland.................	35	23	18	16*	13	204	182	25	95	3.88	2	1
Andy Cooper..............	25	22	16	14	5	153	132	21	43	3.71	4	0
William Force	28	19	14	10	7	176.2	125	30	108	3.87	2	2
Jack Marshall..............	18	12	7	5	6	101	92	24	38	4.63	0	0
Charles Wilson	15	7	3	5	4	65.1	72	9	21	5.65	0	0
Everett Nelson.............	1	—	—	—	—	—	—	—	—	—	—	—
Totals		83	58	50	35	700	603	109	305	4.11	8	3

BATTING

Position	Player	Games	AB	H	Avg.	2B	3B	HR	SB
1B	Edgar Wesley	61	218	75	.344	10	5	12	6
2B-3B	Frank Warfield	58	228	78	.342	10	3	0	10
SS	Mule Riggins	61	215	56	.260	6	2	2	7
3B	I. S. Lane	46	189	57	.302	6	4	3	8
OF	John Jones	49	166	47	.283	8	1	2	2
2B-OF	Clint Thomas	60	231	79	.346	15	7	7	7
OF	Clarence Smith	60	224	81	.362	14	5	4	12
C-OF	Poindexter Williams	47	143	40	.280	6	1	3	0
C	Bruce Petway	30	82	22	.268	2	0	2	3
OF	Jess Barbour...........	16	67	19	.284	1	2	4	4
P-OF	William Force.........	28	56	17	.304	1	2	3	0
P	Bill Holland	35	54	7	.130	0	0	0	0
P	Andy Cooper	25	37	5	.135	0	0	0	0
P	Jack Marshall	18	30	3	.100	0	0	0	0
P-OF	Charles Wilson.......	15	20	3	.150	0	0	0	0
OF	Johnny Watson.......	9	19	2	.105	0	0	0	1
OF	George Bennette.....	5	17	2	.118	0	1	0	0
C	Pepper Daniels	2	3	1	.333	0	0	0	0
P	Everett Nelson	1	1	1	1.000	0	0	0	0
OF	——— Johnson	1	1	0	.000	0	0	0	0
Totals			2001	595	.297	89	33	42	60

1923 Negro National League

	Won	Lost	Pct.
Kansas City Monarchs	57	33	.633
Chicago American Giants	41	29	.586
Detroit Stars	41	29	.586
Indianapolis ABCs	45	34	.570
Cuban Stars (West)	27	31	.466
*Toledo Tigers	11	15	.423
St. Louis Stars	25	40	.385
*Milwaukee Bears	14	32	.304

*The Toledo and Milwaukee franchises did not finish the season.

1923 Detroit Stars
Manager: Bruce Petway
Individual Statistics

PITCHING

Pitcher	GP	GS	CG	Won	Lost	IP	H	BB	SO	RPG	ShO	SV
Andy Cooper	36	20	14	15*	8	172.2	146	42	55	4.07	1	5
William Force........	38	17	10	12	8	165.2	160	47	81	5.11	0	3
Buck Alexander	21	11	2	5	5	76.2	85	42	28	7.51	0	1
Steel Arm Davis	12	9	5	5	3	64.1	59	34	31	4.76	0	1
Jack Combs...........	15	11	2	4	3	60.1	60	21	25	5.37	0	0
——— Haley	2	1	0	0	1	14	15	2	10	7.07	0	0
G. Boggs..............	1	1	0	0	0	6	5	5	3	7.50	0	0
——— Holcomb	1	—	—	0	0	4	3	3	0	4.50	0	0
Turkey Stearnes	1	1	0	0	1	—	—	4	2	—	0	0
Harry Kenyon........	1	—	—	—	—	—	—	—	—	—	0	0
Totals		71	33	41	29	563.2	533	200	235	5.17	1	10

BATTING

Position	Player	Games	AB	H	Avg.	2B	3B	HR	SB
1B	Edgar Wesley	59	218	74	.339	11	0	17*	0
OF-2B	John Jones.............	55	201	54	.269	5	3	3	0
SS	Mule Riggins	57	214	63	.294	8	3	5	1
3B	Harry Jeffries	39	132	26	.197	5	0	0	0
OF	Johnny Watson......	48	185	54	.292	5	3	1	0
OF	Turkey Stearnes	57	232	82	.353	15	13	17*	1
OF	Clarence Smith	52	184	63	.342	3	3	6	0
C	Pepper Daniels	41	108	23	.213	5	2	1	0
C	Bruce Petway	37	86	30	.349	2	1	0	0
2B-3B	——— Phillips	30	79	12	.152	2	0	0	0
P-OF	William Force........	38	71	23	.324	5	1	3	0
P-OF	Steel Arm Davis	27	66	21	.318	6	1	1	0
P	Andy Cooper	36	48	5	.104	2	0	0	0
3B	Boots McClain	9	22	6	.273	0	0	0	0
P	Buck Alexander	21	21	5	.238	0	1	0	0
P	Jack Combs...........	15	18	3	.167	1	1	0	0
2B	Anderson Pryor......	2	6	2	.333	0	0	0	0
P	——— Haley	2	5	1	.200	1	0	0	0
3B	Ernest Gooden	3	5	0	.000	0	0	0	0
P	G. Boggs..............	1	1	0	.000	0	0	0	0
P	——— Holcomb	1	1	0	.000	0	0	0	0
Totals			1903	547	.287	76	32	54	2

1924 Negro National League

	Won	Lost	Pct.
Kansas City Monarchs	55	22	.714
Chicago American Giants	49	24	.671
Detroit Stars	37	29	.561
St. Louis Stars	42	34	.553
*Memphis Red Sox	29	37	.439
Birmingham Black Barons	34	44	.436
Cuban Stars (West)	16	33	.327
Cleveland Browns	15	34	.306

*The Indianapolis ABCs started the season but were replaced in July by Memphis.

Kansas City defeated Hilldale of the Eastern Colored League, 5 games to 4, in the first Colored World Series.

1924 Detroit Stars
Manager: Bruce Petway
Individual Statistics

PITCHING

Pitcher	GP	GS	CG	Won	Lost	IP	H	BB	SO	RPG	ShO	SV
Andy Cooper	30	13	7	12	5	126	122	33	75	4.50	1	6
Buck Alexander	23	15	5	7	11	133.2	132	45	46	5.52	0	0
Lawrence Terrell	27	14	4	7	4	81.1	75	33	36	6.20	1	0
Jack Combs...........	27	14	6	6	7	99.1	117	53	46	8.70	0	2
Julian Bell	5	4	2	2	1	34.1	37	7	9	5.77	0	0
Tom Williams	6	3	0	1	0	21.2	26	9	10	10.80	0	0
——— Coley	1	—	—	1	0	6	—	—	—	1.50	0	0
Charles Brooks	1	—	0	0	0	4	3	2	2	0.00	0	0
Harold Treadwell	1	—	0	0	0	.1	3	2	0	54.00	0	0
Totals		63	24	36	28	506.2	515	184	224	6.18	2	8

BATTING

Position	Player	Games	AB	H	Avg.	2B	3B	HR	SB
1B-OF	Bill Pierce....................	58	230	77	.335	6	13	7	3
2B-3B	Anderson Pryor...........	52	181	54	.298	9	0	4	1
SS	Mule Riggins	58	246	74	.301	7	6	1	5
3B	William Lowe	45	159	48	.302	4	3	1	1
OF-2B	John Jones...................	52	211	64	.303	12	3	0	1
OF	Turkey Stearnes	58	231	80	.346	7	11	10*	3
OF-3B	Clarence Smith	58	238	68	.286	5	6	3	4
C-1B-OF	Bruce Petway..............	30	82	28	.341	3	3	1	1
OF	Johnny Watson............	28	83	21	.253	3	3	0	0
C	Pepper Daniels	25	72	15	.208	1	1	0	0
C	Bobby Roth	20	63	13	.206	3	0	1	1
P-OF	Andy Cooper	32	57	10	.175	1	0	0	0
P	Buck Alexander	23	44	10	.228	1	1	0	0
C	Fat Barnes..................	11	37	10	.270	4	1	1	0
P	Jack Combs..............	27	36	6	.167	0	0	0	0
P	Lawrence Terrell..........	27	27	3	.111	1	0	0	0
3B	Harry Jeffries	7	16	3	.188	1	0	0	0
P	Julian Bell...................	5	12	4	.333	0	1	0	0
P	Tom Williams	6	6	0	.000	0	0	0	0
3B	I. S. Lane	1	4	0	.000	0	0	0	0
2B	Carl Sawyer...............	1	3	2	.667	0	0	0	0
P	Harold Treadwell	2	2	1	.500	0	0	0	0
P	——— Coley	1	3	0	.000	0	0	0	0
P	Charles Brooks	1	1	0	.000	0	0	0	0
Totals			2044	591	.289	68	52	29	19

1925 Negro National League

The league played a split season, with Kansas City winning the first half and St. Louis the second half.

	First Half			Second Half			Total		
	Won	Lost	Pct.	Won	Lost	Pct.	Won	Lost	Pct.
Kansas City Monarchs	31	12	.721	31	11	.738	62	23	.729
St. Louis Stars	31	14	.689	38	12	.760	69	27	.719
*Detroit Stars	29	20	.592	28	21	.571	57	40	.588
*Chicago American Giants	26	22	.542	28	18	.609	54	40	.574
Cuban Stars (West)	12	13	.480	10	12	.455	22	25	.468
Memphis Red Sox	18	24	.429	12	24	.333	30	48	.385
Birmingham Black Barons	14	33	.298	10	16	.384	24	49	.329
Indianapolis ABCs	13	24	.351	4	33	.108	17	57	.230

*Chicago defeated Detroit, 4 games to 2, in a playoff for third place.

Kansas City defeated St. Louis, 4 games to 3, in a playoff for the pennant.

Kansas City lost to Hilldale of the Eastern Colored League, 5 games to 1, in the second Colored World Series.

1925 Detroit Stars
Manager: Bruce Petway
Individual Statistics

PITCHING

Pitcher	GP	GS	CG	Won	Lost	IP	H	BB	SO	RPG	ShO	SV
Andy Cooper........	31	12	6	11	3	126.2	110	24	44	3.41	1	6
Harry Kenyon	23	13	5	8	7	113	132	37	58	6.37	0	0
Yellowhorse Morris	18	9	4	8	2	74	61	34	22	4.50	0	0
Fred Bell..............	22	13	8	7	7	106	115	47	60	6.54	1	0
Jack Combs	23	16	4	6	9	91	86	42	28	6.73	0	0
Lawrence Terrell	13	5	2	6	2	54	56	17	24	7.00	0	0
Lewis Hampton......	10	6	4	5	0	58	58	16	22	4.97	0	0
Finis Branahan	15	9	1	2	4	53.2	58	23	13	7.04	0	0
Omer Newsome....	15	6	1	1	3	53.1	65	12	24	8.10	0	1
Buck Alexander.....	5	3	1	1	0	18	18	8	8	3.00	0	0
Totals		92	36	55	37	747.2	759	260	303	5.78	2	7

BATTING

Position	Player	Games	AB	H	Avg.	2B	3B	HR	SB
1B	Edgar Wesley.......	56	205	87	.424*	13	6	18*	9
2B-3B	Anderson Pryor	81	288	84	.292	22	5	6	17
SS	Mule Riggins.........	84	320	89	.278	15	8	8	18
3B	Ray Sheppard.......	49	172	57	.331	7	3	5	5
OF-2B	John Jones	72	268	74	.276	12	9	4	6
OF	Turkey Stearnes.....	84	324	118	.364	20	10	18*	11
OF-1B	Clarence Smith......	83	341	116	.340	19	11	5	17
C	Pepper Daniels......	63	203	48	.236	6	1	4	9
P-OF	Harry Kenyon	62	196	54	.276	5	2	4	8
INF	Joe Hewitt	33	107	14	.131	5	1	0	3
C	Dan Kennard	36	89	18	.202	1	1	3	1
P-OF	Fred Bell..............	32	73	21	.288	3	3	2	6
P-OF	Lewis Hampton......	21	51	18	.353	2	3	3	1
P	Andy Cooper........	31	45	11	.244	0	2	1	0
P	Jack Combs	23	33	4	.121	0	0	0	1
C-1B	Brue Petway..........	16	32	5	.156	1	0	0	1
P	Finis Branahan	15	24	7	.292	0	1	1	0
P	Yellowhorse Morris	18	22	6	.273	1	0	1	0
3B	Saul Davis	7	19	3	.158	0	0	0	0
P	Lawrence Terrell	13	18	2	.111	1	0	0	0
1B	George McAllister .	5	18	2	.111	0	0	0	0
P	Omer Newsome....	15	17	3	.176	0	0	0	0
P	Buck Alexander.....	5	7	0	.000	0	0	0	0
OF	Chick Harper	1	4	0	.000	0	0	0	0
SS	James Smith	1	3	0	.000	0	0	0	0
Totals			2879	841	.292	133	66	83	113

239

1926 Negro National League

The league played a split season, with Kansas City winning the first half and Chicago the second half.

	First Half			Second Half			Total		
	Won	Lost	Pct.	Won	Lost	Pct.	Won	Lost	Pct.
Kansas City Monarchs	35	12	.745	22	9	.710	57	21	.731
Chicago American Giants	28	16	.636	29	7	.806	57	23	.713
St. Louis Stars	29	18	.617	20	12	.625	49	30	.620
Detroit Stars	34	17	.667	16	25	.390	50	42	.543
Indianapolis ABCs	28	18	.609	15	27	.357	43	45	.489
Cuban Stars (West)	6	27	.182	13	20	.394	19	47	.288
Dayton Marcos	7	32	.179	0	5	.000	7	37	.159
Cleveland Elites	5	32	.135	2	9	.182	7	41	.146

Chicago defeated Kansas City, 5 games to 4, in a playoff for the pennant.

Chicago defeated the Bacharach Giants of the Eastern Colored League, 5 games to 3, in the third Colored World Series.

1926 Detroit Stars
Manager: Candy Jim Taylor
Individual Statistics

PITCHING

Pitcher	GP	GS	CG	Won	Lost	IP	H	BB	SO	RPG	ShO	SV
Andy Cooper........	36*	22	12	12	8	178*	172	21	48	3.99	1	4*
Lewis Hampton......	25	20	13	12	10	147.2	156	26	41	5.97	0	1
Fred Bell..............	18	12	7	7	6	92	72	42	49	4.30	2	0
Yellowhorse Morris	28	15	5	6	8	125.1	132	51	48	6.54	0	1
Harry Kenyon	13	10	5	5	7	76.2	63	10	18	5.87	0	0
John Dixon	8	4	1	4	0	30.1	34	1	8	3.86	0	1
Harold Treadwell...	11	3	2	1	4	35	29	16	16	4.89	0	0
Bob Saunders	7	6	1	1	0	35.1	47	6	4	7.90	0	0
Harry Jeffries.........	1	1	1	1	0	9	7	0	8	3.00	0	0
Omer Newsome....	2	1	0	1	0	1	0	1	1	0.00	0	0
Candy Jim Taylor ..	1	1	0	1	0	8	9	0	2	1.13	0	0
Jack Combs	3	1	0	0	1	3	4	4	1	3.00	0	0
Mule Riggins.........	1	—	0	0	0	.1	1	1	1	27.00	0	0
Totals		96	47	51	44	741.2	726	179	245	5.23	3	7

BATTING

Position	Player	Games	AB	H	Avg.	2B	3B	HR	SB
1B	Edgar Wesley.......	74	257	77	.300	6	1	15	5
2B	Anderson Pryor	34	123	31	.252	4	3	0	2
SS	Mule Riggins..........	80	295	89	.302	16	7	7	16
3B-UT	Harry Jeffries.........	79	275	80	.291	13	1	2	13
OF	Johnny Watson	42	154	31	.201	1	1	3	8
OF	Turkey Stearnes.....	82	301	113	.375	24*	10	20	13
OF	Charles Blackwell ..	73	246	68	.276	11	5	4	11
C	Pepper Daniels......	49	145	38	.262	4	1	2	2
C	Larry Brown	47	135	33	.244	3	4	2	1
P-UT	Harry Kenyon	45	121	38	.314	9	4	2	5
P-OF	Fred Bell...............	27	107	32	.299	4	1	9	3
IF	Ray Sheppard.......	23	81	17	.210	3	1	1	3
OF	John Jones	17	64	22	.344	3	4	0	0
P	Lewis Hampton......	31	61	18	.295	2	0	4	0
IF	Joe Hewitt	16	55	7	.127	2	0	0	1
P	Andy Cooper........	36	50	8	.160	1	0	0	0
P	Yellowhorse Morris	29	46	10	.217	1	1	1	0
OF	——Long	13	44	8	.182	1	1	1	1
3B-P	Candy Jim Taylor ..	10	25	8	.320	0	0	0	0
P	John Dixon	8	12	3	.250	0	0	0	0
P	Harold Treadwell...	11	11	2	.182	0	0	0	0
2B	Robert Baldwin......	5	9	2	.222	0	0	0	1
P	Bob Saunders	7	6	0	.000	0	0	0	0
2B	Perry Hall	2	6	2	.333	0	0	0	0
P	Jack Combs	3	1	0	.000	0	0	0	0
Totals			2630	737	.280	108	45	73	85

241

1927 Negro National League

The league played a split season, with Chicago winning the first half and Birmingham the second half.

	First Half			Second Half			Total		
	Won	Lost	Pct.	Won	Lost	Pct.	Won	Lost	Pct.
Chicago American Giants	32	14	.696	24	15	.615	56	29	.659
Kansas City Monarchs	36	18	.667	18	11	.621	54	29	.635
St. Louis Stars	32	19	.627	—	—	—	32	19	.627
Birmingham Black Barons	25	29	.463	29	15	.659	54	44	.551
Detroit Stars	29	22	.569	24	24	.500	53	46	.535
Memphis Red Sox	19	25	.432	—	—	—	19	25	.432
Cuban Stars (West)	15	23	.395	—	—	—	15	23	.395
Cleveland Hornets	10	37	.213	—	—	—	10	37	.213

*Chicago defeated Birmingham, 4 games to 0, in a playoff for the pennant.

Chicago defeated the Bacharach Giants of the Eastern Colored League, 5 games to 3, in the fourth, and final, Colored World Series between the two leagues. The following spring the Eastern Colored League disbanded.

1927 Detroit Stars
Manager: Bingo DeMoss
Individual Statistics

PITCHING

Pitcher	GP	GS	CG	Won	Lost	IP	H	BB	SO	RPG	ShO	SV
Yellowhorse Morris	29	19	17	14	8	186.2	171	53	74	4.87	3	3
Ed Rile	21	19	17	14	6	163.1	139	47	51	3.47	2	0
Bill Drake	15	14	8	8	6	113.1	110	43	29	5.72	0	0
Andy Cooper........	13	11	6	7	3	80.1	87	3	34	4.93	0	1
Albert Davis..........	12	11	9	3	6	82.1	69	13	16	5.25	1	0
William Ross.........	10	8	5	3	5	59	71	16	23	6.71	1	0
Lewis Hampton......	12	6	5	3	3	58.1	57	18	22	5.40	0	0
Harry Kenyon	10	8	6	2	5	61.1	67	18	11	5.58	0	1
C. Torrienti	3	3	3	2	1	28	31	8	9	4.50	0	0
Fred Bell...............	2	1	0	1	0	4	2	3	2	2.25	0	0
Totals		100	76	56	43	846.2	804	222	271	4.89	7	4

BATTING

Position	Player	Games	AB	H	Avg.	2B	3B	HR	SB
1B-P	Ed Rile	66	234	95	.406	23	6	10	3
2B-3B	G. Johnson...........	78	265	77	.291	9	0	4	11
SS-OF	Hallie Harding......	80	312	90	.288	9	2	3	10
3B-C	Harry Jeffries	65	231	59	.255	10	3	1	3
OF-P	Christobel Torrienti	78	276	90	.326	17	2	4	6
OF	Turkey Stearnes	80	292	99	.339	22	12	20*	11
C-1B-OF	Stack Martin.........	54	196	53	.270	8	4	8	7
C	Pepper Daniels	73	265	71	.268	11	1	4	5
2B-1B	Bingo DeMoss	35	124	26	.210	3	2	1	0
OF	John Jones............	27	112	36	.321	8	1	1	2
SS-OF	Clarence Everett....	26	83	15	.181	1	1	0	0
P-OF	Yellowhorse Morris	29	70	14	.200	2	0	1	0
P-OF	Harry Kenyon.......	21	65	20	.308	3	2	0	2
P	William Drake	15	37	5	.135	0	0	0	0
P	Lewis Hampton	12	22	5	.227	1	1	2	0
P	Andy Cooper	13	22	5	.227	0	0	0	0
P	Albert Davis	12	20	3	.150	0	0	0	0
P	William Ross	10	17	5	.294	0	0	0	0
1B	Edgar Wesley	4	13	3	.231	0	0	0	1
3B	Anderson Pryor.....	2	7	2	.286	0	0	0	0
P	Fred Bell	2	2	0	.000	0	0	0	0
Totals			2665	773	.290	127	37	59	61

1928 Negro National League

The league played a split season, with St. Louis winning the first half and Chicago declared the winner of the second half. A playoff between St. Louis and Chicago for the pennant apparently was never held.

	First Half			Second Half			Total		
	Won	Lost	Pct.	Won	Lost	Pct.	Won	Lost	Pct.
St. Louis Stars	32	8	.800	34	18	.654	66	26	.717
Kansas City Monarchs	24	15	.615	26	16	.619	50	31	.617
Chicago American Giants	24	20	.545	30	17	.638	54	37	.593
Detroit Stars	29	13	.690	25	24	.510	54	37	.593
Birmingham Black Barons	19	28	.404	25	26	.490	44	54	.449
Memphis Red Sox	16	25	.390	14	23	.378	30	48	.385
Cleveland Hornets	—	—	—	—	—	—	19	53	.264
Cuban Stars (West)	—	—	—	—	—	—	12	37	.245

1928 Detroit Stars
Manager: Bingo DeMoss
Individual Statistics

PITCHING

Pitcher	GP	GS	CG	Won	Lost	IP	H	BB	SO	RPG	ShO	SV
George Mitchell	32	20	16	14	11	163.1	162	44	44	5.13	1	2
Ted Shaw.........	29	23	15	12	8	164.1	176	51	70	6.30	1	2
Jack Marshall....	25	19	10	11	6	154	162	54	44	5.67	0	0
C. Torrienti	16	10	4	7	3	83.2	106	17	13	6.78	1	2
Rube Currie	19	12	7	6	5	95.2	99	17	21	4.80	1	0
Albert Davis......	16	8	5	5	2	81.1	86	22	16	4.87	1	0
Ed Rile	4	4	3	2	2	14	10	2	3	4.09	1	0
Stack Martin	1	—	—	0	1	7	6	4	2	3.86	0	0
Totals		96	60	57	38	763.1	807	211	213	5.61	6	6

BATTING

Position	Player	Games	AB	H	Avg.	2B	3B	HR	SB
1B-P	Ed Rile.................	83	298	111*	.372	27*	2	8	7
INF	Grady Orange	68	245	60	.245	7	5	1	6
SS	Hallie Harding......	47	171	55	.322	11	3	3	6
3B-2B	Claude Johnson	76	278	92	.331	10	1	5	2
OF	Wade Johnston.....	79	327	96	.294	14	5	5	7
OF	Turkey Stearnes	81	309	100	.324	18	7	24*	5
OF	Hurley McNair	67	237	65	.274	8	6	3	6
C	Ted Radcliffe	66	253	67	.265	12	4	8	1
C-UT-P	Stack Martin.........	52	172	54	.314	11	3	2	3
2B	Bingo DeMoss	43	129	20	.155	5	1	0	0
OF-P	Christobel Torrienti	39	114	38	.333	5	3	2	3
P	Ted Shaw	29	63	12	.190	4	0	0	0
P	George Mitchell....	32	55	12	.218	1	1	1	0
P	Jack Marshall	25	47	9	.191	0	0	0	0
P	Rube Currie..........	19	38	11	.289	0	0	1	0
P	Albert Davis	16	29	4	.138	0	0	0	0
Totals			2765	806	.292	133	41	66	46

1929 Negro National League

The league played a split season, with Kansas City winning both halves. No play-off was held.

	First Half			Second Half			Total		
	Won	Lost	Pct.	Won	Lost	Pct.	Won	Lost	Pct.
Kansas City Monarchs	28	11	.718	34	6	.850	62	17	.785
St. Louis Stars	30	14	.682	29	19	.604	59	33	.641
Chicago American Giants	22	29	.431	27	11	.711	49	40	.551
Detroit Stars	25	18	.581	13	24	.351	38	42	.475
Cuban Stars (West)	6	14	.300	12	12	.500	18	26	.409
Birmingham Black Barons	20	24	.454	9	27	.250	29	51	.363
Memphis Red Sox	14	22	.389	5	22	.185	19	44	.302

1929 Detroit Stars
Manager: Bingo DeMoss
Individual Statistics

PITCHING

Pitcher	GP	GS	CG	Won	Lost	IP	H	BB	SO	RPG	ShO	SV
Charlie Henry ...	26	17	11	10	8	135	145	42	28	5.80	3	0
Albert Davis......	25	14	12	9	10	160.2	192	28	27	6.50	1	0
Ted Shaw.........	23	13	9	9	7	141.1	136	52	48	5.10	0	0
Bill Tyler..........	20	19	9	7	7	112.1	92	34	56	5.29	0	0
George Mitchell	19	15	9	4	8	105.2	113	50	36	8.51	1	0
Johnny Edwards	4	4	2	1	2	15.1	21	5	1	9.39	0	0
Ed Rile	3	2	0	0	2	6.2	19	1	1	21.59	0	0
Totals		84	52	40	44	677	718	212	197	6.03	5	0

BATTING

Position	Player	Games	AB	H	Avg.	2B	3B	HR	SB
B-P	Ed Rile	68	251	75	.299	12	2	10	2
2B	Grady Orange ..	53	187	52	.278	6	3	5	2
SS	Bobbie Robinson	68	282	87	.309	12	7	4	7
3B	Claude Johnson .	68	252	72	.286	7	3	4	1
OF	Wade Johnston..	68	249	89	.357	13	4	14	5
OF	Turkey Stearnes..	69	259	98	.378	15	5	19	12
OF	John Jones.........	70	302	103	.341	13	6	11	6
C	Ted Radcliffe	32	126	39	.310	7	2	3	4
C	———Stevens ...	24	80	26	.325	4	2	1	0
P	Albert Davis	27	67	20	.299	4	0	1	1
P	Ted Shaw.........	23	57	14	.246	1	0	0	0
2B	Bingo DeMoss ...	13	51	16	.314	1	0	0	4
P	Charlie Henry	26	51	13	.255	2	1	0	1
P-1B	George Mitchell.	22	41	11	.268	0	1	1	0
C	Louis English	12	35	8	.229	0	2	0	1
C	———Stevenson	1	4	1	.250	0	0	0	0
C	Barney Jenkins ...	1	4	1	.250	0	0	0	0
C	———Foote	1	2	0	.000	0	0	0	0
C	———Wyatt	1	2	0	.000	0	0	0	0
P	Johnny Edwards.	4	1	0	.000	0	0	0	0
Totals			2303	725	.315	97	38	73	46

1930 Negro National League

The league played a split season, with St. Louis winning the first half and Detroit the second half.

	First Half			Second Half			Total		
	Won	Lost	Pct.	Won	Lost	Pct.	Won	Lost	Pct.
St. Louis Stars	41	15	.732	24	7	.774	65	22	.747
Detroit Stars	26	26	.500	24	7	.774	50	33	.602
Kansas City Monarchs	31	14	.689	8	12	.400	39	26	.600
Birmingham Black Barons	30	27	.526	14	21	.400	44	48	.478
Chicago American Giants	24	39	.381	23	14	.622	47	56	.456
Memphis Red Sox	21	22	.488	8	23	.258	29	45	.392
Cuban Stars (West)	17	25	.405	6	12	.333	23	37	.383
Nashville Elite Giants	13	35	.271	7	16	.304	20	51	.282

St. Louis defeated Detroit, 4 games to 3, in a playoff for the pennant.

1930 Detroit Stars
Manager: Bingo DeMoss

Individual Statistics

PITCHING

Pitcher	GP	GS	CG	Won	Lost	IP	H	BB	SO	RPG	ShO	SV
Andy Cooper	27	20	16	15	6	161	161	9	50	4.97	2	2
Ted Shaw	24	18	13	11	5	130.1	114	31	80	3.38	3	0
Nelson Dean.	20	14	10	10	8	136.2	117	11	64	3.29	2	0
Willie Powell.	25	19	12	9	10	143.1	145	26	60	5.15	1	1
Albert Davis..	22	17	12	9	7	137	134	25	36	4.73	2	0
Ed Rile	3	2	1	2	0	7	8	—	—	2.57	0	0
Bill Tyler	9	3	1	0	2	25.2	21	11	11	5.61	0	0
Totals		93	65	56	38	741	700	113	301	4.37	10	3

BATTING

Position	Player	Games	AB	H	Avg.	2B	3B	HR	SB
1B-2B-P	Ed Rile	61	226	73	.323	17	9	8	6
2B-SS	Grady Orange ..	55	190	44	.232	6	0	3	2
SS	Jake Dunn	65	240	67	.279	11	7	4	7
3B	Bobbie Robinson	62	231	60	.260	9	4	0	4
OF	Wade Johnston..	63	242	78	.322	10	13*	3	7
OF	Turkey Stearnes..	36	127	43	.339	12	10	3	6
OF	Crush Holloway .	63	256	64	.250	9	8	0	10
C-1B	Pepper Daniels ..	40	113	30	.265	7	1	0	4
C-3B	Spoony Palm	41	127	40	.315	8	3	5	4
2B-1B-OF	William Love	26	86	24	.279	7	0	2	2
1B-OF	Lou Dials	29	80	22	.275	6	4	3	3
2B	Bingo DeMoss ...	11	39	10	.256	2	0	0	1
P	Ted Shaw	24	38	12	.316	1	2	0	0
P	Nelson Dean	20	37	7	.189	0	2	1	0
P	Albert Davis	22	36	8	.222	1	0	0	0
P	Andy Cooper.....	27	34	4	.118	0	0	0	0
P	Willie Powell	25	33	5	.152	0	0	0	0
P-OF	Bill Tyler...........	9	6	1	.167	0	0	0	0
SS	James Smith.......	1	1	0	.000	0	0	0	0
Totals			2142	592	.276	106	63	32	56

249

1931 Negro National League

The league played a split season. Although no official standings were published, St. Louis was declared the winner of both halves. No playoff was held. The standings below were reconstructed from surviving boxscores.

	First Half			Second Half			Total		
	Won	Lost	Pct.	Won	Lost	Pct.	Won	Lost	Pct.
Cleveland Cubs	24	22	.522	—	—	—	24	22	.522
Indianapolis ABCs	25	23	.521	—	—	—	25	23	.521
St. Louis Stars	11	11	.500	—	—	—	11	11	.500
Detroit Stars	25	26	.490	—	—	—	25	26	.490
Louisville White Sox	18	19	.486	—	—	—	18	19	.486
Chicago American Giants	10	11	.476	—	—	—	10	11	.476

The Negro National League disbanded in late summer.

1931 Detroit Stars
Manager: Bingo DeMoss
Individual Statistics

PITCHING

Pitcher	GP	GS	CG	Won	Lost	IP	H	BB	SO	RPG	ShO	SV
Nelson Dean	12	10	9	8	3	97.1	100	10	31	4.16	1	0
Willie Powell	14	11	9	4	7	79.2	71	20	30	5.65	2	0
Bill McCall	12	10	6	3	7	72	81	25	30	5.75	0	0
Vet McDonald	8	5	4	2	3	42	54	3	16	4.71	0	0
Ted Radcliffe	3	2	2	2	0	19.1	22	3	11	6.05	0	0
John Dixon	5	3	2	1	1	25.2	38	6	7	7.71	0	0
Elbert Williams ...	2	2	2	1	1	18	18	8	6	5.50	0	0
Arthur Henderson	4	2	1	0	2	19.2	32	7	6	8.24	0	0
———— Jackson ...	1	—	—	0	1	—	—	—	—	—	0	0
———— Kelly	1	—	—	0	1	—	—	—	—	—	0	0
Bill Pryor	1	—	0	0	0	3	3	4	2	6.00	0	0
James Winston ...	1	—	0	0	0	3	4	0	1	3.00	0	0
Turkey Stearnes...	1	—	—	0	0	—	—	—	—	—	0	0
Totals		45	35	21	26	379.2	423	86	140	5.45	3	0

BATTING

Position	Player	Games	AB	H	Avg.	2B	3B	HR	SB
1B-OF	Lou Dials	35	134	35	.261	7	3	4	1
2B	Bob Saunders	18	64	15	.234	1	0	1	0
SS	Saul Davis	18	67	19	.284	5	1	0	1
3B	Bobbie Robinson .	37	136	33	.243	7	1	0	2
OF	Wade Johnston ...	36	128	38	.297	5	1	2	4
OF-1B	Turkey Stearnes...	34	120	45	.375	9	1	8*	5
OF	Jelly Gardner	27	88	17	.193	2	0	0	6*
C	Spoony Palm	34	120	36	.300	6	1	2	3
1B-C	Andy Love	26	81	10	.123	2	0	1	2
SS-2B	Anderson Pryor ...	18	60	11	.183	1	0	0	3
SS	William Owens...	9	31	8	.258	1	0	0	0
P	Nelson Dean	12	29	4	.138	0	0	1	0
P	Bill McCall	12	25	3	.120	0	1	0	0
P	Willie Powell	14	20	3	.150	0	1	0	0
P	Vet McDonald	8	15	3	.200	0	0	0	1
P	John Dixon	5	10	5	.500	0	1	1	0
1B	William Gill........	3	10	2	.200	0	0	0	0
P	Arthur Henderson	4	8	1	.125	0	0	0	0
P	Ted Radcliffe	4	5	1	.200	0	0	0	0
P	Elbert Williams ...	2	5	0	.000	0	0	0	0
1B	———— Gales......	2	4	1	.250	0	0	0	0
2B	Grady Orange ...	1	3	0	.000	0	0	0	0
P	Bill Pryor	1	1	0	.000	0	0	0	0
P	James Winston ...	1	1	0	.000	0	0	0	0
Totals			1165	290	.249	46	11	20	28

251

1932 East-West League

No standings were published for the league, which disbanded in July. The partial standings below were reconstructed from surviving boxscores.

	Won	Lost	Pct.
Detroit Wolves	29	13	.690
Homestead Grays	29	19	.604
Pittsburgh Crawfords	32	26	.552
Baltimore Black Sox	—	—	—
Cleveland Stars	—	—	—
Cuban Stars	—	—	—
Hilldale	—	—	—
Newark Browns	—	—	—

1932 Detroit Wolves
Manager: Dizzy Dismukes
Individual Statistics

PITCHING

Pitcher	GP	GS	CG	Won	Lost	IP	H	BB	SO	RPG	ShO	SV
Bertrum Hunter	16	12	12	11	4	108	91	2	10	3.42	1	1
Lefty Williams	8	5	3	5	0	42.1	43	8	9	2.98	1	0
Ted Trent	8	6	3	4	2	48	48	7	15	2.63	1	0
Ray Brown.............	7	7	6	4	3	49	40	3	4	3.67	1	0
William Bell..........	5	4	2	4	0	25	22	—	—	2.88	0	0
Quincy Trouppe	2	2	2	2	0	16	4	—	—	1.13	1	0
Chippy Britt	3	2	2	0	2	16	16	—	—	5.63	0	0
Harry Salmon	2	2	0	0	1	—	—	—	—	—	0	0
Smoky Joe Williams	2	1	0	0	0	6.2	10	—	—	9.45	0	0
Dizzy Dismukes......	1	1	0	0	0	—	—	—	—	—	0	0
Totals		42	30	30	12	311	274	20	38	3.44	5	1

BATTING

Position	Player	Games	AB	H	Avg.	2B	3B	HR	SB
1B	Mule Suttles.........	8	23	8	.348	5	0	2	1
2B	Newt Allen..........	5	20	6	.300	0	0	0	0
SS	Willie Wells	16	54	16	.296	7	1	1	5
3B	Dewey Creacy.....	10	33	8	.242	0	0	0	0
OF	Vic Harris............	11	44	18	.409	1	1	1	1
OF	Cool Papa Bell.....	14	52	19	.365	4	0	1	3
OF-P-C	Quincy Trouppe...	13	47	14	.298	1	0	0	0
C	Tom Young..........	12	41	17	.415	0	1	2	2
1B	George Giles	6	23	8	.348	2	0	0	1
P-OF	Ray Brown	8	21	4	.190	1	0	1	0
2B	John Henry Russell	5	17	4	.235	2	0	0	0
P	Bertrum Hunter.....	16	16	1	.063	0	0	0	0
P	Lefty Williams......	8	15	1	.067	1	0	0	0
P	William Bell	5	6	2	.333	0	0	0	1
OF	Leroy Taylor	1	5	2	.400	0	0	0	1
P	Chippy Britt.........	3	4	3	.750	2	1	0	0
2B	Ray Sheppard	1	3	0	.000	0	0	0	0
P	Ted Trent............	8	3	0	.000	0	0	0	0
Totals			427	131	.306	26	4	8	15

1933 Negro National League

The league played a split season, but the second-half schedule was not completed. No playoff was held. Cole's American Giants claimed the pennant, although Pittsburgh owner and league president W. A. (Gus) Greenlee later awarded it to his club.

	First Half			Second Half			Total		
	Won	Lost	Pct.	Won	Lost	Pct.	Won	Lost	Pct.
Cole's American Giants	21	7	.750	—	—	—	21	7	.750
Pittsburgh Crawfords	20	8	.714	—	—	—	20	8	.714
Baltimore Black Sox	10	9	.526	—	—	—	10	9	.526
Nashville Elite Giants	12	13	.480	—	—	—	12	13	.480
*Detroit Stars	13	20	.394	—	—	—	13	20	.394
†Columbus Blue Birds	11	18	.379	—	—	—	11	18	.379

*the Indianapolis ABCs started the season but were replaced in May by Detroit.
†Columbus was replaced in August by the Cleveland Giants.

1933 Detroit Stars
Manager: Candy Jim Taylor

Individual Statistics

PITCHING

Pitcher	GP	GS	CG	Won	Lost	IP	H	BB	SO	RPG	ShO	SV
Columbus Vance	16	10	7	6	7	72.2	60	10	27	4.83	2	2
Slap Hensley	6	6	5	4	2	47.2	34	4	8	4.53	0	0
Percy Bailey...........	7	6	4	4	1	40	21	10	15	1.80	0	0
——— Snowden	8	6	3	1	4	36	31	6	14	7.00	0	0
Lefty Waddy	7	4	1	1	4	21	18	7	3	6.86	0	0
George Mitchell	4	3	1	1	2	13	11	1	2	8.31	0	0
Granville Lyons	4	1	1	0	2	14.1	16	4	2	5.02	0	0
Everett Nelson........	3	2	1	0	1	9.2	21	2	3	12.10	0	0
——— Stokes	1	1	1	0	0	8	5	—	—	2.25	0	0
Hulan Stamps	1	1	0	—	—	—	—	—	—	—	0	0
——— Armour.......	1	—	—	—	—	7.1	10	0	0	7.37	0	0
Candy Jim Taylor ...	1	—	0	0	0	1	5	0	0	36.00	0	0
Sam Thompson	1	—	—	—	—	—	—	—	—	—	—	—
Black Bottom Buford	1	—	—	—	—	—	—	—	—	—	—	—
Totals	40	24	17	23		270.2	232	44	74	5.32	2	2

BATTING

Position	Player	Games	AB	H	Avg.	2B	3B	HR	SB
1B	Granville Lyons	17	67	19	.284	3	4	0	0
2B-SS	Black Bottom Buford	12	43	9	.209	0	1	0	0
SS	Ray Dandridge.......	9	35	9	.257	1	2	0	0
3B	Jimmy Binder	14	49	18	.367	3	1	0	1
OF	John Williams	14	47	17	.362	3	3	0	2
OF	Jerry Benjamin	22	73	25	.342	2	2	0	10
OF	Clarence Smith.......	17	56	15	.268	2	1	0	5
C-1B	Paul Hardy	15	42	7	.167	2	0	0	0
2B	Anderson Pryor	13	37	5	.135	0	1	0	1
3B	William Gill...........	9	31	10	.323	2	0	0	0
OF	Wade Johnston	7	29	7	.241	0	0	0	0
C	Spoony Palm	8	26	8	.308	3	1	0	0
1B	Rainy Bibbs	7	22	8	.364	0	0	0	0
P	Percy Bailey..........	7	13	2	.154	0	0	0	0
P-3B	——— Armour.......	4	12	2	.167	1	0	0	0
P-OF	George Mitchell	4	11	1	.091	0	0	1	0
OF	Leroy Taylor..........	3	10	3	.300	2	1	0	0
C	Jim Webster...........	4	10	0	.000	0	0	0	0
P	——— Snowden	8	9	2	.222	0	0	0	1
2B	——— Jackson	2	8	4	.500	0	0	0	0
3B	——— Busby.........	2	8	2	.250	0	0	0	0
P	Slap Hensley	6	7	2	.286	0	0	0	0
P	Everett Nelson........	4	7	0	.000	0	0	0	0
P	Candy Jim Taylor ...	3	6	4	.667	1	1	0	0
SS	Willie Owens	2	5	1	.200	0	0	0	0
OF	J. Kerner................	1	5	0	.000	0	0	0	0
P	Lefty Waddy	7	3	0	.000	0	0	0	0
Totals			671	186	.277	26	18	1	20

255

Appendix C

Career Pitching and Batting Statistics

Pitching

Player	Yrs	GP	GS	CG	Won	Lost	IP	H	BB	SO	RPG	ShO	SV
Buck Alexander	3	49	29	8	13	16	228.1	235	95	82	5.99	0	1
———Armour	1	1	—	—	—	—	7.1	10	0	0	7.37	0	0
Percy Bailey	1	7	6	4	4	1	40	21	10	15	1.80	0	0
Fred Bell	3	42	26	15	15	13	202	209	92	111	5.44	3	0
Julian Bell	1	5	4	2	2	1	34.1	37	7	9	5.77	0	0
William Bell	1	5	4	2	4	0	25	22	—	—	2.88	0	—
G. Boggs	1	1	1	0	0	0	6	5	5	3	7.50	0	0
Finis Branahan	1	15	9	1	2	4	53.2	58	23	13	7.04	0	0
Chippy Britt...........	1	3	2	2	0	2	16	16	—	—	5.63	0	0
Charles Brooks	1	1	—	—	0	0	4	3	2	2	0.00	0	0
Edward Brown	1	2	1	0	0	1	5	5	2	0	3.60	0	0
Ray Brown	1	7	7	6	4	3	49	40	3	4	3.67	1	0
Black Bottom Buford	1	1	—	—	—	—	—	—	—	—	—	—	—
———Chase..........	1	1	1	0	0	0	8	4	—	—	7.88	0	0
———Coley	1	1	—	—	1	0	6	—	—	—	1.50	0	0
Jack Combs	4	68	42	12	16	20	253.2	267	120	100	7.13	0	2
Andy Cooper	9	229	139	87	91	48	1151.1	1083	185	388	4.24	11	24
Rube Currie...........	1	19	12	7	6	5	95.2	99	17	21	4.80	1	0
Albert Davis	4	75	50	38	26	25	461.1	481	88	95	5.46	5	0
Steel Arm Davis	1	12	9	5	5	3	64.1	59	34	31	4.76	0	1
Nelson Dean	2	32	24	19	18	11	234	217	21	95	3.65	3	0

Pitching (continued)

Player	Yrs	GP	GS	CG	Won	Lost	IP	H	BB	SO	RPG	ShO	SV
Dizzy Dismukes	1	1	1	0	—	—	—	—	—	—		0	0
John Dixon	2	13	7	3	5	1	56	72	7	15	5.63	0	1
Bill Drake	1	15	14	8	8	6	113.1	110	43	29	5.72	0	0
Johnny Edwards	1	4	4	2	1	2	15.1	21	5	1	9.39	0	0
William Force	3	93	55	35	35	21	490.1	412	90	218	4.52	2	6
Bill Gatewood	2	39	30	16	20	13	247	214	49	93	4.37	2	0
——Green	1	1	—	—	—	—	—	—	—	—		0	0
——Haley	1	2	1	0	0	1	14	15	2	10	7.07	0	—
Lewis Hampton	3	47	32	22	20	13	264	271	60	85	5.63	0	1
Chick Harper	2	2	1	1	0	1	11	12	3	2	5.73	0	0
Arthur Henderson	1	4	2	1	0	2	19.2	32	7	6	8.24	0	0
Charlie Henry	1	26	17	11	10	8	135	145	42	28	5.80	3	0
Slap Hensley	1	6	6	5	4	2	47.2	34	4	8	4.53	0	0
——Holcomb	1	1	—	—	0	0	—	4	3	3	4.50	0	—
Bill Holland	3	87	59	48	39	30	531.2	460	89	249	3.77	4	7
——Howard	1	1	—	—	—	—	.1	1	0	0	0.00	0	0
Bertrum Hunter	1	16	12	12	11	4	108	91	2	10	3.42	1	1
——Jackson	1	1	1	0	0	1	—	—	—	—	—	0	0
Harry Jeffries	3	1	1	1	1	0	9	7	0	8	3.00	0	0
Dicta Johnson	1	2	2	2	2	0	18	5	3	3	3.00	0	0
——Kelly	1	1	1	0	0	1	—	—	—	—	—	—	—
Harry Kenyon	4	47	31	16	15	19	251	262	65	87	6.02	0	1
I. S. Lane	3	1	1	—	0	1	—	—	0	0	—	0	0
Granville Lyons	1	4	1	1	0	2	14.1	16	4	2	5.02	0	0
Jimmy Lyons	1	5	1	0	1	1	20.1	22	11	6	5.32	0	0
Jack Marshall	2	43	31	17	16	12	255	254	78	82	5.26	0	0
Stack Martin	2	1	—	—	0	1	7	6	4	2	3.86	0	0
Bill McCall	1	12	10	6	3	7	72	81	25	30	5.75	0	0
Vet McDonald	1	8	5	4	2	3	42	54	3	16	4.71	0	0
Webster McDonald	1	9	8	4	3	4	49.1	46	21	12	6.39	0	0
George Mitchell	3	55	38	26	19	21	282	286	95	82	6.54	2	2
Yellowhorse Morris	3	75	43	26	28	18	386	364	138	144	5.34	3	4
Everett Nelson	2	4	2	1	0	1	9.2	21	2	3	12.10	0	0
Omer Newsome	2	17	7	1	2	3	54.1	65	13	25	7.95	0	0
Willie Powell	2	39	30	21	13	17	223	216	46	90	5.33	3	1
Bill Pryor	1	1	—	0	0	0	3	3	4	2	6.00	0	0
Ted Radcliffe	3	3	2	2	2	0	19.1	22	3	11	6.05	0	0
Mule Riggins	7	1	—	—	0	0	.1	1	1	1	27.00	0	0
Ed Rile	4	31	27	21	18	10	199	180	50	55	4.12	3	0
William Ross	1	10	8	5	3	5	59	71	16	23	6.71	1	0
Harry Salmon	1	2	2	0	0	1	—	—	—	—	—	0	—
Bob Saunders	2	7	6	1	1	0	35.1	47	6	4	7.90	0	0

Pitching (continued)

Player	Yrs	GP	GS	CG	Won	Lost	IP	H	BB	SO	RPG	ShO	SV
Ted Shaw	3	76	54	37	32	20	436	426	134	198	5.04	4	2
——Snowden	1	8	6	3	1	4	36	31	6	14	7.00	0	0
——Spencer	1	—	—	—	—	—	—	—	—	—	—	—	—
Hulan Stamps	1	1	—	—	—	—	—	—	—	—	—	—	—
Turkey Stearnes	9	2	1	0	0	1	—	—	4	2	—	0	0
——Stokes..........	1	1	1	1	0	0	8	5	—	—	2.25	0	0
Candy Jim Taylor....	2	2	1	0	1	0	9	14	0	2	5.00	0	0
Lawrence Terrell	2	40	19	6	13	6	135.1	131	50	60	6.52	1	0
Gunboat Thompson.	1	8	6	2	3	2	37.1	31	22	13	6.03	0	0
Sam Thompson.......	1	1	—	—	—	—	—	—	—	—	—	—	—
Christobel Torrienti..	2	19	13	7	9	4	111.2	137	25	22	6.21	1	2
Harold Treadwell....	2	12	3	2	1	4	35.1	32	18	16	5.35	0	0
Ted Trent	1	8	6	3	4	2	48	48	7	15	2.63	1	0
Quincy Trouppe	1	2	2	2	2	0	16	4	—	—	1.13	1	0
Bill Tyler	2	29	22	10	7	9	138	113	45	67	5.35	0	0
Columbus Vance	1	16	10	7	6	7	72.2	60	10	27	4.83	2	2
Lefty Waddy	1	7	4	1	1	4	21	18	7	3	6.86	0	0
Elbert Williams	1	2	2	2	1	1	18	18	8	6	5.50	0	0
Lefty Williams.........	1	8	5	3	5	0	42.1	43	8	9	2.98	1	0
Smokey Joe Williams..............	1	2	1	0	0	0	6.2	10	—	—	9.45	0	—
Tom Williams	1	6	3	0	1	0	21.2	26	9	10	10.80	0	—
Charles Wilson.......	2	16	8	4	5	5	74.1	86	12	22	5.69	0	0
James Winston	1	1	—	0	0	0	3	4	0	1	3.00	0	—
Doc Ziegler	1	1	—	—	—	—	2	2	—	—	9.00	0	—

Batting

Player	Yrs	Games	AB	H	Avg.	Slug.	2B	3B	HR	SB
Buck Alexander......	3	49	72	15	.208	.278	1	2	0	0
Newt Allen	1	5	20	6	.300	.300	0	0	0	0
——Armour........	1	4	12	2	.167	.250	1	0	0	0
Percy Bailey..........	1	7	13	2	.154	.154	0	0	0	0
Robert Baldwin	1	5	9	2	.222	.222	0	0	0	1
Jess Barbour	1	16	67	19	.284	.537	1	2	4	4
John Barnes	1	11	37	10	.270	.514	4	1	1	0
Cool Papa Bell	1	14	52	19	.365	.500	4	0	1	3
Fred Bell................	3	61	182	53	.291	.555	7	4	11	9
Julian Bell	1	5	12	4	.333	.500	0	1	0	0
William Bell..........	1	5	6	2	.333	.333	0	0	0	1
Jerry Benjamin	1	22	73	25	.342	.425	2	2	0	10
George Bennette	1	5	17	2	.118	.176	0	1	0	0
Rainy Bibbs	1	7	22	8	.364	.364	0	0	0	0
Jimmy Binder	1	14	49	18	.367	.469	3	1	0	1
Charles Blackwell ...	1	73	246	68	.276	.411	11	5	4	11
Finis Branahan	1	15	24	7	.292	.500	0	1	1	0
Chippy Britt	1	3	4	3	.750	1.750	2	1	0	0

259

Batting (continued)

Player	Yrs	Games	AB	H	Avg.	Slug.	2B	3B	HR	SB
Charles Brooks.......	1	1	1	0	.000	.000	0	0	0	0
Edward Brown	1	2	2	0	.000	.000	0	0	0	0
George Brown	1	4	15	1	.067	.067	0	0	0	1
Larry Brown	1	47	135	33	.244	.370	3	4	2	1
Ray Brown............	1	8	21	4	.190	.429	1	0	1	0
Black Bottom Buford	1	12	43	9	.209	.256	0	1	0	0
———Busby..........	1	2	8	2	.250	.250	0	0	0	0
William Carter	1	7	16	1	.067	.125	1	0	0	0
———Coley..........	1	1	3	0	.000	.000	0	0	0	0
Jack Combs	4	68	88	13	.148	.182	1	1	0	1
Andy Cooper........	9	231	335	55	.164	.212	5	4	1	0
Dewey Creacy	1	10	33	8	.242	.242	0	0	0	0
Rube Currie	1	19	38	11	.289	.368	0	0	1	0
Ray Dandridge.......	1	9	35	9	.257	.429	1	2	0	0
Pepper Daniels.......	8	296	910	227	.249	.341	34	8	11	20
Albert Davis..........	4	75	152	35	.230	.283	5	0	1	1
Saul Davis	2	25	86	22	.256	.326	5	1	0	1
Steel Arm Davis......	1	27	66	21	.318	.485	6	1	1	0
Nelson Dean	2	32	66	11	.167	.318	0	2	2	0
Bingo DeMoss	4	102	343	72	.210	.268	11	3	1	5
Lou Dials	2	64	214	57	.266	.491	13	7	7	4
John Dixon	2	13	22	8	.364	.591	0	1	1	0
Bill Drake	1	15	37	5	.135	.135	0	0	0	0
Jake Dunn	1	65	240	67	.279	.433	11	7	4	7
Johnny Edwards	1	4	1	0	.000	.000	0	0	0	0
Mack Eggleston	1	24	74	20	.270	.446	7	3	0	0
Lou English	1	12	35	8	.229	.343	0	2	0	1
Clarence Everett.....	1	26	83	15	.181	.217	1	1	0	0
———Foote	1	1	2	0	.000	.000	0	0	0	0
William Force	3	93	169	50	.296	.497	8	4	6	0
———Gales..........	1	2	4	1	.250	.250	0	0	0	0
Jelly Gardner	1	27	88	17	.193	.216	2	0	0	6
Bill Gatewood........	2	40	59	25	.424	.644	6	2	1	0
George Giles.........	1	6	23	8	.348	.435	2	0	0	1
William Gill..........	2	12	41	12	.293	.341	2	0	0	0
Ernest Gooden	1	3	5	0	.000	.000	0	0	0	0
———Haley..........	1	2	5	1	.200	.400	1	0	0	0
Perry Hall	1	2	6	2	.333	.333	0	0	0	0
Lewis Hampton	3	64	134	41	.306	.604	5	4	9	1
Hollie Harding	2	127	483	145	.300	.400	20	5	6	16
Paul Hardy	1	15	42	7	.167	.214	2	0	0	0
Chick Harper........	2	17	60	14	.233	.333	1	1	2	0
Vic Harris	1	11	44	18	.409	.545	1	1	1	1
Arthur Henderson ...	1	4	8	1	.125	.125	0	0	0	0
Charlie Henry	1	26	51	13	.255	.333	2	1	0	1
Slap Hensley	1	6	7	2	.286	.286	0	0	0	0
Joe Hewitt	3	80	266	43	.162	.214	10	2	0	10
Charley Hill	2	46	139	31	.223	.252	4	0	0	6
Johnson Hill	1	42	153	42	.275	.451	5	5	4	0

Batting (continued)

Player	Yrs	Games	AB	H	Avg.	Slug.	2B	3B	HR	SB
Pete Hill	2	68	215	74	.344	.512	9	6	5	7
———Holcomb	1	1	1	0	.000	.000	0	0	0	0
Bill Holland............	3	87	130	14	.108	.000	0	0	0	0
Crush Holloway	1	63	256	64	.250	.348	9	8	0	10
———Howard.......	1	2	9	3	.333	.444	1	0	0	0
Bertrum Hunter	1	16	16	1	.063	.063	0	0	0	0
———Jackson	1	2	8	4	.500	.500	0	0	0	0
Harry Jeffries	3	190	654	168	.257	.327	29	4	3	16
———Jenkins	1	1	4	1	.250	.250	0	0	0	0
———Johnson	1	1	1	0	.000	.000	0	0	0	0
Claude Johnson......	3	222	795	241	.303	.395	26	4	13	14
Dicta Johnson	1	2	4	1	.250	.250	0	0	0	0
Wade Johnston	5	253	975	308	.316	.489	42	23	27	23
John Jones	7	342	1324	400	.302	.437	61	27	21	16
Dan Kennard	1	36	89	18	.202	.337	1	1	3	1
Harry Kenyon	4	129	382	112	.293	.427	17	8	6	15
J. Kerner................	1	1	5	0	.000	.000	0	0	0	0
I. S. Lane...............	3	48	193	57	.295	.415	6	4	3	8
———Long	3	29	88	21	.239	.511	6	3	4	1
———Longware	1	19	62	10	.161	.177	1	0	0	0
Andy Love	1	26	81	10	.123	.185	2	0	1	2
William Love..........	1	26	86	24	.279	.430	7	0	2	2
William Lowe.........	1	45	159	48	.302	.384	4	3	1	1
Granville Lyons	1	17	67	19	.284	.448	3	4	0	0
Jimmie Lyons..........	1	37	136	55	.404	.699	10	3	8	22
Jack Marshall.........	2	43	77	12	.156	.156	0	0	0	0
Stack Martin	2	106	368	107	.291	.462	19	7	10	10
George McAllister ..	1	5	18	2	.111	.111	0	0	0	0
Bill McCall.............	1	12	25	3	.120	.200	0	1	0	0
Boots McClain	1	9	22	6	.273	.273	0	0	0	0
Vet McDonald........	1	8	15	3	.200	.200	0	0	0	1
Webster McDonald	1	8	6	0	.000	.000	0	0	0	0
Hurley McNair.......	1	67	237	65	.274	.397	8	6	3	6
George Mitchell	3	58	107	24	.224	.355	1	2	3	0
Nat Moore	2	21	71	14	.197	.282	6	0	0	3
Yellowhorse Morris.	3	75	138	30	.217	.326	4	1	3	0
Everett Nelson........	2	5	8	1	.125	.125	0	0	0	0
Omer Newsome.....	2	17	17	3	.176	.176	0	0	0	0
Grady Orange.......	4	177	625	156	.250	.349	19	8	9	9
Willie Owens	2	11	36	9	.250	.278	1	0	0	0
Spoony Palm	3	83	273	84	.308	.484	17	5	7	7
Carl Perry.............	1	22	72	17	.236	.375	2	1	2	0
Bruce Petway	6	178	490	141	.288	.371	14	6	5	18
———Phillips	1	30	79	12	.152	.177	2	0	0	0
Bill Pierce	1	58	230	77	.335	.565	6	13	7	3
Willie Powell	2	39	53	8	.151	.189	0	1	0	0
Anderson Pryor	7	201	702	189	.269	.389	36	9	10	24
Bill Pryor	1	1	1	0	.000	.000	0	0	0	0

Batting (continued)

Player	Yrs	Games	AB	H	Avg.	Slug.	2B	3B	HR	SB
Ted Radcliffe.........	3	102	384	107	.279	.445	19	6	11	5
Andrew Reed........	1	19	80	10	.125	.138	1	0	0	0
John Reese	1	8	31	7	.226	.258	1	0	0	0
Mule Riggins..........	7	424	1603	473	.295	.429	79	30	25	52
Ed Rile	4	280	1009	354	.351	.574	79	19	36	18
Bobbie Robinson	3	167	649	180	.278	.376	28	12	4	13
Bobby Roth...........	1	20	63	13	.206	.302	3	0	1	1
John Henry Russell..	1	5	17	4	.235	.353	2	0	0	0
Bob Saunders	2	25	70	15	.214	.271	1	0	1	0
———Sawyer........	1	1	3	2	.667	.667	0	0	0	0
———Scott	1	6	18	3	.167	.167	0	0	0	0
Ted Shaw	3	76	158	38	.241	.304	6	2	0	0
Ray Sheppard........	3	73	256	74	.289	.430	10	4	6	8
Clarence Smith.......	6	271	1046	345	.330	.472	43	26	18	38
James Smith...........	2	2	4	0	.000	.000	0	0	0	0
———Snowden	1	8	9	2	.222	.222	0	0	0	1
Turkey Stearnes......	9	585	2217	783	.353	.678	143	79	140	67
———Stevens........	2	25	84	27	.321	.429	4	2	1	0
———Stevenson	1	1	4	1	.250	.250	0	0	0	0
Mule Suttles	1	8	23	8	.348	.826	5	0	2	1
Candy Jim Taylor ...	2	13	31	12	.387	.484	1	1	0	0
Leroy Taylor..........	2	4	15	5	.333	.600	2	1	0	1
Lawrence Terrell	2	40	45	5	.111	.156	2	0	0	0
Clint Thomas..........	1	60	231	79	.346	.558	15	7	7	7
Gunboat Thompson	1	8	15	3	.200	.267	1	0	0	0
Christobel Torrienti .	2	117	390	128	.328	.456	22	5	6	9
Harold Treadwell ...	2	12	13	3	.231	.231	0	0	0	0
Ted Trent	1	8	3	0	.000	.000	0	0	0	0
Quincy Trouppe	1	13	47	14	.298	.319	1	0	0	0
Bill Tyler	2	29	39	6	.207	.345	1	0	1	0
Columbus Vance	1	16	24	6	.250	.292	1	0	0	0
Lefty Waddy	1	7	3	0	.000	.000	0	0	0	0
Frank Warfield.......	3	149	578	174	.301	.403	28	11	3	23
Johnny Watson	4	127	441	108	.245	.324	9	7	4	9
Jim Webster...........	1	4	10	0	.000	.000	0	0	0	0
Speck Webster	1	20	49	12	.245	.327	1	0	1	0
Willie Wells	1	16	54	16	.296	.519	7	1	1	5
Edgar Wesley........	7	330	1185	400	.338	.613	57	13	79	27
John Williams	1	14	47	17	.362	.553	3	3	0	2
Lefty Williams	1	8	15	1	.067	.133	1	0	0	0
Poindexter Williams	2	51	155	42	.271	.381	6	1	3	0
Tom Williams.........	1	6	6	0	.000	.000	0	0	0	0
Charles Wilson	2	20	51	8	.157	.176	1	0	0	0
———Wingfield	1	14	56	15	.268	.286	1	0	0	0
James Winston.......	1	1	1	0	.000	.000	0	0	0	0
———Wyatt	1	1	2	0	.000	.000	0	0	0	0
Tom Young	1	12	41	17	.415	.610	0	1	2	2

Appendix D

All-Time Regular Season Records

Service

Seasons Played

MOST SEASONS PLAYED

9   Andy (Lefty) Cooper, 1920–27, 1930
    Norman (Turkey) Stearnes, 1923–31
8   Leon (Pepper) Daniels, 1921–27, 1930
    Edgar Wesley, 1919–23, 1925–27
7   John Jones, 1922–27, 1929
    Anderson Pryor, 1923–27, 1931, 1933
    Orville (Mule) Riggins, 1920–26

Games Played

MOST GAMES PLAYED, SEASON

84   Orville (Mule) Riggins, 1925
     Norman (Turkey) Stearnes, 1925
83   Clarence Smith, 1925
     Ed Rile, 1928
82   Norman (Turkey) Stearnes, 1926

MOST GAMES PLAYED, CAREER

585 Norman (Turkey) Stearnes, 1923–31
424 Orville (Mule) Riggins, 1920–26
342 John Jones, 1922–27, 1929

Pitching

Games Pitched

MOST GAMES PITCHED, SEASON

38   William Force, 1923
36   Andy (Lefty) Cooper, 1923
     Andy (Lefty) Cooper, 1926
35   Bill Holland, 1922

MOST GAMES PITCHED, CAREER

229 Andy (Lefty) Cooper, 1920–27, 1930
 93 William Force, 1921–23
 87 Bill Holland, 1920–22

Games Started

MOST GAMES STARTED, SEASON

23   Bill Holland, 1922
     Ted Shaw, 1928
22   Andy (Lefty) Cooper, 1922
     Andy (Lefty) Cooper, 1926

MOST GAMES STARTED, CAREER

139 Andy (Lefty) Cooper, 1920–27, 1930
 59 Bill Holland, 1920–22
 55 William Force, 1921–23

Complete Games

MOST COMPLETE GAMES, SEASON

18 Bill Holland, 1921
   Bill Holland, 1922
17 Harold (Yellowhorse) Morris, 1927
   Ed Rile, 1927

MOST COMPLETE GAMES, CAREER

87 Andy (Lefty) Cooper, 1920–27, 1930
48 Bill Holland, 1920–22
37 Ted Shaw, 1928–30

Games Won

MOST GAMES WON, SEASON

16 Bill Holland, 1922
15 Andy (Lefty) Cooper, 1923
   Andy (Lefty) Cooper, 1930

MOST CONSECUTIVE GAMES WON

9 Andy (Lefty) Cooper, 1925
7 Andy (Lefty) Cooper, 1922

MOST GAMES WON, CAREER

91 Andy (Lefty) Cooper, 1920–27, 1930
39 Bill Holland, 1920–22
32 Ted Shaw, 1928–30

Games Lost

MOST GAMES LOST, SEASON

13 Bill Holland, 1922
11 Bill Holland, 1921
   Buck Alexander, 1924
   George Mitchell, 1928

MOST GAMES LOST, CAREER

48 Andy (Lefty) Cooper, 1920–27, 1930
30 Bill Holland, 1920–22
21 William Force, 1921–23

Winning Percentage

HIGHEST WINNING PERCENTAGE, SEASON (MINIMUM 10 DECISIONS)

.800 Harold (Yellowhorse) Morris, 1925 (Won 8, Lost 2)
.786 Andy (Lefty) Cooper, 1925 (Won 11, Lost 3)
.778 Bill Gatewood, 1920 (Won 14, Lost 4)

HIGHEST WINNING PERCENTAGE, CAREER (MINIMUM 30 DECISIONS)

.655 Andy (Lefty) Cooper, 1920–27, 1930 (Won 91, Lost 48)
.625 William Force, 1921–23 (Won 35, Lost 21)
.615 Ted Shaw (Won 32, Lost 20)

Innings Pitched

MOST INNINGS PITCHED, SEASON

204 Bill Holland, 1922
186.2 Harold (Yellowhorse) Morris, 1927
178 Andy (Lefty) Cooper, 1926

MOST INNINGS PITCHED, CAREER

1,151.2 Andy (Lefty) Cooper, 1920–27, 1930
531.2 Bill Holland, 1920–22
461.1 Albert Davis, 1927–30

Base Hits

MOST BASE HITS, SEASON

192 Albert Davis, 1929
182 Bill Holland, 1922
176 Ted Shaw, 1928

MOST BASE HITS, CAREER

1,083 Andy (Lefty) Cooper, 1920–27, 1930
481 Albert Davis, 1927–30
460 Bill Holland, 1920–22

Bases On Balls

MOST BASES ON BALLS, SEASON

54 Jack Marshall, 1928
53 Jack Combs, 1924
   Harold (Yellowhorse) Morris, 1927
52 Ted Shaw, 1929

MOST BASES ON BALLS, CAREER

185 Andy (Lefty) Cooper, 1920–27, 1930
138 Harold (Yellowhorse) Morris, 1925–27
134 Ted Shaw, 1928–30

Strikeouts

MOST STRIKEOUTS, SEASON

108 William Force, 1922
95 Bill Holland, 1922
86 Bill Holland, 1921

MOST STRIKEOUTS, CAREER

388	Andy (Lefty) Cooper, 1920–27, 1930
249	Bill Holland, 1920–22
218	William Force, 1921–23

Runs Per Game

LOWEST RUNS PER GAME, SEASON
(MINIMUM 60 INNINGS)

3.29	Nelson Dean, 1930
3.32	Bill Holland, 1920
3.38	Ted Shaw, 1930

LOWEST RUNS PER GAME, CAREER (MIN-
IMUM 150 INNINGS)

3.65	Nelson Dean, 1930–31
3.77	Bill Holland, 1920–22
4.12	Ed Rile, 1927–30

Shutouts

MOST SHUTOUTS, SEASON

4	Andy (Lefty) Cooper, 1922
3	Harold (Yellowhorse) Morris, 1927
	Charlie Henry, 1929
	Ted Shaw, 1930

MOST CONSECUTIVE SHUTOUTS

2	William Force, 1922
	Charlie Henry, 1929

MOST SHUTOUTS, CAREER

11	Andy (Lefty) Cooper, 1920–27, 1930
5	Albert Davis, 1927–30
4	Ted Shaw, 1928–30

Saves

MOST SAVES, SEASON

6	Andy (Lefty) Cooper, 1924
	Andy (Lefty) Cooper, 1925
5	Andy (Lefty) Cooper, 1923
4	Bill Holland, 1921
	Andy (Lefty) Cooper, 1926

MOST SAVES, CAREER

24	Andy (Lefty) Cooper, 1920–27, 1930
7	Bill Holland, 1920–22
6	William Force, 1921–23

Batting

At-Bats

MOST AT-BATS, SEASON

341	Clarence Smith, 1925
327	Wade Johnston, 1928
324	Norman (Turkey) Stearnes, 1925

MOST AT-BATS, CAREER

2,217	Norman (Turkey) Stearnes, 1923–31
1,603	Orville (Mule) Riggins, 1920–26
1,324	John Jones, 1922–27, 1929

Base Hits

MOST BASE HITS, GAME

6	Stack Martin, April 28, 1928 vs. Cleveland
	Hollie Harding, May 30, 1928 vs. Birmingham
	Ed Rile, July 31, 1928 vs. St. Louis

MOST BASE HITS, SEASON

118	Norman (Turkey) Stearnes, 1925
116	Clarence Smith, 1925
113	Norman (Turkey) Stearnes, 1926

MOST BASE HITS, CAREER

783	Norman (Turkey) Stearnes, 1923–31
473	Orville (Mule) Riggins, 1920–26
400	John Jones, 1922–27, 1929
	Edgar Wesley, 1920–23, 1925–27

MOST CONSECUTIVE GAMES WITH A
BASE HIT

19	Norman (Turkey) Stearnes, 1924
18	Edgar Wesley, 1925 (twice)
17	Norman (Turkey) Stearnes, 1923
	Norman (Turkey) Stearnes, 1924

Batting Average

HIGHEST BATTING AVERAGE, SEASON
(MINIMUM 100 AT-BATS)

.424	Edgar Wesley, 1925
.406	Ed Rile, 1927
.404	Jimmy Lyons, 1920

HIGHEST BATTING AVERAGE, CAREER
(MINIMUM 300 AT-BATS)

.353	Normay (Turkey) Stearnes, 1923–31
.351	Ed Rile, 1927–30
.338	Edgar Wesley, 1920–23, 1925–27

Two-Base Hits

MOST TWO-BASE HITS, SEASON

27	Ed Rile, 1928
24	Norman (Turkey) Stearnes, 1926
23	Ed Rile, 1927

MOST TWO-BASE HITS, CAREER

143	Norman (Turkey) Stearnes, 1923–31
79	Orville (Mule) Riggins, 1920–26
	Ed Rile, 1927–30
61	John Jones, 1922–27, 1929

Three-Base Hits

MOST THREE-BASE HITS, GAME

3	Norman (Turkey) Stearnes, June 17, 1923 vs. Milwaukee (2nd game)

MOST THREE-BASE HITS, SEASON

13	Norman (Turkey) Stearnes, 1923
	Bill Pierce, 1924
	Wade Johnston, 1930
12	Norman (Turkey) Stearnes, 1927
11	Norman (Turkey) Stearnes, 1924
	Clarence Smith, 1925

MOST THREE-BASE HITS, CAREER

79	Norman (Turkey) Stearnes, 1923–31
27	Orville (Mule) Riggins, 1920–26
	John Jones, 1922–27, 1929

Home Runs

MOST HOME RUNS, GAME

3	Norman (Turkey) Stearnes, September 3, 1927 vs. Cuban Stars (West)

MOST CONSECUTIVE GAMES HITTING A HOME RUN

5	Norman (Turkey) Stearnes, 1928
4	Edgar Wesley, 1923
	Edgar Wesley, 1925
	Norman (Turkey) Stearnes, 1928
	Norman (Turkey) Stearnes, 1929

MOST HOME RUNS, SEASON

24	Norman (Turkey) Stearnes, 1928
20	Norman (Turkey) Stearnes, 1926
	Norman (Turkey) Stearnes, 1927
19	Norman (Turkey) Stearnes, 1929

MOST HOME RUNS, CAREER

140	Norman (Turkey) Stearnes, 1923–31
79	Edgar Wesley, 1920–23, 1925–27
36	Ed Rile, 1927–30

Extra-Base Hits

MOST EXTRA-BASE HITS, SEASON

54	Norman (Turkey) Stearnes, 1926
	Norman (Turkey) Stearnes, 1927
49	Norman (Turkey) Stearnes, 1928
48	Norman (Turkey) Stearnes, 1925

MOST EXTRA-BASE HITS, CAREER

362	Norman (Turkey) Stearnes, 1923–31
149	Edgar Wesley, 1920–23, 1925–27
134	Orville (Mule) Riggins, 1920–26
	Ed Rile, 1927–30

Total Bases

MOST TOTAL BASES, SEASON

217	Norman (Turkey) Stearnes, 1926
216	Norman (Turkey) Stearnes, 1927
212	Norman (Turkey) Stearnes, 1925

MOST TOTAL BASES, CAREER

1,504	Norman (Turkey) Stearnes, 1923–31
726	Edgar Wesley, 1920–23, 1925–27
687	Orville (Mule) Riggins, 1920–26

Slugging Percentage

HIGHEST SLUGGING PERCENTAGE, SEASON (MINIMUM 100 AT-BATS)

.810	Edgar Wesley, 1925
.741	Norman (Turkey) Stearnes, 1923
.721	Norman (Turkey) Stearnes, 1926

HIGHEST SLUGGING PERCENTAGE, CAREER (MINIMUM 300 AT-BATS)

.678	Norman (Turkey) Stearnes, 1923–31
.613	Edgar Wesley, 1920–23, 1925–27
.574	Ed Rile, 1927–30

Stolen Bases

MOST STOLEN BASES, SEASON

22	Jimmy Lyons, 1920
18	Orville (Mule) Riggins, 1925
17	Anderson Pryor, 1925
	Clarence Smith, 1925

MOST STOLEN BASES, CAREER

67	Norman (Turkey) Stearnes, 1923–31
52	Orville (Mule) Riggins, 1920–26
38	Clarence Smith, 1921–25, 1933

Team Records

Games Played

MOST GAMES PLAYED

99	1927
97	1925

LONGEST GAME PLAYED

17 in- August 6, 1921 vs. Columbus (Detroit
nings won, 5–4)

Games Won

MOST GAMES WON

57	1925
54	1928

MOST CONSECUTIVE GAMES WON

21	July 16 to August 17 (1st game), 1930
17	May 26 to June 16, 1926

Games Lost

MOST GAMES LOST

46	1927
42	1926
	1929

MOST CONSECUTIVE GAMES LOST

8	June 21 to June 30, 1924
7	July 30 to August 11 (1st game), 1929

Winning Percentage

HIGHEST WINNING PERCENTAGE

.690	1932 (Won 29, Lost 13)
.614	1920 (Won 35, Lost 22)

LOWEST WINNING PERCENTAGE

.394	1933 (Won 13, Lost 20)
.490	1931 (Won 25, Lost 26)

Scoring

MOST RUNS SCORED, GAME

21	May 31, 1927 vs. Cleveland
20	July 20, 1929 vs. Chicago
18	May 14, 1922 vs. Kansas City
	May 26, 1923 vs. Cleveland
	May 27, 1923 (2nd game) vs. Cleveland
	May 1, 1928 vs. Cleveland

MOST RUNS SCORED, DOUBLEHEADER

28	May 27, 1923 vs. Cleveland

GREATEST MARGIN OF VICTORY

16 runs May 26, 1929 vs. Nashville (Detroit
won, 17–1)

MOST RUNS ALLOWED, GAME

29	June 12, 1933 vs. Chicago
21	July 11, 1928 vs. St. Louis
20	June 26, 1923 vs. Chicago
	August 17, 1928 vs. Memphis

GREATEST MARGIN OF DEFEAT

20 runs June 26, 1923 vs. Chicago (Chicago
won, 20–0)
June 12, 1933 vs. Chicago (Chicago
won, 29–9)

MOST RUNS SCORED, BOTH TEAMS, GAME

38	Chicago (29) vs. Detroit (9), June 12, 1933
34	Memphis (20) vs. Detroit (14), August 17, 1928
33	Indianapolis (18) vs. Detroit (15), June 1, 1922
	St. Louis (17) vs. Detroit (16), May 19, 1926
	Birmingham (17) vs. Detroit (16), August 19, 1929

Pitching

Runs Per Game

LOWEST RUNS PER GAME, SEASON

3.44	1932
4.11	1922

HIGHEST RUNS PER GAME, SEASON

6.18	1924
6.03	1929

Shutouts

MOST SHUTOUTS, SEASON

10	1930
8	1922

Saves

MOST SAVES, SEASON

10	1923

Batting

Batting Average

HIGHEST BATTING AVERAGE, SEASON

.315   1930

LOWEST BATTING AVERAGE, SEASON

.249   1931

Home Runs

MOST HOME RUNS, SEASON

83   1925

Appendix E

Career Playoff Statistics

Pitching

Player	GP	GS	CG	Won	Lost	IP	H	BB	SO	RPG	ShO	SV
Fred Bell	1	1	1	0	1	9	8	7	6	7.00	0	0
Andy Cooper	3	1	1	0	1	11.2	15	1	1	6.94	0	1
Albert Davis	2	2	2	0	2	17	24	7	7	5.82	0	0
Nelson Dean	3	3	2	1	2	25	29	9	9	6.84	0	0
Lewis Hampton	2	2	1	1	1	18	11	3	7	2.50	1	0
Yellowhorse Morris	1	1	1	0	1	9.1	7	1	4	5.79	0	0
Omer Newsome	1	1	1	1	0	9	2	1	1	0.00	1	0
Willie Powell	2	1	0	2	0	10.1	10	0	0	6.97	0	0
Ted Shaw	1	1	0	0	0	5	6	3	3	5.40	0	0

Batting

Player	Games	AB	H	Avg.	2B	3B	HR	SB
Fred Bell	6	21	4	.190	0	0	1	1
Andy Cooper	3	4	1	.250	0	0	0	0
Pepper Daniels	9	27	6	.222	1	0	0	0
Albert Davis	4	10	1	.100	0	0	0	0
Nelson Dean	2	6	0	.000	0	0	0	0
Bingo DeMoss	1	4	0	.000	0	0	0	0
Lou Dials	5	14	3	.214	0	1	0	0
Jake Dunn	7	26	8	.308	1	1	0	0
Lewis Hampton	5	21	0	.000	0	0	0	0
Crush Holloway	7	29	11	.379	0	0	0	1
Wade Johnston	7	30	6	.200	2	0	0	0
John Jones	6	19	4	.210	1	1	0	0

Batting (continued)

Player	Games	AB	H	Avg.	2B	3B	HR	SB
Dan Kennard	2	4	1	.250	0	0	0	0
William Love	1	5	1	.200	0	0	0	0
Yellowhorse Morris	1	4	2	.500	0	0	0	0
Omer Newsome	1	3	1	.333	0	0	0	0
Grady Orange	6	18	5	.278	1	0	0	0
Spoony Palm	6	25	8	.320	1	0	0	0
Bruce Petway	1	4	1	.250	0	0	0	0
Willie Powell	2	2	0	.000	0	0	0	0
Anderson Pryor	6	25	5	.200	0	0	0	0
Mule Riggins	6	25	3	.120	0	1	0	0
Ed Rile	6	23	8	.348	1	0	1	2
Bobbie Robinson	4	12	3	.250	0	0	0	0
Ted Shaw	1	2	1	.500	0	0	0	0
Clarence Smith	6	25	7	.280	2	0	0	2
Cleo Smith	1	1	1	1.000	0	0	0	0
Turkey Stearnes	12	50	21	.420	6	2	4	1
Edgar Wesley	3	10	2	.200	0	0	0	0

Notes

Introduction. A Distant Diamond

1. Interview with Fred Guinyard.
2. *Detroit News,* Aug. 11, 1982.
3. *Detroit News,* Sept. 16, 1992.
4. Richard Bak, *Cobb Would Have Caught It: The Golden Age of Baseball in Detroit* (Detroit: Wayne State University Press, 1991), pp. 98–99.
5. The term "Negro leagues" refers collectively to the various black leagues that existed between 1920 and the early 1950s. Up until 1920, when the first truly professional black league—the Negro National League (NNL)—started regularly scheduled play, there was no formal network of black teams. The NNL, of which the Detroit Stars were a charter member, disbanded in 1931. A second major black league, the Eastern Colored League (ECL), operated from 1923 to 1928. For several years the NNL and ECL staged a Colored World Series. A reorganized Negro National League survived from 1933 to 1948 (with the Detroit Stars a member in 1933). The third major association, the Negro American League, was created in 1937 and lasted until 1960, although it was in a state of decline during its last eight or ten years. Generally speaking, by 1950 or so the major leagues' rapid desegregation had stripped the Negro leagues of most of their prestige and fan support.
6. *Detroit News,* Sept. 16, 1992.
7. Ibid.

Chapter 1. Following the North Star

1. The best primer on American slavery remains Kenneth M. Stampp, *The Peculiar Institution* (New York: Knopf, 1956). Another excellent survey is Nathan Irvin Huggins, *Black Odyssey: The African-American Ordeal in Slavery* (New York: Pantheon, 1977).

2. Howard Zinn, *A People's History of the United States* (New York: Harper & Row, 1980), p. 28.
3. Ibid., p. 33.
4. Silas Farmer, *History of Detroit and Wayne County and Early Michigan* (Detroit: Gale Research, [reprint of 1890 edition] 1969), p. 344.
5. Ibid., pp. 344–45.
6. Ibid., p. 344.
7. Ibid. Detroit's population included several free blacks at the time, as well. A farmhand named William Lee was employed by the Macomb family, while a woman known as "Black Betty" was a cook for several prominent families.
8. Harriet A. Jacobs (ed. Jean Fagan Yellin), *Incidents in the Life of a Slave Girl* (Cambridge: Harvard University Press, 1987), pp. 27–28. A good general study of slavery and abolition in Michigan is contained in John C. Dancy, "The Negro People in Michigan," *Michigan History* (Spring 1940), pp. 211–40.
9. Farmer, *History of Detroit and Wayne County,* p. 345.
10. Ibid., pp. 345–46.
11. Ibid., p. 346.
12. Arthur M. Woodford, *Detroit: American Urban Renaissance* (Tulsa, Okla.: Continental Heritage Press, 1979), pp. 51–53.
13. Scott McGehee and Susan Watson (eds.), *Blacks in Detroit* (Detroit: Detroit Free Press, 1980), pp. 20–25.
14. Interview with Tom Dietz, director of the Detroit Historical Society.
15. David M. Katzman, *Before the Ghetto: Black Detroit in the Nineteenth Century* (Urbana: University of Illinois Press, 1973), p. 71. In 1884 the *Detroit Post* called the area a "plague spot."
16. Woodford, *Detroit: American Urban Renaissance,* pp. 53–54. Webb's house was on the north side of Congress, near St. Antoine. A state marker identifies the site today. Another important historical event can be linked to Detroit's anti-slavery activities: In 1854 local merchant Zachariah Chandler helped organize political rallies in response to the Fugitive Slave Act. A larger meeting of similar committees from around the state was scheduled for summer in Jackson. It was there that the Republican Party was founded "under the oaks" on July 6, 1854.
17. Alexis de Tocqueville (ed. and rev. Phillips Bradley), *Democracy in America* (New York: Knopf, 1980), p. 359.
18. Ibid., p. 356.
19. "A Thrilling Narrative from the Lips of the Sufferers of the Late Detroit Riot, March 6, 1863," in Melvin G. Holli (ed.), *Detroit* (New York: New Viewpoints, 1976), pp. 86–92.
20. Woodford, *Detroit: American Urban Renaissance,* p. 53.
21. C. Vann Woodward, *The Strange Career of Jim Crow* [3rd rev. ed.] (New York: Oxford University Press, 1974), pp. 69–74.
22. For an overview of caste relations in Detroit, see Katzman, *Before the Ghetto,* pp. 81–103.

23. Ibid., p. 99.
24. The city's first black policeman, Joseph Stowers, was hired May 1, 1890. He was fired two months later, the victim of a smear campaign waged by white officers. According to his brother, prominent attorney Walter Stowers, white officers had written "anonymous letters, charging him with improper conduct toward white women and all sorts of dishonorable acts." In 1920 only fifteen of the city's 3,000 policemen were black. See McGehee and Watson, *Blacks in Detroit,* pp. 70–74.
25. Katzman, *Before the Ghetto,* pp. 116–18. In 1870, 55 percent of Detroit's barbers were black. By 1910 the percentage had dropped to 7.3.
26. *Detroit News,* Jan. 31, 1992.
27. Ibid.
28. Woodward, *The Strange Career of Jim Crow,* p. 73.
29. *Detroit News-Tribune,* Sept. 20, 1896.
30. Katzman, *Before the Ghetto,* pp. 135–205.
31. Ibid., p. 164.
32. Ibid., pp. 199–200.
33. In 1905 Pelham invented the first tabulating machines used in the census of manufactures. Among his other activities, he ran a black news service and published and edited the *Washington Tribune.* He died in 1943 in Washington at age eighty-four.
34. Frank B. Woodford and Arthur M. Woodford, *All Our Yesterdays: A Brief History of Detroit* (Detroit: Wayne State University Press, 1969) pp. 254–69; Steve Babson *Working Detroit* (New York: Adama Books, 1984), pp. 18–28.
35. Two excellent studies of this historic exodus from the South are Nicholas Lemann, *The Promised Land: The Great Black Migration and How It Changed America* (New York: Knopf, 1991) and Carole Marks, *Farewell, We're Good and Gone: The Great Black Migration* (Bloomington: Indiana University Press, 1989).
36. Babson, *Working Detroit,* pp. 41–42.
37. Ibid., p. 42; David L. Lewis, "Working Side by Side," *Michigan History* (Jan./Feb. 1993), pp. 25–30.
38. Ford was practical about his benevolence. The Rouge plant was the only Ford factory he integrated, and even there half of the black workers remained in the foundry. And instead of attempting to desegregate the all-white suburb of Dearborn, he created a black settlement west of the city, Inkster. His paternalism was to serve him well, however. Blacks, who had historically served as strikebreakers during labor-management battles, listened to their preachers and resisted unionization as stubbornly as old Henry himself. Ford finally capitulated to the United Auto Workers in 1941. When he died six years later, the black press eulogized him as "a great benefactor of the Negro race, probably the greatest that ever lived."
39. Olivier Zunz, *The Changing Face of Inequality: Urbanization, Industrial Development, and Immigrants in Detroit, 1880–1920* (Chicago: University of Chicago Press, 1982), pp. 372–98.

40. Babson, *Working Detroit,* p. 41.
41. John C. Dancy, *Sand Against the Wind: The Memoirs of John C. Dancy* (Detroit: Wayne State University Press, 1966), p. 55.
42. *Detroit Free Press,* Feb. 17, 1991. Oral histories of several Detroiters who migrated during this period are found in Elaine Latzman Moon, *Untold Tales, Unsung Heroes: An Oral History of Detroit's African American Community* (Detroit: Wayne Sate University Press, 1994).

Chapter 2. The Father of Black Baseball

1. John B. Holway, *Blackball Stars: Negro League Pioneers* (Westport, Conn.: Meckler Books, 1988), p. 8.
2. The profile of Foster is primarily drawn from Holway, *Blackball Stars,* and Robert Peterson, *Only the Ball Was White* (Englewood Cliffs, N.J.: Prentice-Hall, 1970). A secondary source is an uneven biography by Charles E. Whitehead, *A Man and His Diamonds* (New York: Vantage Press, 1980), which is best for its details of the Chicago American Giants' operations.
3. Holway, *Blackball Stars,* p. 8.
4. Jules Tygiel, "Black Ball," in John Thorn and Pete Palmer (eds.), *Total Baseball* (New York: Warner, 1989), p. 549; Peterson, *Only the Ball Was White,* pp. 28–30.
   The term "organized baseball," often abbreviated to "O. B.," refers to the various major and minor leagues signatory to the National Agreement, a mutual pact among club owners to honor players' contracts. Beyond preventing players from jumping clubs, it also made it more convenient for owners to blacklist certain players, including (but not limited to) those with the wrong skin color. Outlaw leagues and independent teams operated outside of the National Agreement, but those run by whites bowed to precedent and their own racist tendencies and barred blacks as well.
5. Tygiel, "Black Ball," p. 548; Peterson, *Only the Ball Was White,* pp. 16–17.
6. Peterson, *Only the Ball Was White,* p. 37.
7. The first black league, the League of Colored Base Ball Clubs, was organized in 1887 with teams in Baltimore, Boston, Cincinnati, Louisville, New York, Philadelphia, Pittsburgh, and Washington. It collapsed after just six weeks of play. Subsequent start-ups included the Inter-State League in 1890 and the International League of Independent Professional Baseball Clubs in 1906. Neither lasted more than one season. The Negro National Baseball League, formed in Chicago in 1910, folded before playing a single league-sanctioned game.
8. Tygiel, "Black Ball," p. 548.
9. Ibid., p. 549.
10. Thomas E. Powers, "The Page Fence Giants Play Ball," *Chronicle: The Quarterly Magazine of the Historical Society of Michigan* (Spring 1983), pp. 14–18.
11. *Detroit News,* Oct. 10, 1895.
12. Ibid.
13. Powers, "The Page Fence Giants Play Ball," p. 18.

14. Tygiel, "Black Ball," p. 550.
15. Peterson, *Only the Ball Was White,* pp. 54–57. Grant closed out his career playing for the Columbia Giants. In 1932 he was working as a janitor in Cincinnati when he was struck and killed by an automobile.
16. Holway, *Blackball Stars,* p. 14.
17. Ibid., p. 18.
18. For descriptions of Foster's managerial style, see Holway, *Blackball Stars,* pp. 22–31.
19. Janet Bruce, *The Kansas City Monarchs: Champions of Black Baseball* (Lawrence: University Press of Kansas, 1985), pp. 9, 14–17.
20. *Indianapolis Freeman,* Jan. 27, 1917. Cited in Bruce, *The Kansas City Monarchs,* p. 9.
21. Interviews with James Jenkins, president of the Graystone Jazz Museum in Detroit, and Haywood T. Henderson; *Detroit News,* June 23, 1929.
22. Holway, *Blackball Stars,* pp. 251–52.
23. *Detroit News,* June 20, 1935, July 20, 1954; interviews with Ruth Porter and Joyce Roesink.
24. Interview with Bob Sampson.
25. The description of Mack Park is pieced together from the reminiscences of several players, fans, and sportswriters.
26. Reproductions of the Stars' 1920 uniform, as well as other Negro-league jerseys, are available through Ebbets Field Flannels, P. O. Box 19685, Seattle, Washington 98109; 800/377–9777. The Cooperstown Ball Cap Company (Box 1003, Cooperstown, New York 13326; 607/264–8294) offers reproductions of Negro-league caps, including the Detroit Stars.
27. Peterson, *Only the Ball Was White,* p. 244.
28. Several major-league teams made the annual winter trip to Cuba to play exhibitions with the powerful all-Cuban Almendares team and the Havana Reds, who typically were strengthened by the addition of several black stars from the states. The three-time pennant-winning Tigers, missing Cobb, Sam Crawford, and several other starters, did poorly in their first trip in 1909, winning just four of twelve games. Detroit redeemed itself the following winter, however, winning seven games, losing four, and typing one. Cobb, who arrived late and played only the final five games, hit .370 for the series. Petway hit .390. These games are the only recorded instances of Cobb taking the field against blacks.
29. Ibid., pp. 209–10, 220–21, 223; Holway, *Blackball Stars,* pp. 50–59. Some accounts have Cobb being thrown out once by Petway; others say three times. Since "caught stealing" statistics were not kept in those days, twice seems to be the prevailing compromise.
30. Zunz, *The Changing Face of Inequality,* p. 373.
31. Joe Grimm (ed.), *Michigan Voices: Our State's History in the Words of the People Who Lived It* (Detroit: Wayne State University Press, 1987), p. 139.
32. Joanne Grant (ed.), *Black Protest: History, Documents, and Analyses, 1619 to the Present* (New York: Fawcett, 1968), p. 178. Between 1882 and 1927 there were 3,513 recorded lynchings of blacks across the country.

33. James T. Farrell, *Studs Lonigan* (New York: Avon, 1977), p. 214. Farrell's novel originally was published as a trilogy by Vanguard Press: *Young Lonigan* (1932), *The Young Manhood of Studs Lonigan* (1934), and *Judgment Day* (1935). Much of Farrell's prodigious output, which includes hundreds of short stories and more than fifty books, revolves around the changing ethnic neighborhoods of his native Chicago, particularly during the years of the Great Migration. Farrell, a lifelong baseball fan, also wrote *My Baseball Diary* in 1957. For an excellent overview, see Charles Fanning and Ellen Skerrett, "James T. Farrell and Washington Park: The Novel as Social History," *Chicago History* (Summer 1979), pp. 80–91.
34. Peterson, *Only the Ball Was White*, p. 113. Chicago was scheduled to host the Bacharach Giants; instead they headed back East for several games.

Chapter 3. A League for Every Race-Loving Man

1. Peterson, *Only the Ball Was White*, pp. 83–84; Bruce, *The Kansas City Monarchs*, pp. 13–15. In 1954 Elisha Scott's sons would argue for school desegregation in the landmark civil rights case, *Brown v. Board of Education.*
2. Holway, *Blackball Stars*, p. 15.
3. Bruce, *The Kansas City Monarchs*, p. 33. It was customary for visiting teams to ask for a guarantee of expenses from the home club since 35 percent of the gate receipts often didn't cover the cost of travel.
4. *Indianapolis Freeman*, Jan. 17, 1920. Cited in Bruce, *The Kansas City Monarchs*, p. 13.
5. John Holway, *Voices from the Great Black Baseball Leagues* (New York: De Capo Press, 1992), p. 212.
6. One game between Chicago and Kansas City drew 18,000 fans to South Side Park.
7. Interview with John Glover.
8. *Detroit News*, Aug. 11, 1982.
9. Glover interview.
10. Guinyard interview.
11. *Detroit Contender*, May 7, 1921.
12. *Chicago Defender*, July 8, 1933. Cited in Bruce, *The Kansas City Monarchs*, p. 53.
13. Detroit's first several pro football franchises, the Heralds (1920–21), Panthers (1925–26), and Wolverines (1928), all came and went with little media fanfare. The first permanent franchise, the Lions, started play in 1934.
14. Interview with Edgar Hayes.
15. Bak, *Cobb Would Have Caught It*, p. 194.
16. Bruce, *The Kansas City Monarchs*, p. 53.
17. *Kansas City Call*, Jan. 7, 1922. Cited in Bruce, *The Kansas City Monarchs*, p. 36.
18. Peterson, *Only the Ball Was White*, p. 90; Bruce, *The Kansas City Monarchs*, pp. 29–30. The expense of having a league umpiring staff, combined with charges of incompetence and a salary dispute, led the NNL to revert to the

old system of hiring umpires locally in 1927. This time, the majority of those used were black.

19. Peterson, *Only the Ball Was White,* p. 88.
20. The sportswriter quoted is Al Monroe, writing in *Abbot's Monthly in* 1932. Cited in Peterson, *Only the Ball Was White,* p. 113.
21. Holway, *Voices from the Great Black Baseball Leagues,* pp. 119–20.
22. Ibid., p. 29.
23. Ibid., p. 117.
24. John B. Holway, *Black Diamonds: Life in the Negro Leagues from the Men Who Lived It* (New York: Stadium Books, 1991), p. 51.

Chapter 4. The Way It Was: Eddie Batchelor

1. Interviews with Eddie Batchelor, Jr., and Eddie Batchelor III. Edward Armistead Batchelor, son of a career army officer, was born in North Carolina in 1883 and raised on a succession of western military outposts. His father, a much-decorated captain of infantry, died of cholera in the Philippines in 1900. Unable to get into West Point because one of his legs was shorter than the other, Batchelor "refused to let his lameness be a detriment," recalled his only child, Eddie, Jr. The short but heavily muscled Batchelor attended Brown University (where he established a school record for push-ups), then started his journalism career with the *Providence Journal.* He came to Detroit in 1906, serving at various times as a general assignment reporter, sportswriter, editor, and war correspondent for the *Free Press* and the *News.* For financial reasons, Batchelor quit daily journalism for advertising in 1927. He died in 1968. Eddie Jr., who was born in 1915 and often accompanied his father to Mack Park, worked for all three major Detroit dailies from 1934 to 1976 before retiring to South Carolina. His son, Eddie Batchelor III, is an attorney.
2. *Detroit Saturday Night* began publishing in 1907 and was an immediate success, due largely to its glossy picture pages and the vigorous, pro-business stance of its editor, Harry M. Nimmo. See Norman Beasley and George W. Stark, *Made in Detroit* (New York: G. P. Putnam's Sons, 1957), pp. 142–44.
3. E. A. Batchelor, "Afro-American Rooters Are the Best Part of the Show at Mack Park." *Detroit Saturday Night,* Aug. 19, 1922, p. 17.

Chapter 5. Shining Bright

1. Peterson, *Only the Ball Was White,* p. 89. Total league attendance in 1923 was 402,436.
2. Bruce, *The Kansas City Monarchs,* p. 37.
3. Peterson, *Only the Ball Was White,* pp. 89–90.
4. Bruce, *The Kansas City Monarchs,* p. 32.
5. Holway, *Blackball Stars,* p. 250.
6. The Southern Negro League (SNL) was organized in 1920 and existed in one form or another through the 1940s. The circuit included some of the

biggest cities in the South, but local Jim Crow laws prevented interracial matches, thus depriving SNL teams of a primary source of revenue. The low salaries made it easier for northern clubs to either buy or trade for top-flight SNL players like Leroy "Satchel" Paige and George "Mule" Suttles. At various times the Birmingham Black Barons, Memphis Red Sox, Nashville Elite Giants, and Louisville White Sox were made either associate or full-fledged members of the NNL.

7. Ibid., p. 251.
8. Ibid., p. 250.
9. Ibid., p. 252.
10. Ibid., p. 249.
11. Ibid.
12. Ibid., p. 248.
13. *Detroit News,* Aug. 11, 1982.
14. Sampson interview.
15. Holway, *Blackball Stars,* p. 252.
16. Sampson interview.
17. Rube Foster, not an impartial observer to the proceedings, enjoyed a measure of revenge against Hilldale owner Ed Bolden by reportedly sitting on Kansas City's bench and calling Mendez's pitches throughout the game. Mendez, who had played for Foster in Chicago and was a member of the original Detroit Stars in 1919, was thirty-seven years old at the time of this game. He died less than three years later in his native Cuba, probably of tuberculosis. See Holway, *Blackball Stars,* pp. 50–59.
18. Bruce, *The Kansas City Monarchs,* p. 57.
19. Ibid., p. 58.

Chapter 6. Black and White and Red All Over

1. Holway, Blackball Stars, p. 252.
2. *Detroit Times,* Oct. 10, 15, 1923.
3. *Grand Rapids Herald,* May 10, 1928.
4. Ibid., May 11, 12, 1928.
5. For the best descriptions of life on the barnstorming circuit, see Donn Rogosin, *Invisible Men: Life in Baseball's Negro Leagues* (New York: Atheneum, 1983), pp. 118–51; and Peterson, *Only the Ball Was White,* pp. 145–57.
6. Charles C. Alexander, *Ty Cobb* (New York: Oxford University Press, 1983), pp. 179, 185.
7. Ken Sobol, *Babe Ruth and the American Dream* (New York: Ballantine Books, 1974), p. 173. It's illuminating to examine the income of Babe Ruth and Oscar Charleston, the greatest gate attractions of their respective major leagues during the 1920s. In 1921, for example, Ruth made $30,000 in regular season salary. His postseason earnings included a World Series share of $3,510, perhaps $25,000 barnstorming with his own all-star team, and another $50,000 on the vaudeville circuit. That year Charleston, playing for the St. Louis Giants, led the NNL in stolen bases and home runs. He also played close to

150 or so exhibition games, including several against touring big-league squads. For all this he was probably lucky to make $5,000. Small wonder that he held up a St. Louis-Chicago game for five minutes that summer as he retrieved the loose change that appreciative fans had showered on him for hitting his third home run of the afternoon. Of course, Charleston, like all Negro leaguers, couldn't afford to be profligate. While Ruth eased into retirement with career baseball earnings that approached an estimated $2 million, Charleston closed out his life working as a baggage handler.

8. Bak, *Cobb Would Have Caught It,* pp. 193–94.
9. Bruce, *The Kansas City Monarchs,* p. 32. Robert Peterson estimates that by the late 1920s a good journeyman Negro leaguer made about $250 a month.
10. Ibid.
11. *Detroit Times,* Oct. 9, 1923.
12. The Browns' hero that day, pitcher Ray Kolp, "told us he was going to beat us, said he was going to hit his run in," remembered Turkey Stearnes. "And that's what he did." Besides pitching a complete game, Kolp contributed a single, double, and home run to the Browns' total of seventeen hits. Holway, *Blackball Stars,* p. 253.
13. The Stars hit .315 as a team in their three games against the Browns, with the murderers' row of Stearnes, Charleston, Beckwith, and Wesley combining for seven home runs.
14. Ibid., p. 28.
15. Holway, *Voices from the Great Black Baseball Leagues,* pp. xviii-xix.
16. Donald Honig, *Baseball When the Grass Was Real* (New York: Coward, McCann & Geoghagen, 1975), pp. 171–72.
17. Holway, *Black Diamonds,* p. 63.
18. Holway, *Voices from the Great Black Baseball Leagues,* pp. 54–55.
19. Holway, *Black Diamonds,* p. 64.
20. Bak, *Cobb Would Have Caught It,* p. 170.
21. Fred Lieb, *Baseball As I Have Known It* (New York: Coward, McCann & Geoghagen, 1977), pp. 57–58.
22. A more comprehensive examination of Cobb's racial attitudes throughout his life can be found in Richard Bak, *Ty Cobb: His Tumultuous Life and Times* (Dallas: Taylor Publishing Co., 1994).
23. Bak, *Cobb Would Have Caught It,* pp. 229, 265–66.
24. Ibid., pp. 251–59.
25. Greenberg's experiences as a Jewish ballplayer encountering prejudice at times paralleled those of Negro leaguers. See Hank Greenberg (with Ira Berkow), *Hank Greenberg: The Story of My Life* (New York: Times Books, 1989).
26. Bak, *Cobb Would Have Caught It,* pp. 220, 248–49.
27. The Associated Press story was dated July 31, 1938. Cited in *Detroit Free Press,* Feb. 5, 1993.
28. Rogosin, *Invisible Men,* pp. 134–35.
29. Jorge Figuerado, "The Day Torriente Outclassed Ruth," *Baseball Research Journal* (1982), pp. 130–31. In addition to his three home runs, all hit off George Kelly of the New York Giants, Torriente hit a double off Ruth, who

as usual in such games also took a short turn on the mound. Torriente finished with six RBIs in an 11–4 win.

30. Interviews with Willis "Ace" Hudlin and Ted Radcliffe. In addition to Hudlin, who won seventeen games that year with the third-place Cleveland Indians, other members of Gehringer's all-star team included pitchers George Uhle and Earl Whitehill, third baseman Bill Sweeney, first baseman Johnny Neun, and outfielder Harry Heilmann, all with Detroit; shortstop Red Kress, catcher Wally Schang, and outfielder Heinie Manush of St. Louis; and Cleveland pitcher Jake Miller. Since barnstorming teams rarely exceeded a dozen men, members, particularly the pitchers, often played out of position. For a closer look as to how the series unfolded (including a sample boxscore), see Holway, *Blackball Stars,* pp. 271–72.
31. Honig, *Baseball When the Grass Was Real,* p. 171.
32. Bak, *Cobb Would Have Caught It,* p. 194.
33. James Bankes, *The Pittsburgh Crawfords: The Lives and Times of Black Baseball's Most Exciting Team* (DuBuque, Iowa: Wm. C. Brown, 1991), pp. 60–61.
34. Not that prejudice didn't occasionally manifest itself in more subtle ways. Cool Papa Bell, the fastest man in the Negro leagues, remembered once tagging up and scoring from second base on a fly ball to deep center field. Bell was obviously safe, but the white home plate umpire called him out. "I'm not gonna let you do that on major leaguers," the ump said with a laugh. "Maybe you can do that in *your* league, but not against major leaguers."
35. Fred Lieb, *The Detroit Tigers* (New York: G. P. Putnam's Sons, 1946), pp. 141, 175–76.
36. *New York Daily News,* Oct. 10, 1934. The writer is Paul Gallico.
37. Holway, *Voices from the Great Black Baseball Leagues,* pp. 45–46.
38. Interview with Charles "Red" House.
39. Batchelor, Jr., interview.
40. Interview with Bobbie Robinson,
41. Rogosin, *Invisible Men,* p. 180.
42. Holway, *Black Diamonds,* p. 64.

Chapter 7. From Valley to Mountaintop

1. For a lively account of Berry Gordy, Sr.'s, life in George and Detroit, see Berry Gordy, Sr., *Movin' Up* (New York: Harper & Row, 1979).
2. Joe Louis (with Edna and Art Rust, Jr.), *Joe Louis: My Life* (New York: Harcourt Brace Jovanovich, 1978), p. 11.
3. Fine, *Frank Murphy,* p. 99.
4. Ibid., pp. 146–48.
5. Ibid., p. 148.
6. Ibid., pp. 148–50.
7. Milton Meltzer (ed.), *The Black Americans: A History in Their Own Words, 1619–1983* (New York: Harper Trophy, 1984), p. 197.
8. Lowell Cauffiel, "Bittersweet Victory," *Michigan: The Magazine of The Detroit News,* Feb. 15, 1987, p. 16.

9. Ibid., p. 22.
10. Fine, *Frank Murphy,* p. 154.
11. Glover interview. Sweet's personal life fell to pieces after the trials. By 1940 his daughter, wife, and brother Henry had all died of tuberculosis. Two subsequent marriages ended in divorce. He ran for elective office four times and was defeated on each occasion. In 1960 he committed suicide. The house today is owned by Sweet's one-time paperboy.
12. Radcliffe interview.
13. Ibid.
14. James Lincoln Collier, *Duke Ellington* (New York: Oxford University Press, 1987), p. 35.
15. Sidney Bolkosky, *Harmony and Dissonance: Voices of Jewish Identity in Detroit, 1914–1967* (Detroit: Wayne State University Press, 1991), pp. 197–98.
16. Al Stark, "Flashback to Paradise," *Michigan: The Magazine of The Detroit News,* Dec. 4, 1988, p. 7.
17. Holli, *Detroit,* p. 152. The best study of prohibition in Detroit and Michigan is Lawrence Engelmann, *Intemperance: The Lost War Against Liquor* (New York: Free Press, 1979).
18. Timothy Belknap, "Detroit's Purple Gang," *Detroit Free Press Magazine,* June 26, 1983, p. 8; Fine, *Frank Murphy,* p. 102.
19. Belknap, "The Purple Gang," p. 9; Louis (with Rust), *Joe Louis,* p. 12.
20. Fine, *Frank Murphy,* p. 102; *Detroit News,* Aug. 11, 1982.
21. Radcliffe interview.
22. Holway, *Blackball Stars,* p. 131.
23. Robinson interview.
24. Holway, *Blackball Stars,* p. 147.
25. Bruce, *The Kansas City Monarchs,* p. 42.
26. Holway, *Blackball Stars,* pp. 132.
27. *Chicago Defender,* Jan. 8, 1927. Cited in Bruce, *The Kansas City Monarchs,* p. 37.
28. Robinson interview.
29. Radcliffe interview.
30. *Detroit Independent,* June 10, 1927.
31. Hines interview.
32. Bak, *Cobb Would Have Caught It,* p. 97.
33. Holway, *Blackball Stars,* p. 252.
34. Robinson interview.
35. Ibid.
36. Interview with Saul Davis.
37. This account is drawn fully from Richard Bak, "The Toughest Cop Who Ever Lived," *Detroit Monthly* (June 1986), pp. 108–13.
38. See Louis (with Rust), *Joe Louis,* pp. 20–21.
39. Bak, *Cobb Would Have Caught It,* p. 102.
40. Ibid.
41. Robinson interview.

Chapter 8. Of Satch and Oscar and Others Passing Through

1. Undated [August 1941?] *Baltimore Afro-American* clipping in author's possession.
2. Peterson, *Only the Ball Was White,* pp. 141–42. The profile of Paige is drawn primarily from Peterson, pp. 129–44; Bankes, *The Pittsburgh Crawfords,* pp. 30–43; and Richard Donovan, "The Fabulous Satchel Paige" in Charles Einstein (ed.), *The Baseball Reader* (New York: Harper & Row, 1980). Also see Leroy Paige (with David Lipman), *Maybe I'll Pitch Forever* (Garden City, N.J.: Doubleday, 1962).
3. Bankes, *The Pittsburgh Crawfords,* p. 156.
4. Players' profiles are drawn from Peterson, *Only the Ball Was White; Bankes, The Pittsburgh Crawfords;* Holway's three volumes of oral histories; and Jim Riley, *The All-Time All-Stars of Black Baseball* (Cocoa, Fla.: TK Publishers, 1983).
5. Holway, *Blackball Stars,* p. 100.
6. Ibid., p. 101.
7. Bankes, *The Pittsburgh Crawfords,* p. 152.
8. *Detroit Free Press,* March 4, 1984.
9. Bankes, *The Pittsburgh Crawfords,* p. 49. A short but excellent biography of the troubled backstop is Bill Brashler, *Josh Gibson: A Life in the Negro Leagues* (New York: Harper & Row, 1978).
10. Holway, *Blackball Stars,* p. 155.
11. Ibid.
12. Ibid., p. 220.
13. Ibid., p. 217.
14. Ibid., p. 244.
15. Bankes, *The Pittsburgh Crawfords,* p. 60.
16. Bak, *Cobb Would Have Caught It,* p. 194.
17. Peterson, *Only the Ball Was White,* p. 156.
18. Rogosin, *Invisible Men,* p. 42.
19. Peterson, *Only the Ball Was White,* p. 210.
20. Holway, *Blackball Stars,* p. 168.
21. Ibid., p. 193.
22. Ibid., p. 198.
23. According to Dick Clark, the name Dobie Moore appears in recently discovered boxscores of semipro games played in Detroit in the 1930s.

Chapter 9. The Way It Was: Saul Davis

1. During the depression any number of novelty teams and fantasy encounters could be found on the barnstorming circuit. There were, for instance, the Zulus and Ethiopian Clowns, all-black teams that played games in grass skirts, war paint, and bare feet. And the long-haired, bearded House of David team, which represented a religious sect based in Benton Harbor and often played their games on donkey back. Satchel Paige's duels with Dizzy Dean

(and later, Bob Feller) drew large crowds in nearly every part of the country. Other contests might feature Mildred "Babe" Didrikson, an Olympic gold-medal winner in track and field and the leading woman golfer in the country, on the mound. Or Olympic track star Jesse Owens racing a horse before the game. The rule of thumb that promoters and performers followed was: if it drew paying customers, then anything went.

Chapter 10. The End of Something.

1. Peterson, *Only the Ball Was White,* pp. 114–15; Holway, *Blackball Stars,* pp. 32–34.
2. Holway, *Blackball Stars,* p. 32.
3. Poverty, overcrowding, and ignorance made America's ghettos breeding grounds for a host of highly communicable diseases, including tuberculosis, which claimed Negro-league stars Jose Mendez and Ted Trent. A 1930 report showed the rate of venereal disease among Detroit's blacks to be eight times higher than that of whites. In addition, the rates of sterility and infant mortality among blacks typically was two and three times the rates for whites; the result was that deaths actually outstripped births in Black Bottom during the 1920s.
4. Sobol, *Babe Ruth and the American Dream,* pp. 187–90. Another biographer, while acknowledging Ruth's indiscriminate and excessive whoring, believes the best evidence points to an abdominal abscess, not syphilis. See Chapter 25 of Robert W. Creamer, *Babe: The Legend Comes to Life* (New York: Simon & Schuster, 1974).
5. Capone, described as being "nutty as a cuckoo," died January 25, 1947, in Florida. For a description of Capone's losing battle with the disease and his gradual mental deterioration, see Robert J. Schoenberg, *Mr. Capone* (New York: Morrow, 1992), pp. 342–53.
6. Holway, *Blackball Stars,* p. 33.
7. Peterson, *Only the Ball Was White,* pp. 229–30.
8. Holway, *Voices form the Great Black Baseball Leagues,* p. 36.
9. Holway, *Black Diamonds,* p. 51.
10. Bruce, *The Kansas City Monarchs,* pp. 64–66.
11. Walter O. Briggs was born February 27, 1877, the son of a Michigan Central Railroad engineer. Briggs started working in car shops as a body trimmer when he was fifteen. Later he joined a trim and paint shop owned by Barney Everitt, a childhood friend. Briggs bought the company in 1909 and changed its name to Briggs Manufacturing. Briggs usually was sympathetically portrayed by the press, even during his frequent clashes with labor. Sportswriters, in particular, portrayed him as a populist, "the fan who bought a ballpark." For a typical treatment by a long-time Detroit newspaperman, see Malcolm Bingay, *Detroit Is My Own Home Town* (Indianapolis: Bobbs-Merrill, 1946), pp. 137–48.
12. Joyce Shaw Peterson, *American Automobile Workers,* 1900–1933 (Albany: State University of New York, 1987), pp. 66–67, 139–40.

13. Holway, *Blackball Stars,* p. 254.
14. Peterson, *American Automobile Workers,* pp. 139–40; Woodford, *Detroit: American Urban Renaissance,* p. 108.
15. Holway, *Blackball Stars,* p. 254.
16. Robinson interview.
17. *Detroit News,* July 8, 1929.
18. *Detroit Free Press,* July 8, 1929.
19. Ibid. All three major dailies ran complete lists of the injured.
20. Ibid.
21. Fine, *Frank Murphy,* p. 246.
22. Hines interview.
23. Interview with Gene Berlin.
24. Holway, *Voices from the Great Black Baseball Leagues,* p. 62.
25. Bruce, *The Kansas City Monarchs,* pp. 68–72. The Monarchs's custom-built lighting system, which cost between $50,000 and $100,000, proved their salvation during the depression. The large crowds attracted by this electrical curiosity weren't lost on struggling major-league owners. On May 23, 1935, Cincinnati hosted the first major-league night game, and several other clubs quickly followed suit. The Tigers were the last American League club, and second-from-last major-league team, to install lights. On June 15, 1948, Walter O. Briggs finally capitulated to what he termed an "artificial" environment, the Tigers playing their first night game against the Philadelphia Athletics.
26. Robinson interview.
27. Holway, *Voice from the Great Baseball Leagues,* p. 68.
28. On the afternoon of the first night game, Detroit players, claiming that their contracts said nothing about playing under the lights, threatened to go on strike unless they received an extra five dollars per game. The strike threat was relayed to J. L. Wilkinson through Moses Walker. Anticipating a big gate, the Kansas City owner grudgingly agreed to pay the extra money—a total of $240 for sixteen players and three night games—himself.
29. *Detroit News,* Aug. 8, 1988.
30. *Oklahoma Black Dispatch,* Aug. 28, 1930.
31. Dials interview.
32. *Oklahoma Black Dispatch,* Aug. 28, 1930.
33. Robinson and Dials interviews.
34. Holway, *Blackball Stars,* p. 258.
35. Fine, *Frank Murphy,* pp. 246–53; Conot, *American Odyssey,* p. 275.
36. Glover interview.
37. Holway, *Black Diamonds,* p. 51.
38. *Detroit News,* Sept. 18, 1938.
39. Henderson interview; *Detroit News,* June 23, 1929.
40. Bruce, *The Kansas City Monarchs,* p. 68.
41. Holway, *Black Diamonds,* pp. 51–52.
42. Hines interview.
43. In 1933 the Tigers drew less than 4,100 fans a game.

44. Holway, *Black Diamonds*, p. 52.
45. Bruce, *The Kansas City Monarchs*, pp. 83–84.
46. Holway, *Blackball Stars*, pp. 300–07.
47. Conot, *American Odyssey*, pp. 278–79.
48. Holway, *Black Diamonds*, p. 64.
49. Dials interview. An interesting footnote to the Wolves' abbreviated 1932 season concerns a mammoth home run Mule Suttles reportedly hit while playing for Detroit. According to Dials, who was playing first base for Hilldale that afternoon, Suttles unloaded on a spitball from Phil Cockrell and sent it over the center-field fence ("right under the scoreboard"), which was 515 feet from home plate. No boxscore has been found for this game. But if this is true, Suttles would be the only hitter known to have accomplished that feat.
50. Bankes, *The Pittsburgh Crawfords*, pp. 23–29; Holway, *Blackball Stars*, pp. 308–12.
51. The biographical sketch of Dandridge is drawn from Holway, *Blackball Stars*, pp. 353–56; and Rogosin, *Invisible Men*, pp. 36–38.

Epilogue. Come In Out of the Dark

1. Bankes, *The Pittsburgh Crawfords*, p. 28.
2. Louis (with Rust), *Joe Louis: My Life*, pp. 59–60, 73.
3. House interview. For the record, the roster at one time or another included first baseman Alphonse "Blue" Dunn; second basemen Larry Bleach and Charles "Dusty" Decker; shortstops E. "Red" Hale and J. Thomas; third basemen Red House and Roosevelt Cox; and outfielders Turkey Stearnes, Sam Hill, Bill Hoskins, Kermit Dial, Ed Salters, and Ely Underwood. Earl Jones was a utility infielder. The pitching staff included Albert Davis, Charley Justice, Orel Thomas, Walter Thomas, Ray Underwood, and Dempsey "Dimp" Miller. Double Duty Webster, Felton Wilson, Jimmy McIntosh, and Shirley Petway were the catchers. The 1937 season was the extent of most of these players' Negro-league careers, although Cox and Dunn signed with the New York Cubans, and Walter Thomas later caught on with the Kansas City Monarchs. Most of the others continued their lives as full-time factory workers and weekend athletes.
4. *Detroit News*, Sept. 9, 1938, and Nov. 30, 1944.
5. Peterson, *Only the Ball Was White*, pp. 186–87.
6. The best treatment of Robinson's breaking of the color line is Jules Tygiel, *Baseball's Great Experiment: Jackie Robinson and His Legacy* (New York: Oxford University Press, 1983).
7. House interview.
8. Bak, *Cobb Would Have Caught It*, p. 104.
9. Holway, *Blackball Stars*, p. 163.
10. Bak, *Cobb Would Have Caught It*, p. 104.
11. *Detroit Free Press*, July 26, 1953. The players were Roosevelt Evans of Northwestern High School, Dave Mann of Miller, Leonard Green of Pershing, Vir-

gil Woods of Northwestern, and Lawrence Estelle, all signed by St. Louis; Richard Lewis of Wayne, signed by the White Sox; and John Henry of Northwestern, signed by the Cubs.

12. Interview with Willie Horton.
13. *Detroit News,* June 17, 1984.
14. The movie was based on a novel by the same name by William Brashler. Brashler, author of a biography of Josh Gibson, largely based his characters on the Indianapolis Clowns.
15. Bak, *Cobb Would Have Caught It,* p. 96.
16. Ibid., p. 106.
17. Roesink died July 19, 1954, in Detroit. Watson died January 18, 1960, in Detroit. As is often the case with sports teams, the name "Detroit Stars" was too recognizable to bury. Thus the name appeared here and there throughout the postwar years, describing what was usually a semipro team hoping to grab a measure of recognition by resurrecting a familiar name. The most notable version surfaced in the Negro American League in the 1950s. It was owned by Ted Rasberry, a black Grand Rapids promoter who later purchased the Kansas City Monarchs. The six-team association also included the Indianapolis Clowns. At the end of the decade this was not even a good minor-league circuit, the Stars trying to spike the gate by adding off-season basketball players like Nat "Sweetwater" Clifton to the lineup. Only four teams—and a shred of professionalism—were left by 1960, after which the league quietly dissolved.
18. *Detroit News,* May 14, 1982; interview with Janet Bruce.
19. Holway, *Voices from the Great Black Baseball Leagues,* p. 55.

Bibliography

Aaron, Hank (with Lonnie Wheeler). *I Had a Hammer* (New York: Harper Collins, 1991).

Alexander, Charles C. *Ty Cobb* (New York: Oxford University Press, 1984).

Allen, Frederick Lewis. *Only Yesterday* (New York: Harper & Row, 1931).

Babson, Steve. *Working Detroit* (New York: Adama Books, 1984).

Badger, Anthony J. *The New Deal: The Depression Years, 1933–1940* (New York: Noonday Press, 1989).

Bak, Richard. *Cobb Would Have Caught It: The Golden Age of Baseball in Detroit* (Detroit: Wayne State University Press, 1991).

———. *Ty Cobb: His Tumultuous Life and Times* (Dallas: Taylor Publishing Co., 1994).

———. "The Toughest Cop Who Ever Lived." *Detroit Monthly* (June 1986).

Bankes, James. *The Pittsburgh Crawfords: The Lives and Times of Black Baseball's Most Exciting Team* (Dubuque, Iowa: Wm. C. Brown, 1991).

Batchelor, E. A. "Afro-American Rooters Are the Best Part of the Show at Mack Park." *Detroit Saturday Night,* Aug. 19, 1922.

Bauman, John F., and Thomas H. Coode. *In the Eye of the Great Depression: New Deal Reporters and the Agony of the American People* (DeKalb: Northern Illinois University Press, 1988).

Beasley, Norman, and George W. Stark. *Made In Detroit* (New York: G. P. Putnam's Sons, 1957).

Belknap, Tim. "Detroit's Purple Gang." *Detroit Free Press Magazine,* June 26, 1983.

Betzold, Michael and Ethan Casey. *Queen of Diamonds: The Tiger Stadium Story* (West Bloomfield, Mich.: A & M, 1992).

Bingay, Malcolm. *Detroit Is My Own Home Town* (Indianapolis: Bobbs-Merrill, 1946).

Bolkosky, Sidney. *Harmony and Dissonance: Voices of Jewish Identity in Detroit, 1914–1967* (Detroit: Wayne State University Press, 1991).

Botkin, B. A. (ed.). *Lay My Burden Down: A Folk History of Slavery* (Athens: University of Georgia Press, 1989).

Brashler, Bill. *Josh Gibson: A Life in the Negro Leagues* (New York: Harper & Row, 1978).

Bruce, Janet. *The Kansas City Monarchs: Champions of Black Baseball* (Lawrence: University Press of Kansas, 1985).

Buchanan, A. Russell. *Black Americans in World War II* (Santa Barbara, Calif.: Clio Press, 1979).

Bushell, Garvin (as told to Mark Tucker). *Jazz from the Beginning* (Ann Arbor: University of Michigan Press, 1990).

Cauffiel, Lowell. "Bittersweet Victory." *Michigan: The Magazine of the Detroit News*, Feb. 15, 1987.

Clive, Alan. *State of War: Michigan in World War II* (Ann Arbor: University of Michigan Press, 1979).

Collier, James Lincoln. *Duke Ellington* (New York: Oxford University Press, 1987).

Conot, Robert. *American Odyssey* (New York: Bantam, 1974).

Creamer, Robert W. *Babe: The Legend Comes to Life* (New York: Simon & Schuster, 1974).

Dancy, John C. "The Negro People in Michigan." *Michigan History* (Spring 1940).

———. *Sand Against the Wind: The Memoirs of John C. Dancy* (Detroit: Wayne State University Press, 1966).

Denby, Charles. *Indignant Heart: A Black Worker's Journal* (Detroit: Wayne State University Press, 1978).

Dixon, Phil, and Patrick J. Hannigan, *The Negro Baseball Leagues: A Photographic History* (Mattituck, N.Y.: Amereon House, 1992).

Einstein, Charles (ed.). *The Baseball Reader* (New York: Harper & Row, 1980).

Engelmann, Lawrence. *Intemperance: The Lost War Against Liquor* (New York: Free Press, 1979).

Falls, Joe. *Detroit Tigers* (New York: Collier, 1975).

Farmer, Silas. *History of Detroit and Wayne County and Early Michigan* (Detroit: Gale Research, 1969).

Farrell, James T. *Studs Lonigan* (New York: Avon, 1977).

Figueredo, Jorge S. "The Day Torriente Outclassed Ruth." *Baseball Research Journal* (1982).

Fine, Sidney. *Frank Murphy: The Detroit Years* (Ann Arbor: University of Michigan Press, 1975).

Gordy, Berry, Sr. *Movin' Up* (New York: Harper & Row, 1979).

Grant, Joanne (ed.). *Black Protest: History, Documents and Analyses, 1619 to the Present* (New York: Fawcett, 1968).

Grimm, Joe (ed.). *Michigan Voices: Our State's History in the Words of the People Who Lived It* (Detroit: Wayne State University Press, 1987).

Harms, Richard. "Jess Elster and the Grand Rapids Athletics." *Michigan History* (Jan./Feb. 1993).

Holli, Melvin G. (ed.). *Detroit* (New York: New Viewpoints, 1976).

Bibliography

Holway, John B. *Blackball Stars: Negro League Pioneers* (Westport, Conn.: Meckler Books. 1988).

———. *Black Diamonds: Life in the Negro Leagues from the Men Who Lived It* (New York: Stadium, 1991).

———. *Voices from the Great Black Baseball Leagues* (New York: De Capo Press, 1992).

Honig, Donald. *Baseball When the Grass Was Real* (New York: Coward, McCann & Geoghagen, 1975).

Huggins, Nathan Irvin. *Black Odyssey: The African-American Ordeal in Slavery* (New York: Pantheon, 1977).

Jacobs, Harriet A. (ed. Jean Fagan Yellin). *Incidents in the Life of a Slave Girl* (Cambridge: Harvard University Press, 1987).

Katzman, David M. *Before the Ghetto: Black Detroit in the Nineteenth Century* (Urbana: University of Illinois Press, 1973).

Kleinknecht, Merl. "Integration of Baseball After World War II." *Baseball Research Journal* (1983).

Lemann, Nicholas. *The Promised Land: The Great Black Migration and How It Changed America* (New York: Knopf, 1991).

Levine, David Allan. *Internal Combustion: The Races in Detroit, 1915–1926* (Westport, Conn.: Greenwood Press, 1976).

Lewis, David L. *The Public Image of Henry Ford* (Detroit: Wayne State University Press, 1976).

———. "Working Side by Side." *Michigan History* (Jan./Feb. 1993).

Lieb, Fred. *Baseball As I Have Known It* (New York: *Coward, McCann & Geoghagen, 1977*).

———. *The Detroit Tigers* (New York: G. P. Putnam's Sons, 1946).

Louis, Joe (with Edna and Art Rust, Jr.). *Joe Louis: My Life* (New York: Harcourt Brace Jovanovich, 1978).

Manchester, William. *The Glory and the Dream: A Narrative History of America, 1932–1972* (Boston: Little, Brown & Co., 1973).

Marks, Carole. *Farewell, We're Good and Gone: The Great Black Migration* (Bloomington: Indiana University Press, 1989).

McGehee, Scott, and Susan Watson (eds.). *Blacks in Detroit* (Detroit: Detroit Free Press, 1980).

Mead, Chris. *Champion: Joe Louis, Black Hero in White America* (New York: Charles Scribner's Sons, 1985).

Meltzer, Milton (ed.). *The Black Americans: A History in Their Own Words, 1619–1983* (New York: Harper Trophy, 1984).

Moon, Elaine. *Untold Tales, Unsung Heroes: An Oral History of Detroit's African American community* (Detroit: Wayne State University Press, 1994).

Motley, Mary Penick. *The Invisible Soldier: The Experience of the Black Soldier, World War II* (Detroit: Wayne State University Press, 1975).

Oestreicher, Richard Jules. *Solidarity and Fragmentation: Working People and Class Consciousness in Detroit, 1875–1900* (Urbana: University of Illinois Press, 1986).

Paige, Leroy (as told to David Lipman). *Maybe I'll Pitch Forever* (Garden City, N.J.: Doubleday, 1962).

Peterson, Joyce Shaw. *American Automobile Workers, 1900–1933* (Albany: State University of New York, 1987).

Peterson, Robert. *Only the Ball Was White* (Englewood Cliffs, N.J.: Prentice-Hall, 1970).

Powers, Thomas E. "The Page Fence Giants Play Ball." *Chronicle: The Quarterly Magazine of the Historical Society of Michigan* (Spring 1983).

Reichler, Joseph L. (ed.). *The Baseball Encyclopedia: The Complete and Official Record of Major League Baseball* (8th ed.) (New York: Macmillan, 1990).

Riess, Steven A. *City Games: The Evolution of American Urban Society and the Rise of Sports* (Urbana: University of Illinois Press, 1989).

Riley, Jim. *The All-Time All-Stars of Black Baseball* (Cocoa, Fla.: TK Publishers, 1983).

Robinson, Jackie (as told to Alfred Duckett). *I Never Had It Made* (New York: G. P. Putnam's Sons, 1972).

Rogosin, Donn. *Invisible Men: Life in Baseball's Negro Leagues* (New York: Atheneum, 1983).

Ruck, Rob. *Sandlot Seasons: Sport in Black Pittsburgh* (Urbana: University of Illinois Press, 1986).

Rust, Art, Jr. *"Get That Nigger Off the Field!"* (New York: Delacorte Press, 1976).

Serafino, Frank. *West of Warsaw* (Hamtramck, Mich.: Avenue, 1983).

Seymour, Harold. *Baseball: The Early Years* (New York: Oxford University Press, 1960).

———. *Baseball: The Golden Years* (New York: Oxford University Press, 1971).

Sobol, Ken. *Babe Ruth and the American Dream* (New York: Ballantine, 1974).

Spear, Alan. *Black Chicago: The Making of a Negro Ghetto, 1890–1920* (Chicago: University of Chicago Press, 1967).

Stampp, Kenneth M. *The Peculiar Institution* (New York: Knopf, 1956).

Stark, Al. "Flashback to Paradise." *Michigan: The Magazine of The Detroit News,* Dec. 4, 1988.

Thomas, Richard W. *Life For Us Is What We Make It: Building Black Community in Detroit, 1915–1945* (Bloomington: Indiana University Press, 1992).

Thorn, John, and Pete Palmer (eds.). *Total Baseball* (New York: Warner, 1989).

Tocqueville, Alexis de (ed. and rev. Phillips Bradley). *Democracy in America* (New York: Knopf, 1980).

Trouppe, Quincy. *Twenty Years Too Soon* (Los Angeles: S & S Enterprises, 1977).

Turner, Arthur, and Earl R. Moses. *Colored Detroit: A Brief History of Detroit's Colored Population and a Directory of Their Businesses, Organizations, Professions, and Trades* (Detroit, 1924).

Tuttle, William M., Jr. *Race Riot: Chicago in the Red Summer of 1919* (New York: Oxford University Press, 1970).

Tygiel, Jules. *Baseball's Great Experiment: Jackie Robinson and His Legacy* (New York: Oxford University Press, 1983).

Bibliography

Voigt, David Q. *American Baseball: From the Commissioners to Continental Expansion* (University Park: Pennsylvania State University Press, 1983).

Washington, Forrest B. "The Negro in Detroit: A Survey of the Conditions of a Negro Group in a Northern Industrial Center During the War Prosperity Period." (Detroit, 1920).

Weiss, William J. "The First Negro in 20th Century O. B." *Baseball Research Journal* (1979).

Whitehead, Charles E. *A Man and His Diamonds* (New York: Vantage Press, 1980).

Woodford, Arthur M. *Detroit: American Urban Renaissance* (Tulsa, Okla.: Continental Heritage Press, 1979).

Woodford, Frank B., and Arthur M. Woodford. *All Our Yesterdays: A Brief History of Detroit* (Detroit: Wayne State University Press, 1969).

Woodward, C. Vann. *The Strange Career of Jim Crow* (3d. rev. ed.) (New York: Oxford University Press, 1974).

Wytrwal, Joseph A. *Polish Experience in Detroit* (Detroit: Endurance, 1992).

Zinn, Howard. *A People's History of the United States* (New York: Harper & Row, 1980).

Zunz, Olivier. *The Changing Face of Inequality: Urbanization, Industrial Development, and Immigrants in Detroit, 1880–1920* (Chicago: University of Chicago Press, 1982).

Index

293

Titles in the Great Lakes Books Series

Detroit: City of Race and Class Violence, revised edition, by B. J. Widick, 1989

Deep Woods Frontier: A History of Logging in Northern Michigan, by Theodore J. Karamanski, 1989

Orvie, The Dictator of Dearborn, by David L. Good, 1989

Seasons of Grace: A History of the Catholic Archdiocese of Detroit, by Leslie Woodcock Tentler, 1990

The Pottery of John Foster: Form and Meaning, by Gordon and Elizabeth Orear, 1990

The Diary of Bishop Frederic Baraga: First Bishop of Marquette, Michigan, edited by Regis M. Walling and Rev. N. Daniel Rupp, 1990

Walnut Pickles and Watermelon Cake: A Century of Michigan Cooking, by Larry B. Massie and Priscilla Massie, 1990

The Making of Michigan, 1820–1860: A Pioneer Anthology, edited by Justin L. Kestenbaum, 1990

America's Favorite Homes: A Guide to Popular Early Twentieth-Century Homes, by Robert Schweitzer and Michael W. R. Davis, 1990

Beyond the Model T: The Other Ventures of Henry Ford, by Ford R. Bryan, 1990

Life after the Line, by Josie Kearns, 1990

Michigan Lumbertowns: Lumbermen and Laborers in Saginaw, Bay City, and Muskegon, 1870–1905, by Jeremy W. Kilar, 1990

Detroit Kids Catalog: The Hometown Tourist, by Ellyce Field, 1990

Waiting for the News, by Leo Litwak, 1990 (reprint)

Detroit Perspectives, edited by Wilma Wood Henrickson, 1991

Life on the Great Lakes: A Wheelsman's Story, by Fred W. Dutton, edited by William Donohue Ellis, 1991

Copper Country Journal: The Diary of Schoolmaster Henry Hobart, 1863–1864, by Henry Hobart, edited by Philip P. Mason, 1991

John Jacob Astor: Business and Finance in the Early Republic, by John Denis Haeger, 1991

Survival and Regeneration: Detroit's American Indian Community, by Edmund J. Danziger, Jr., 1991

Steamboats and Sailors of the Great Lakes, by Mark L. Thompson, 1991

Cobb Would Have Caught It: The Golden Age of Baseball in Detroit, by Richard Bak, 1991

Michigan in Literature, by Clarence Andrews, 1992

Under the Influence of Water: Poems, Essays, and Stories, by Michael Delp, 1992

The Country Kitchen, by Della T. Lutes, 1992 (reprint)

The Making of a Mining District: Keweenaw Native Copper 1500–1870, by David J. Krause, 1992

Kids Catalog of Michigan Adventures, by Ellyce Field, 1993

Henry's Lieutenants, by Ford R. Bryan, 1993

Lake Erie and Lake St. Clair Handbook, by Stanley J. Bolsenga and Charles E. Herdendorf, 1993

Historic Highway Bridges of Michigan, by Charles K. Hyde, 1993

Pontiac and the Indian Uprising, by Howard H. Peckham, 1994 (reprint)

Queen of the Lakes, by Mark Thompson, 1994

Iron Fleet: The Great Lakes in World War II, by George J. Joachim, 1994

Charting the Inland Seas: A History of the U.S. Lake Survey, by Arthur M. Woodford, 1994 (reprint)

Turkey Stearnes and the Detroit Stars: The Negro Leagues in Detroit, 1919–1933, by Richard Bak, 1994